D0796952

Sustainable Agriculture

Sustainable Agriculture

A Christian Ethic of Gratitude

Mark E. Graham

WIPF & STOCK · Eugene, Oregon

For My Daughter,
Hannah Emerling Graham

and

For My Parents,
Michael and Laurie Graham

Wipf and Stock Publishers
199 W 8th Ave, Suite 3
Eugene, OR 97401

Sustainable Agriculture
A Christian Ethic of Gratitude
By Graham, Mark E.
Copyright©2005 Pilgrim Press
ISBN 13: 978-1-60608-806-7
Publication date 5/18/2009
Previously published by Pilgrim Press, 2005

This limited edition licensed by special permission of The Pilgrim Press.

Contents

Chapter Three
AN ALTERNATIVE VISION FOR AMERICAN AGRICULTURE: INCARNATING A CHRISTIAN ETHIC OF GRATITUDE
140

Acknowledgments

My thanks to those who have contributed in various ways to this book. Villanova University generously granted me a sabbatical to finish my manuscript, and without this freedom from my ordinary professional responsibilities this book would still be in process. The Theology and Religious Studies Department provided me with a graduate assistant every semester since my arrival at Villanova. For the past two years, Sara Leader has been an invaluable assistant, spending many hours in the library locating books and articles, using her formidable research skills to gather a great deal of pertinent information, and compiling the index.

The faculty of the Theology and Religious Studies Department is a supportive group of scholars that has enriched my life considerably. My thanks especially to William Werpehowski and Suzanne Toton for their friendship, humor, lively conversations, and professional advice.

For over a decade, James Keenan, S.J., my former professor and dissertation director, has encouraged and helped me in many ways, and I have benefited enormously from his insights, guidance, and friendship. His commitment to the ethics of everyday life is well represented in this book, and it will continue to occupy my attention for the foreseeable future — a seed well planted!

Writing a book while raising two young children is no easy feat, and my wife, Laura, has been patient and encouraging throughout the process. My daily periods of self-imposed isolation meant that Laura assumed more than her fair share of childcare responsibilities, and I am grateful for her support. Laura also proofread the entire manuscript. Our children, Peter and Hannah, are constant sources of enjoyment, delight, unpredictability, and energy in our lives, and we are blessed to have such wonderful kids.

My parents, Michael and Laurie Graham, provided a loving, nurturing home for their children, and I have benefited from the many ways they have formed me. Parents are probably the most formative influence in a person's life, and I am lucky and thankful to have been raised by these two. They have given me much — more, I am sure, than they will ever imagine.

My sister and brother-in-law, Angela and Stephen Koop, and their children, Thomas, Rachel, and Timothy, have provided much laughter and enjoyable family gatherings over the years, and their sense of hospitality is enviable. They always make our all-too-infrequent trips to Iowa memorable events, and we are grateful for their friendship over the years.

Finally, this book is an extended "thank you" to a place and people I cherish: Iowa and its farmers. I was born, raised, and spent a sizeable chunk of my adult life in Iowa, where I befriended and became familiar with many farmers and their families. I have always admired their neighborliness, charitableness, self-discipline, decency, and earthiness. I thrived in a culture created and sustained by farmers and I hope this book is a fitting requital to a noble group of people who deserve a sincere thanks for the food they provide, the children they raise, and the type of community they foster. While much of this book is highly critical of the dominant form of agriculture in the Corn Belt, this criticism is borne by respect and love.

Introduction

While browsing through a bookstore several years ago, I stumbled across Wes Jackson's *New Roots for Agriculture*. The title was piquant and my puzzlement considerable: Why would agriculture need "new roots"? I had witnessed firsthand the enormous productivity of American agriculture, with elevator bins filled to capacity with corn and soybeans, and mountains of grain piled stories high in adjacent parking lots at the end of the harvest season due to lack of storage space. I had also internalized the litany of praises emanating from the popular media about American agriculture being the "breadbasket to the world" and a beacon of light to be emulated by Third World countries struggling to feed their citizens. More laudable thoughts popped into my head: record yearly production levels; the most inexpensive food in the world; synthetic chemicals to boost production levels and to compensate for nature's deficiencies; powerful machinery to produce grain more efficiently; specialization that confers a comparative advantage; fewer and fewer farmers to feed more and more people. What in the world could be wrong with American agriculture? Convinced that the pages of *New Roots for Agriculture* would be filled with little more than the ramblings of a malcontent, I decided to buy it anyway — and what a moment of grace!

Jackson's trenchant attack on conventional American agriculture exploded my preconceptions about our Corn Belt agricultural system. More than a little unnerved by Jackson's ominous predictions and secretly hoping that his assessment was seriously flawed, I immersed myself in the agricultural literature for the next few years. The more I read, however, the more I became convinced that the broad lineaments of Jackson's critique were right on target. As currently

1

practiced, American agriculture is sowing the seeds of its own destruction and slowly, but inexorably, grinding its way to an ignominious conclusion. As American agriculture continues its death march like a lemming to the sea, it is leaving a wake of destruction in its path in the form of ghost towns that were once thriving rural communities, topsoil erosion, chemical pollution of the countryside, genetic homogeneity of our major cash crops, poverty in rural areas, and disenfranchised and powerless farmers, to mention but a few. Moreover, as American agriculture continues to undermine the natural and social capital upon which its health depends, it is foreclosing possibilities for future generations and making it more and more difficult to transition to another type of agricultural system.

The theological implications of the state of contemporary American agriculture are momentous. Americans have been blessed through God's creative power with some of the most fertile farmland in the world. Yet our current agricultural practices and policies are clearly undermining this divine gift, pitting us against the creative forces that forged our bountiful farmland and placing us in sharp opposition to God's desire that the land nourish and sustain everyone, both present and future generations. In many ways, our agricultural system is unraveling God's benevolent work that has been in process for millennia, placing us in the theologically uncomfortable position of deconstructing a vital aspect of creation.

Fortunately, the forces responsible for American agriculture's development are reversible, and the damage to our agricultural system is repairable. The construction of a more theologically palatable agricultural system, however, will demand a new — and very different — moral vision for American agriculture that will require a substantial and lengthy structural overhaul. Yet I am hopeful that as the best elements of the Christian moral tradition are brought to bear on agricultural issues, the new moral vision it provides will unmask the moral dubiousness of business as usual in the agricultural sector and offer a powerful stimulus to understand the laborious structural adjustments awaiting us as redemptive tasks expressing our love for

God and neighbor, our desire to cooperate with God's creative activity, and our willingness to make God's kingdom a little more present in the world.

This book is a conscious attempt to promote an "ethics of everyday life." I believe that God's action of creating, sustaining, redeeming, and saving — the central mysteries of the Christian faith — converge in the mundane, pedestrian events of my daily life: talking with my wife, raising and nurturing our children, writing, teaching, talking to students, praying, watching my dog hunt and point birds, gardening, fishing, experiencing the seasons changing, interacting with colleagues, and probably the most mundane event of all — eating food — which we materially fortunate Americans do several times a day. These everyday events are pervaded by sacredness, meaning, and value, and they constitute the arena in which God bestows grace and expresses love, care, and concern, challenge, and sometimes reproach.

When placed in this context, food consumption assumes an entirely new meaning. Eating food is not simply a matter of caloric or nutritional intake. Eating food creates a demand for certain agricultural products, which in turn explicitly or implicitly supports, encourages, and legitimizes a wide array of farming methods, practices, policies, and institutions that either promote or undermine God's wishes for creation. Day after day, year after year, decade after decade we consume food and in the process help construct a coordinated network of relationships and behavioral patterns, all of which are, and should be, legitimate objects of moral concern. Like it or not, eating food is a moral and theological activity whereby we define ourselves; construct political, social, and economic institutions; and respond to God.

This book, then, is an invitation to all Christians to begin constructing a food ethics. To the consumer, it raises awareness of the ethical ramifications of purchasing food and supporting a certain kind of agricultural industry. To the farmer, it questions — and criticizes — the dominant type of agricultural production in the Corn Belt and offers a hopeful, alternative vision for American agriculture that restores communities and creates genuine freedom for individual farmers. To the politician, it recommends legislative initiatives that counteract decades of neglect and abuse. To the academic Christian ethicist, it presents an opportunity to join a discussion on a topic relevant in so many ways to the life of every American. Finally, to the Christian for whom the spark of the divine is detectable in the daily life, it is a chance to begin making ethical sense out of something done every day for the entirety of one's natural life — participating in agriculture.

One final note. American agriculture is an incredibly diverse industry — far too diverse to be treated adequately in one volume. To make the subject manageable and to avoid scores of inapplicable generalizations, I will limit my analysis to grain production in the Corn Belt, even though many of my comments and conclusions are equally applicable to other forms of agriculture in the United States. Thus, the phrase "American agriculture" and cognates refer only to agriculture in the Corn Belt, unless specified otherwise. To a certain degree, I lament this self-imposed limitation since many other agricultural production systems are equally worthy of sustained deliberation. Yet the requirement to present accurate, informed, relatively detailed and comprehensive, and fair assessments is best attained by restricting the investigation's scope.

Chapter One

Theology, Ethics, and Agriculture

Natural History and Giftedness

Nearly 2 million years ago began the Ice Age, a period dominated by glaciers advancing and retreating across the area now known as the Corn Belt. Imagining a more inhospitable environment for human life during this glacial activity is difficult, but what a boon this activity would become for later residents of this area! As the glaciers began their southward descent from the Arctic, they functioned as massive bulldozers, lifting debris and rocks from underneath the ground, and their weight was more than sufficient to crush and pulverize everything in their path. Four times during the Ice Age this phenomenon was repeated, in cycles of approximately one hundred thousand years, each time culminating in a precious resource: a thick layer of dust left behind by the retreating glaciers that formed the foundation for our topsoil today.[1]

The accumulated sediment proved to be a welcome home to the tallgrass prairie, an ecosystem dominated by grasses that can grow upward of seven or eight feet. American literature is replete with stories of awestruck settlers moving westward from the eastern hardwood forests and encountering a sea of grass as far as the eye could see, thick, chock full of wildlife, and reaching higher than the backs of their sizeable draft horses.

While the majestic spectacle of the unbroken tallgrass prairie is surely inspiring fodder for the literary imagination, of more import is the tallgrass prairie's ability to accumulate and enrich soil unlike any other ecosystem in the world. The tallgrass prairie comprises primarily

5

perennial plants that devote much of their energy to root production. The surface area of a single rye plant's primary roots, for example, is approximately twenty-five hundred square feet; its 14 billion root hairs add another four thousand square feet. Compared to its total above-ground surface area, the rye plant's network of roots is 130 times larger![2] The remarkably robust and widespread root structure of the tallgrass prairie's plants continually adds nutrient-rich organic matter to the soil as roots are dispersed, eventually die and decay, and thereby provide food for other plants. The dense mat of sod characteristic of the tallgrass prairie also minimizes erosion by holding and keeping soil in place during wind and rainstorms. In consequence, the tallgrass prairie continually accumulates an essential ingredient for its ongoing flourishing: fertile topsoil.

The tallgrass prairie's fecundity, however, is attributable not only to its plants; its complex web of interdependencies with animals and natural occurrences also contributed to its ability to attain the requisite conditions that maximize survivability. Buffalo, which roamed the tallgrass prairie in almost unimaginable numbers before the arrival of Euro-Americans, provided two beneficial services. Their manure provided a valuable source of organic matter that enriched the soil and fostered plant growth. Grazing also stimulated plant growth by inducing the production of lateral shoots that branched outward, then upward, to form new plants. In both instances, the activity of buffalo increased the tallgrass prairie's total biomass, which was eventually returned to the soil as precious organic matter.[3]

Fire, too, played a crucial role in the tallgrass prairie's life. While humans typically regard naturally occurring fires as nothing more than destroyers of valuable natural resources, fires help ensure the long-term health of the tallgrass prairie. The most immediate physical effect of fire is the elimination of standing dead material and litter that has accumulated above ground since the previous fire, which provides more space for plants, especially seedlings, to capture sunlight and grow. Fire also functions similarly to microbial decomposers by releasing nutrients trapped in dead plant matter into the soil, which then contribute to the growth of new plants. Absent dead stems and leaves that trap rainfall and prevent it from entering plants through their root systems, the amount of water available to the tallgrass prairie increases after a fire, and along with it the nutrients, especially nitrogen, it needs. Most important, these functions of fire increase the tallgrass prairie's biomass enormously; compared to prairies that never experience fire, the plant production of prairies that are burned every other year can be up to 75 percent greater.[4] This increase in biomass eventually translates into more topsoil accumulating on the tallgrass prairie.

Any discussion of the tallgrass prairie would be exceedingly deficient without mention of those tiny, often inconspicuous creatures, the daily activities of which contribute vitally to the prairie's health. While certainly not as awe inspiring as a fire consuming large chunks of tallgrass prairie, or as grandiose as a large herd of buffalo meandering and grazing, these creatures provide unique and indispensable services. Gophers and ground squirrels dig tunnels through the prairie's thick network of roots, aerating the soil and chopping plant matter into small pieces that are more easily decomposed.[5] Earthworms, reaching astonishing densities of up to 5 million per acre on the tallgrass prairie, ingest soil and expel excreta that "serve as nutritional hotspots for microbes" and stimulate plant growth.[6] Bacteria and fungi, which represent the final stages of the process of decomposition, break down organic matter further and fix and create nutrients beneficial to the tallgrass prairie's numerous plants.

This cursory presentation, of course, only scratches the surface of the tallgrass prairie's manifold relationships, processes, dependencies, cycles, animals and insects, geological events, climatic and hydrological patterns, nutrient recycling activities, and natural occurrences too numerous to catalogue. The point of this brief snippet of natural history, however, is to underscore the fact that the complex phenomenon of the tallgrass prairie has provided Americans with some of the best agricultural land in the world. The cumulative effect of the tallgrass prairie has been to create a thick layer of soil stretching westward from

Indiana, through Illinois, Iowa, southern Minnesota and Wisconsin, northern Missouri, and the eastern parts of North and South Dakota, Nebraska, and Kansas. Commonly called the "Corn Belt," this large swath of the American heartland is renowned worldwide for its topsoil: deep, rich in minerals and nutrients, chock full of organic matter, porous, with the granular structure necessary to support a broad array of plant life — this topsoil is a near-perfect environment for a thriving grain production system. The possibility offered by the tallgrass prairie has been realized by Corn Belt farmers: Iowa farmers alone produce about 12 percent of the world's supply of corn, and a slightly lower percentage of the world's supply of soybeans.

Describing the benefits conferred by glaciers, buffalo, fires, earthworms, rodents, grasses, and the hundreds of other important components of the tallgrass prairie as a "blessing" seems almost too tame to capture the enormity of the gift of good land.[7] While some countries struggle mightily to feed their citizens because of soil ill-suited for crop production, Corn Belt farmers consistently produce abundant harvests that stretch our national storage capacity to the limit every fall. In fact, overproduction of grain in the Corn Belt has bedeviled policy makers and legislators for well-nigh half a century. The somewhat sterile words "production" and "harvest," however, should not disguise the most pertinent aspect of this blessing: because of the Corn Belt's fertile soil, Americans (and others) are able to fill their bellies with food. Not only does the fecundity of the American heartland militate against hunger, starvation, and the many deleterious effects of malnutrition — bloated stomachs, emaciated bodies, depressed immune systems, headaches, dizziness, lethargy, and diseases — but it also helps provide Americans with a sufficient daily supply of energy and nutrition that enable us in turn to pursue a wide array of social, political, economic, cultural, familial, and personal goods.

The blessing enjoyed by contemporary Americans as a result of scores of natural forces and processes occurring over millions of years and culminating in a parcel of land second to none in its grain-producing ability raises an intriguing theological question: How should

Christians respond to this gift? One reason for this question's piquancy stems from the fact that the gift of good land confronts us with God's creative power that is both awe-inspiring and majestic. Faced with the grandeur, perhaps even incomprehensibility, of God's activity that began with the "Big Bang" and culminated 15 billion years later in abundant, fertile topsoil, we are appropriately awestruck and stupefied. Confronted similarly with the spectacular reality of God's creative activity, Job found it best to remain silent — a silence that betokened wonder, amazement, and humility (Job 40:3–5). While Job's response is understandable, even laudable, the gift of good land should be met with a different response: gratitude. A Christian agricultural ethic needs to be motivated and given content by gratitude for God's benevolent activity to be theologically and morally sufficient. Before making good on this assertion, however, a few words about the nature of gratitude are in order.

Gratitude

Many Christian ethicists regard gratitude as one of the basic, enduring sensibilities that should characterize Christian existence and our lifelong response to God. James Gustafson, a noted American theologian, claims that "Gratitude to God is a fundamental reason for being moral in Judaism and Christianity."[8] Brian Childs speaks in similar glowing terms about the religious importance of gratitude: "gratitude, as the truly appropriate and comprehensive response to God's grace in Jesus Christ, is the fundamental orientation for Christian life, the basic motive and perspective for all true worship and faithful living."[9] Others have opined that gratitude is the foundational Christian attitude with which our lives should be imbued,[10] "the pivotal virtue of the moral life,"[11] and that the entirety of Christian ethics should be characterized as a response of thanksgiving and gratitude to God.[12]

Gratitude's pride of place in Christian ethics, as some of these accolades suggest, stems from the belief that God has gifted us in myriad ways. If gratitude is the appropriate reaction to the benevolent conferral of some benefit, and if many of these benefits or gifts stem either proximately or remotely from God, either by God causing or being the condition for the gift to exist or by God actually delivering the gift immediately and directly (such as grace), then it is fitting to be grateful to God for these benefits. Understood in this manner, it is clear why gratitude is so foundational to the moral-theological enterprise: our lives are replete with God's gifts. Indeed, in some branches of popular piety and academic theology, it has been thought that since literally everything originates in God and comes from God, and thus is considered a divine gift, then we should be grateful for everything. This theological conviction underlies St. Paul's exhortation to give thanks for all that exists and happens, "always and everywhere."[13] This undifferentiated tendency to regard everything as a gift simply because it ultimately originates in God is seriously mistaken, however, since many aspects of God's creation are not beneficial to us, which is a necessary prerequisite for classifying something as a gift.[14] As James Gustafson points out forcefully, one aspect of our lives with which we have to contend — the natural world — is sometimes inimical to our existence and welfare:

> [A]spects of the natural world also threaten human interests. Carcinogenic cells, germs, viruses, and other causes of diseases and death are natural. Earthquakes, typhoons, droughts, and floods are natural.... We properly fear certain features of the natural world; it is not always a "friend" which serves our interests. Its threats provoke awe and respect; its destructive as well as sustaining powers bear down on us. We are a part of the natural world; it brings us into life and sustains life; it also creates suffering and pain and death.[15]

Especially if human agency is understood as being created and supported in existence by God, and thus causally linked to God's activity, then added to the ambiguity and sometimes hostility of the natural world is the vast realm of evil human actions that have added, sometimes substantially, to the amount of suffering, pain, and death humans have inflicted upon one another. But this point needs to be belabored no longer. Not all of creation is rightly conceived as a gift to us, even though it originates in God, but this does not undermine my contention that God has bestowed innumerable gifts upon us, gifts that are cherished and meaningful, which make life worth living.

This point is well illustrated by many aspects of our lives that are commonly regarded as enriching and enlivening. Whether Christian or not, people almost universally value loving parents and siblings; opportunities for leisure and recreation; a supportive network of friends; neighbors, coworkers, and other members of the community who are kind, truthful, and willing to work for the common good; clean air to breathe and water to drink; a stable political order; physical and psychological health; opportunities to perfect one's individual talents; and a host of others. From a specifically Christian context, however, the layers of meaning accumulate even more. Even the most cursory examination of events or beliefs integral to the Christian self-identity reveals many aspects around which we order our lives and give thanks through prayer and worship: the incarnation, through which the God-man, Jesus, enters the world, redeems the universe, and reveals in the clearest way possible the nature of God; justification, whereby our sins are remitted and we are made right with God; forgiveness, whereby God graciously and lovingly accepts our repentance; and grace, through which God encourages, directs, gives strength, comforts, clarifies, and sometimes reproves for our own good, among others.

The fact remains, however, that the opportunity to enjoy these gifts depends upon our ability to secure sufficient sustenance to continue living, which is further contingent on the health and fertility of our agricultural system and its ability to produce a necessary ingredient for life, food. In this sense, good agricultural land not only is the necessary precondition for the enjoyment of a wide array of human goods, but it is one of the most basic, foundational, and important gifts we can be given. While Christians commonly associate the phrase "original blessing" with the idyllic conditions and sinless state of humans in the

Garden of Eden, this phrase is equally applicable to the gift of good land, albeit in a different way, since it makes possible physical life and everything to which we aspire.

This is precisely why it is so fitting to situate the gift of good agricultural land within the context of an ethic of gratitude. While our lives are replete with God's gifts, not all these gifts are equally important, nor should our feelings of thankfulness or expressions of gratitude be the same for all the benefits God confers on us. Things that fulfill trivial desires like the innumerable gadgets and trinkets that adorn our desks, cabinets, countertops, and walls might accurately be classified as gifts for which thanks should be given, but they surely pale in comparison to the gift of good land. Rarely does anyone pause, reflect, and say a prayer of thanksgiving for the opportunity to enjoy a new stapler or kitchen knife; yet Christians worldwide on a daily basis routinely stop before meals, offer a sincere "thanks" to God for the food provided, and acknowledge their dependence on God's creative power that sustains and nourishes. This common, longstanding, ritualized, and emotionally laden practice of saying "grace" before meals, moreover, speaks volumes about the importance of food, and by extension, of the good land from which it comes.

For these reasons, good land and the food it provides are subjects that almost yearn for an ethic of gratitude. How, then, does a theological ethic of gratitude help us understand God's gift of good land and the appropriate moral response to it? Let me answer this question by breaking down the phenomenon of gratitude into two broad categories that represent conceptually distinct moments, namely, gift giving and the recipient's response, and specifying what each component entails.

The Benefactor: The Act of Gift Giving

Gratitude, generally speaking, is a person's appropriate attitudinal response to a gift, or some unearned benefit.[16] The movement toward gratitude begins with a benevolent action that attempts to bestow some benefit, or something valuable, on another. While in the vast majority of cases a benevolent action will result practically in some tangible benefit accruing to someone, the word "attempts" in the preceding sentence is important, since it signifies that the action need not culminate in an actual benefit being delivered. A firefighter's vain effort to pull a child from a burning building, a lifeguard's inability to locate a drowning person underwater, and a physician's failure to save a shooting victim all fall short of delivering the intended benefit: saving someone's life. In many other ways the objectives of benevolent actions can be thwarted, resulting in no actual, direct benefit being delivered to anyone.[17] This, however, does not undermine the feeling of gratefulness that those near and dear to the deceased almost assuredly would (and should) have toward those who strove to save their beloved, which shows that gratitude is primarily a response to benevolence.[18]

As the preceding examples illustrate, gratitude need not be confined to benevolence directed at oneself.[19] Ethicists commonly use the phrase "special relations" to designate relationships characterized by a high degree of emotional attachment, loyalty, and personal satisfaction for all parties involved. While most frequently used in reference to familial relations, the phrase could also legitimately be extended to include intimate friendships. An undeniable fact about human beings is that we forge close, long-lasting bonds with a select group of people toward whom we direct a disproportionate amount of attention, care, and concern. Our lives become intertwined on multiple levels; we wish them well, pray for them, try to nurture them, and often make sacrifices — sometimes small, sometimes momentous and painful — to enhance their well-being. Through these special relations we become linked to, and more important share in and are affected by, the successes or failures of those to whom we are attached. This melding of lives and emotional bonding create a unity through which benevolent acts directed toward those with whom we share special relations elicit gratitude, just as if the acts were directed toward oneself. Probably the paradigm case for this phenomenon is the parent-child relationship, where parents experience rather intense feelings of gratitude toward those who enrich their children's lives, such as friends, teachers, neighbors, grandparents, etc.[20]

To elicit gratitude from the recipient, a benevolent act must also be performed freely and intentionally. A bevy of factors — ranging from force to coercion, to fear, to compulsions, to delusions — undermine, and sometimes completely extinguish, the voluntariness of the action. I should not be grateful, for example, when a person gives me something valuable because a gun is held to his or her head. While the gift might be beneficial, it certainly lacks the benevolence necessary to evoke gratitude.[21] The criterion that a benevolent act be performed intentionally precludes mistaken or accidental benefits being sufficient to evoke gratitude. It is important to note that intentionality is a supple and varied phenomenon that goes far beyond the typical case of one benefactor benefiting a single recipient. A benefactor can intend a gift to benefit one individual, small or large groups of people, people the benefactor has never met (or never will meet), or unborn generations of people, and the gift can be given all at once, incrementally over a period of time, or sometime in the future.

Another necessary characteristic of the benevolent action is the relative absence of self-serving motives.[22] In other words, the gift must be given primarily to benefit the recipient.[23] I say "primarily" because human motivation is complex, and an action might be motivated by a number of considerations.[24] Psychologists have long documented the reality of multiple layers of consciousness, each of which might subtly influence actions on different levels of awareness. Common human experience frequently confirms this point, especially when sufficient knowledge about a person is possessed to be able to detect a discrepancy between the stated and actual motive for an action. Who has not encountered someone who feigns a benevolent motive, while it is apparent to knowledgeable bystanders that this is nothing more than a convenient rationalization? A full-blown discussion of motivation would be lengthy and complicated, and I am unsure whether articulating criteria to determine whether a motivation is properly considered primary, secondary, tertiary, etc., would be helpful for our purposes. The only point I wish to make is that a certain purity of motive is necessary to warrant gratitude, even though in practice it might be exceedingly difficult to separate self-regarding from other-regarding motives (even for the benefactor).

One notable exception to the criterion that an action must be relatively free of self-interested motives occurs when the benefactor makes some substantial sacrifice or puts himself or herself at considerable risk in offering a benefit, or when the gift is enormously beneficial to the recipient, even when self-interest is the primary impetus for acting.[25] In these instances, the motive does not disqualify an action from warranting gratitude. The importance of pure other-regarding motives decreases, sometimes to the point of being irrelevant, when basic human needs are at stake. The phrase "basic human needs" indicates something essential for human flourishing, without which humans either cannot survive or would consider life intolerable if the needs went unmet. These can range from the need for adequate nutrition and hydration to shelter from the elements, to a lack of violence, to a minimal degree of contact with other human beings. Gift giving involving the satisfaction of basic needs, I think, can involve a considerable amount of self-interested motives and still warrant gratitude. Consider being pulled from a burning car by someone trying only to impress passersby. While the benefactor's motive is clearly self-interested, I suspect gratitude would be the almost universal response, even if the recipient were well aware of the benefactor's motive. In situations involving the satisfaction of basic needs, recipients simply do not care whether the benefactor acted out of self-interest or not; they are glad to have their basic need fulfilled, and feelings of gratitude are readily forthcoming regardless of the degree of self-interest that motivated the action.

The benefactor's action must also possess the following two features: it cannot be performed to fulfill a preexisting obligation, and it must be unearned and undeserved by the recipient. A preexisting obligation means that the recipient has a legitimate legal, moral, or some other type of claim upon the valuable object, and thus the object is due to the recipient. Fulfilling one's part of a contractual agreement, for example, should not evoke gratitude in the recipient, since the valuable object was owed to the recipient. The purpose of contracts is to promote the interests of each respective party, not to help another,[26] and thus the benevolence required to elicit gratitude is absent.[27] The same line of reasoning underlies the second criterion. Gratitude directed at an employer for paying a person an agreed-upon weekly wage is out of place, since the worker earned the money and is entitled to the paycheck. The example also involves a lack of benevolence, insofar as the paycheck was not, and would not have been, given absent the worker's input of time, energy, and effort.

Before moving on to discuss the recipient's response to a gift, it is important to note the rich moral dynamics accompanying the act of gift giving. A benefactor's benevolent act is not only the conferral of a benefit; implicit in the act of gift giving is an affirmation of the recipient's worth and his or her status as an object of care, concern, and sometimes affection. The psychological effects of this affirmation can be quite momentous. Jean Valjean, the destitute, wretched, callous criminal in Victor Hugo's *Les Misérables*, for instance, undergoes a dramatic moral conversion as a result of Bishop Bienvenu's gift of silver utensils and candlesticks. Describing the gift's effect on Jean Valjean, Hugo writes, the bishop "filled the whole soul of this miserable man [Valjean] with a magnificent radiance."[28] Confronted with such generosity, Valjean vows to treat others similarly and becomes a benevolent force enriching the lives of others throughout the remainder of the novel.

The affirmation implicit in a gift, however, need not only engender once-in-a-lifetime existential moments to possess considerable moral value. The type of social fabric necessary for human flourishing, which includes trust, cooperation, respect, and fidelity, is fostered by benevolent acts. In the familial sphere, gifts solidify existing relationships by deepening levels of intimacy, expressing enjoyment, and celebrating existing bonds. Gifts also frequently function as invitations to friendship, which are forged, grow, and blossom into nurturing, caring relationships that benefit all parties involved.[29] Even in the context of mild acquaintances or complete strangers, however, benevolent acts serve to stimulate reciprocity and to create a climate of goodwill that is contagious and beneficial on a broad scale. Probably everyone has been in the situation of needing assistance desperately, being helped by a passerby, and subsequently feeling moved to help others in need. On a mundane, daily level, gift giving functions as social cement that brings people together, creates an attitude of thankfulness, and fosters harmonious relationships in all aspects of life.

The Recipient: Proper Reception of a Gift

The first moment of gratitude is thankfulness for the offer of a gift. While initial reactions to a gift given might range from pleasant surprise to borderline shock, these eventually give way to a sense of appreciation that someone has extended the offer of a gift. Gratitude, in other words, begins as a positive emotional response. Commentators have noted that this attitudinal component of gratitude raises a conceptual difficulty, because many recipients fail to recognize the gift's value, and thus they do not immediately appreciate the gift and experience the appropriate positive feelings.[30] Alcoholics in denial, rebellious adolescents, and the perpetually cantankerous, for instance, are likely to meet an act of gift giving with indifference, mild annoyance, or perhaps even anger. Indeed, in retrospect most people can regretfully recall instances of being offered gifts, sometimes highly valuable gifts that required considerable sacrifices from the benefactors, which went unappreciated and unacknowledged. While subjective impediments sometimes stifle the attitudinal response appropriate to a gift that fulfills the aforementioned criteria, this should in no way undermine the normative assertion that gratitude requires an emotional, appreciative reaction to the gift.[31]

A positive attitudinal response to the gift need not imply that the gift must be accepted, however. Nor should the act of rejecting a gift necessarily imply anything negative about the benefactor or the recipient. Of course, a recipient might question the benefactor's reasons for offering the gift and whether they were motivated by self-aggrandizement, a desire to make the recipient indebted, malice, or some other unsavory reason. But even absent any suspicions about the benefactor's motives, there might be legitimate reasons to refuse the offer. Contrary to the benefactor's belief, the gift might not actually be beneficial to the recipient. Gift giving intended to begin or deepen a friendship might also be rejected if the recipient does not desire a new or more intimate friendship. Certain stipulations articulated by the benefactor regulating the use of the gift might be unpalatable to the recipient. Perhaps the recipient is in no position to return the favor, and thus would feel guilty about the unrequited benevolence. For these and many other reasons, gifts can — and sometimes should — be rejected without reflecting poorly on the benefactor or recipient. This does not negate, however, the proper thankful attitude toward the benefactor for offering the gift.

Upon accepting the gift, the recipient is obligated "to provide the benefactor willingly with a commensurate benefit if the proper occasion for doing so arises"[32] and to use the gift gratefully.[33] The language of obligation, it has been noted, seems misplaced in the sphere of gift giving in which benefactors are under no obligation to offer gifts or to give specific gifts, feelings of gratitude arise spontaneously and freely, and the recipient is likewise under no obligation to accept gifts. As Paul Camenisch writes, "Talk of obligation and duty obscures the fact that gift, at least ideally, is a freer, more open, less constraining and more personally involving relation than are contractual or other kinds of explicit, precisely defined, and narrowly limited obligations."[34] Camenisch adds that while the sphere of gift giving is mostly characterized by nonobligatory components, it would be erroneous to evacuate any sense of obligation from the act of accepting gifts:[35]

If there are no strings attached to gifts, why have so many of us wanted to decline gifts from persons with whom we wished to have no further relations? Was it not precisely because we perceived that, in accepting the gift, we were consenting to such relations in a morally significant way? And if there are no obligations attached to gifts and their acceptance, why is ingratitude so universally and so vehemently condemned as a moral failure or defect?[36]

Camenisch and others are correct that while the concepts of deontological ethical theory such as "duty," "ought," and "obligation" have very limited applicability when applied to gifts and gratitude, there is no denying that being benefited by a gift requires something in turn from the recipient. In most cases, this desire to requite is a natural reaction to benevolence, and thus there is little need to invoke the language of obligation to elicit an appropriate response. But even absent this typical reaction, it is quite reasonable — and common in everyday life — to express moral disapproval, even condemnation, toward someone who accepts a gift without acknowledging some kind of debt to the benefactor.[37]

The recipient's obligation to return a commensurate benefit to the benefactor if the right opportunity arises allows for, and almost seems to require, a great deal of creativity and originality. The adjective "commensurate" is not intended to foster a calculative, balance-sheet mentality that seeks to return a gift of exactly the same value.[38] Its purpose is to correct both excesses and deficiencies in acts of requital and to counteract the narcissistic tendency to shirk one's obligation to requite a benefit conferred, especially when the gift caused considerable sacrifice on the benefactor's part, and thus would require something substantial from the recipient. Just as it would be out of place to give someone a new car for the favor of an opened door, so too would it be disproportionate to give a benefactor a cheap box of chocolates for rescuing the recipient from a burning building. Moreover, the appropriateness of the gift depends on the benefactor's needs,[39] which means that every act of requital will hinge upon a number of subjective factors that make each person different and make each gift different in the benefit it confers on the benefactor. The practical upshot is that the recipient's obligation can be fulfilled in myriad ways, ranging from an acknowledgment of the gift's value or a simple "thank you," to something that might take the remainder of one's life to complete.

The last component of the recipient's response, namely, proper use of the gift, is determined by two factors: the nature of the gift and the benefactor's intention for the gift's use.[40] The religious, social, and cultural web of meaning attached to most gifts specifies, in greater or lesser detail, appropriate uses of a gift, which both prohibit and mandate using the gift in certain ways. Some gifts might lend to only one or maybe two proper uses. Other gifts, however, because of the variable conventions regulating their use, can be used in a variety of ways. In some instances, as commentators have shown, identifying an appropriate use, or even a range of appropriate uses, is bedeviling at best, and virtually impossible at worst.[41] The ambiguity and considerable flexibility sometimes surrounding the use of gifts, however, is no reason to doubt the contention that gifts are embedded in a network of meaning that often conveys normative direction for persons using the gifts.

How the benefactor intended the gift to be used is also relevant in determining proper use.[42] Explicit written or verbal declarations provide the clearest expression of intentionality, and many gifts, especially highly valuable ones, are frequently given with precise stipulations or conditions regulating their use. In the absence of unambiguous declarations, it is often possible to infer the benefactor's intention by examining the way he or she treats similar things, the moral values espoused by the benefactor, his or her general lifestyle and the goods he or she pursues frequently, or particular actions the benefactor regrets or frowns upon, to mention but a few.[43] Although inferences often have limited applicability in situations involving gifts between strangers due to the paucity of information about the benefactor and the necessity of making assumptions about human beings in general to determine the benefactor's likely intention for using the gift, inferences can be highly reliable and valuable in the context of family, friends, coworkers, colleagues, and others with whom one has considerable familiarity.

To summarize the argument thus far, gratitude is the appropriate response to a benefactor when the following conditions are met:

1. The gift was given intentionally.

2. The gift was given freely.

3. The gift was given primarily to benefit the recipient, although self-interested motives do not disqualify an action from warranting a grateful response if basic needs are fulfilled.

4. The gift was given to oneself or to someone with whom one shares a special relationship.

5. The benefactor was under no obligation to give the gift.

6. The recipient did not earn or deserve the gift.

A grateful response to the benefactor, in turn, requires the following elements:

7. A positive emotional response of thankfulness for and appreciation of the offer of the gift.

8. If the gift is accepted, a willingness to return a gift of comparable value, that meets the benefactor's needs, if the proper occasion arises.

9. Grateful use of the gift, which depends on either the gift's nature or the benefactor's intention for using the gift.

As I show below, God's gift of good land fulfills conditions 1 through 6, and therefore the appropriate response to the gift is specified in conditions 7 through 9. Let me examine each condition in turn and show exactly how the gift of good land fulfills each one as well as the normative moral conclusions consistent with each respective condition.

God's Gift of Good Land

Condition 1 states that God must have intended to give good land, or the Corn Belt, to us. Christian theologians are quick to assert that an adequate theology of the land must recognize that even if it can be substantiated that God intended to give us good land to use, we never "own" that land, as many contemporary theories of private property assume. God alone is the perpetual owner of all land because God is exclusively responsible for calling creation into being.[44] While humans might possess the ingenuity to reconfigure, manipulate, and enhance the land for human benefit, this is a far cry from actually making the land by willing creation into existence, a feat accomplished by God alone.[45] This conviction underlies biblical passages that forcefully assign the right of ultimate possession and disposal only to God.[46] Thus, God's intention to give good land to anyone must be understood only as the charge to tend a portion of the earth, similar to a tenant being allowed to use a particular piece of property as long as the owner's wishes for the property are observed.[47]

This being said, the conviction that God has given us good land to provide sustenance for ourselves is strongly represented in biblical theology,[48] official Christian church statements,[49] and the writings of notable theologians on agriculture and land use.[50] The main line of reasoning supporting this conviction is that the primary purpose of creation is to secure everyone's needs, especially "basic needs." Commonly called the universal destination of creation's goods, this claim is grounded in the belief that God desires every person's needs to be fulfilled and allows us to use creation's bounty to provide the requisite material goods. As stated by the National Catholic Rural Life Conference, "The universal destination of goods is clear: all of us, each person in the world, is meant to receive enough to eat and drink, enough to clothe and house themselves, and enough to live in dignity."[51] Thus by working the land and providing sufficient nourishment for every person, one of the main objectives of creation is fulfilled.

The universal destination of creation's goods is linked to the fulfillment of "needs," not "desires." This terminological distinction is based on the fact that certain goods are more pivotal to human fulfillment than others. As I explained earlier, some goods are necessary for the maintenance of life itself, such as food, water, and shelter from the elements; others such as psychological health are highly desirable, although not necessary to live; and other goods, while desirable, are more peripheral to a life well lived. Quite clearly, not all goods are equally central to human well-being, and the order of importance dictates how creation's goods are to be appropriated: everyone's "basic" needs are to be satisfied first, since these are necessary for the enjoyment of all other human goods, and only after these needs are fulfilled can creation's goods be directed toward the satisfaction of less pressing interests.

Given the fact that food is a foundational human good upon which access to all other goods depends, it is reasonable to endorse a robust protectionist attitude toward good land and the agricultural system dependent on it, which might not be considered applicable to other industries. It is one thing for humans to do without many modern conveniences commonly considered to be goods, such as airplane travel, microwave ovens, televisions, and electric shavers; it is another thing entirely to envision shortages of food and the untold suffering it would cause, especially on the poor. The goal of this protectionist posture would generally attempt to insulate agriculture from various vicissitudes that have the potential to disrupt, undermine, or inhibit the health of our agricultural system and it would prefer policies making agriculture more adaptable, less dependent on undependable inputs, more forgiving of human folly and error, and less likely to be affected by circumstances beyond our control. While it might be disputable which policy or practice best insulates agriculture from certain vicissitudes, it is beyond doubt that an agricultural system capable of functioning uninterruptedly through adverse political, natural, economic, or other circumstances is best able to supply the goods necessary to satisfy the basic human good of food.

Lest this protectionist attitude seem unduly conservative or alarmist, let us remember that civilizations once considered advanced, technologically sophisticated, politically strong, and economically dominant — just like the United States is considered today — have crumbled and disappeared due to the fragility of their agricultural systems. Sometimes this disintegration was incremental and gradual; other times it was sudden and calamitous. Whatever the case, the common factor underlying the collapse of agricultural systems is some type of structural flaw, usually resulting from lack of human foresight, which was eventually exposed and proved to be insuperable.[52]

While the universal destination of creation's goods and the derivative theological mandate to till the earth to satisfy basic needs are highly persuasive ideas, it is important to temper the robust anthropocentrism often assumed in both. For instance, Pope John Paul II writes, "The land is God's gift entrusted to *people* from the very beginning. It is God's gift, given by a loving creator as a means of sustaining the life which He had created."[53] Nor is the pope's anthropocentrism an isolated aberration; for several decades theologians have debated at length whether and in what ways God gives preference to humans over the rest of creation, especially animals.[54] While it is impossible to recount this debate in any detail, let me outline why it is necessary to affirm that creation, and thus good land, is not intended to provide sustenance for humans alone, but for other creatures as well.

Creation exists for God, to serve God's purposes and to make possible the unfolding and final realization of God's plan for all that exists. Our calling as Christians is to help realize these purposes as far as humanly possible, either by cooperating with God's attempts to bring these purposes to fruition or by not resisting them, actively or passively. Without question, these purposes and this plan include humans insofar as God values our existence and unique attributes and also our ability to cooperate with God to bring God's project to fruition. Moreover, God frequently acts to secure human welfare, both by providing daily necessities and by acting momentously in history to liberate, save, instruct, befriend, heal, suffer, and die for our benefit. Thus humans are not only objects of divine delight, love, compassion, care, and concern, but we are frequently the object of God's benevolent action.

Other creatures, however, are also objects of divine affection and action. God creates sea monsters apparently for play or delight;[55] God revels in the splendor and power of Behemoth and Leviathan;[56] God establishes a covenant with "every living creature," a promise repeated five other times;[57] lowly animals such as sparrows are not forgotten by God;[58] God's shalom, or the eventual state of universal peace, extends to the animal kingdom where wolf and lamb, leopard and goat, and lion and calf will live and rest together;[59] the saving power of Christ's suffering, death, and resurrection extends to "all things, whether on earth or in heaven," and not only to humankind;[60] and as one commentator notes about the Priestly author's account of creation in Genesis 1, "all the communities of created beings, from the creeping things to the stars, are created and continue to be created because the Creator wishes to bring these creatures into being and to fulfillment. Hence the cadence: 'and God saw that it was good.' "[61]

These considerations indicate that God's affection, care, and salvific activity extend beyond the human realm and that God's purposes and benevolent activity are not aimed at human welfare alone. To be sure, the evidence is incontrovertible that humans figure prominently in the unfolding of God's purposes for creation; it is also clear that God desires and acts to secure human flourishing in many instances. But it is mistaken to assume that God's purposes and human welfare always coincide, or when human welfare and the welfare of nonhuman creation truly conflict that God will always desire the former to be realized. As James Gustafson asserts, "If one's basic theological perception is of a Deity who rules all of creation,... then the good that God values must be more inclusive than one's normal perceptions of what is good for me, what is good for my community, and even what is good for the human species."[62]

For these reasons, it is vital to underscore the adjective "universal" in the phrase "universal destination of creation's goods." Creation is a banquet to which all beings are invited, and access is granted by God to all those creatures, large or small, simple or complex, common or rare, that serve divine purposes in bringing creation to fruition. In a very practical sense, this means that good land, the Corn Belt, is not a gift given exclusively to humans. As a part of creation that serves God's purposes above and beyond contributing to human welfare, the Corn Belt is also intended to nourish and sustain the lives of nonhuman creatures so that they, too, can play their respective parts in God's plan for creation.

This theological understanding of good land supports several moral considerations. First, it sharply curtails the pervasive tendency to regard fertile farmland as nothing more than a repository of resources to produce food for humans. Whether implicit or explicit, this belief, which often gets translated as a moral imperative to bring as much land as possible into cultivation, has permeated the agricultural sector since our country's inception. As a result, we have drained wetlands, plowed under the native prairie, cleared woodlands, diverted waterways, and done everything possible to bring almost every tillable acre of fertile land into production. In fact, at one time farmers were exhorted by the Secretary of the United States Department of Agriculture to farm "fencerow to fencerow," meaning that no strip of arable ground should be left untouched.[63] The only portions of the Corn Belt spared from our appetite for bringing land into agricultural production are those too infertile, steep, rocky, sandy, or wet to farm.

Of course, this state of affairs might be morally unproblematic if the type of agricultural production predominant in the Corn Belt were conducive to creating beneficial habitats for a wide range of nonhuman creatures. But, as currently practiced, the only nonhumans to benefit from agricultural production in the Corn Belt are a few opportunistic species (the ring-necked pheasant, white-tailed deer, and certain bug species come readily to mind) that thrive on large-scale grain production. In fact, from the perspective of the vast majority of nonhuman creatures, agriculture as currently practiced is one of the most destructive forces ever to appear on our planet. Wes Jackson, for instance, writes, "So destructive has the agricultural revolution been that, geologically speaking, it surely stands as the most significant and explosive event to appear on the face of the earth."[64] The monocultures of corn and soybeans characteristic of contemporary Corn Belt farming have destroyed millions of acres of native tallgrass prairie, the home to an almost unimaginable array of creatures, and replaced them with simplified, homogeneous, and impoverished ecosystems that support only a minute fraction of nonhuman life compared to the native prairie. To honor the theological conviction, then, that creation is a banquet intended for all, human and nonhuman, it behooves us not only to reject the "garden mentality" that considers untilled land to be unproductive or wasteful, but also to embrace the moral mandate to develop an agricultural system that sets more chairs at creation's table by providing more habitats conducive to the thriving of nonhuman creatures.

Another important dimension of the universal destination of creation's goods is its transtemporal character. The goods of creation are intended to succor everyone, past, present, and future, from the Native Americans who occupied the region now called the Corn Belt before the arrival of the Europeans, to the early pioneers who first plowed under the native prairie, to the contemporary American, to those who will be birthed, live, and die far into the future. Good land was neither created for nor given only to one generation to use; good land is a common gift intended to enrich the lives of anyone who happens to exist now or will exist in the future.[65]

This position accords well with other foundational Christian beliefs. God's love is commonly thought to be universal in scope, embracing everyone at all times. Other divine gifts, motivated by love and the derivative desire to bring us into intimate communion with God — the incarnation, redemption, salvation, the resurrection, grace — are understood to be directed toward everyone. God simply does not discriminate against any individuals or groups of people when distributing these gifts, and God intends the effects of these gifts to be experienced and embraced by everyone. To assert that the gift of good land, then, was intended to benefit everyone is simply to acknowledge the foundational Christian conviction that God's love, and the gifts flowing from this love, are universal in scope, excluding no one. Understood in this context, it becomes imperative to construct a sustainable agricultural system that can fulfill the nutritional needs of future generations, since the gift of good land was intended for them, too. (More on sustainability later in this chapter.)

Returning to the conditions necessary to elicit gratitude, let me discuss conditions 2, 5, and 6 together, all of which concern whether God's gift of good land was given freely or whether God was obligated to give it because we earned or deserve the gift. Christian theologians of all stripes have long maintained the freedom of God.[66] Karl Barth, for instance, perhaps the most uncompromising proponent of divine freedom, maintained that God is supremely free, unconditioned by any extrinsic condition or compulsion:[67]

> God is unlimited, unrestricted and unconditioned from without.
> He is the free Creator, the free Reconciler, the free Redeemer.
> ... His divinity is not exhausted in the fact that in His revelation
> it consists throughout in this freedom from external compulsion:
> in free utterance and action, free beginning and ending, free
> judgment and blessing, free power and spirit.[68]

For Barth, then, every divine decision and action is properly considered free, whether intelligible to humans or not, because God is not compelled to do anything.

Catholic theologians, generally speaking, have been harder pressed on the issue of divine freedom because they maintain that God is limited by the divine nature, which functions as "a stable principle of action and preceding and limiting" God's decisions and actions.[69] In other words, if God is loving by nature, meaning that God has no choice but to be loving, then it not only follows that God will never do anything unloving, but God is also determined to act lovingly. An analogy with human behavior, however, will show why having a particular nature and being conditioned by that nature does not preclude free choice.

It is something of a truism in Christian ethics that humans are social by nature. We have a natural inclination to seek social intercourse with others, which becomes manifest in a wide variety of behaviors: forming a family; fostering intimate, long-lasting friendships; and establishing harmonious relations with coworkers, neighbors, and casual acquaintances are among the more obvious illustrations. Yet even though we are naturally programmed, so to speak, to seek out the company of others, we are still capable of rejecting social interaction and living a solitary life in which contact with other humans occurs only accidentally. Of course, such a life would be extremely distasteful. But the point is that having a nature and being conditioned to seek certain goods does not cross over into the sphere of coercion or force, which would obviate the ability to act otherwise. Possessing a nature does not compel us to act in specific ways and eliminate the capacity for free choice; it only creates a strong predisposition that can, ultimately, be resisted if one so chooses. In an analogous way, God's nature, while creating constancy and predictability in God's actions, does not determine God in the sense that God must act in specific ways. Thus, in the context of giving the gift of good land (and also in the case of all God's other gifts to us), it is correctly maintained that God acted freely.

Conditions 5 and 6 focus on the issue of desert in the form of God having a preexistent obligation to give good land to us or that we somehow earned good land. Any talk of entitlement or desert in relationship to God grates on our educated Christian sensibilities, and for good reasons. When considering some of the central categories of Christian theology that have fired the Christian theological imagination for millennia — revelation, justification, salvation, the incarnation, grace — there is virtual unanimity that neither our status nor our actions constitute sufficient grounds to warrant the conclusion that these were not true gifts, unmerited and undeserved. In essence, this issue is simply a variation on the theme of Pelagianism, whereby through good works and moral perfection we are thought to earn eternal life with God. Although the goods at issue are dissimilar (eternal life versus good land), the underlying theological question is the same: What does God owe us? The appropriate answer to this question is "nothing." There is nothing we can do to merit God's self-communication, eternal life, interior renovation through grace, life itself, or the good land that makes possible physical life. God gives these gifts gratuitously out of love and the desire to nourish, sustain, and bring all creatures into the most intimate communion possible with God.

Condition 4 specifies that the gift of good land must benefit oneself, or those with whom one shares special relations such as family, relatives, or close friends. This condition is patently true in a number of ways. Most importantly, good land makes possible one of the necessary goods to sustain human life, food, and allows Americans to avoid the anxiety and suffering caused by hunger and malnutrition. Indirectly, these gifts have given rise to a rural culture lauded by many for its sense of initiative, ingenuity, self-help, and strong communitarianism. They have also contributed to our political stability and economic vitality. Insofar as one benefits from these goods — and it is virtually impossible for every American not to benefit from these goods on a daily basis — condition 4 is fulfilled.

Condition 3, which concerns an other-regarding motive for gift giving, is satisfied in two ways. I argued earlier that gifts satisfying a basic need, need not be motivated by a desire to benefit the recipient. Thus, even if an agent's motive in bestowing a gift that secures a recipient's basic need is less than laudable because it is narcissistic, done for self-aggrandizement, or is intended to bring benefits to oneself, it still warrants a grateful response. In this way the motivation for giving us good land is largely irrelevant since the gift satisfies a basic need.

The irrelevance of the motive for the gift of good land is not the only way condition 3 is satisfied, however. Examining other instances of divine gift giving shows a pattern that strongly indicates that self-interest is not a motivating factor for God. In the Christian tradition, divine love is the principal reason for God acting and bestowing gifts. Creation, for instance, is understood as a self-communicating act of love in which God brings everything into existence in order to convey God's goodness[70] and to bring forth creatures that can know and enjoy God and share fully in God's life. God does not create to display power, to entertain God's self, or to gain some tangible benefit; no, God creates so that the divine goodness can be shared and the blessing of being in intimate fellowship with God can be conferred upon creatures capable of responding to the divine initiative.[71]

Other gifts such as the incarnation and the suffering, death, and resurrection of Jesus corroborate God's other-regarding motivation. The incarnation, described as God's "absolute self-communication,"[72] was not only intended to show us the fullness of life in God and the possibilities that exist for humankind, but also to reconcile all creation with God.[73] Jesus' suffering, death, and resurrection epitomized God's sacrificial love insofar as the God-man, Jesus, willingly submitted to violence, degradation, and crucifixion so that we may be capable of enjoying eternal union with God.

In addition, Jesus is often portrayed as the "compassionate one"[74] who not only is deeply moved by others' suffering, but actively seeks out the poor, destitute, despised, sick, sinners, and outcasts to alleviate their suffering as far as possible. Jesus' actions of healing the sick, raising the dead, restoring sight, and feeding the hungry[75] were not intended as displays of Jesus' power to convince unbelievers, nor were they self-interested actions designed to secure some benefit for him (many of these actions, in fact, were highly offensive to Jesus' critics); Jesus' intention was to rectify a situation or condition inimical to a person's well-being, thereby making that person's life more palatable.

The clear pattern emerging from this brief survey of divine gift-giving is that God distributes gifts out of love, care, and concern for God's creatures, and there is no hint of a self-interested motive behind God's actions. The gift of good land, too, should be understood in a way consistent with this pattern. Good land is an expression of God's love and compassion, through which God creates the conditions necessary for us to avoid the suffering imposed by hunger and malnutrition and, more positively, makes it possible to sustain our physical lives so we can pursue other highly desirable goods. Of course, it could be argued that if some of God's actions of gift giving have multiple levels of motivation, then divine self-interest could be present in some form. This objection, however, while perhaps true, does not prevent condition 3 from being fulfilled since it requires only that the primary motivation for giving a gift, not the secondary or tertiary motivation, be to benefit the recipient.

In summary, I have explained how the gift of good land fulfills all the criteria necessary for eliciting a grateful response. In this process, I have also discussed why a proper theology of the land supports several normative moral positions, including sustainability, the need to insulate and protect our agricultural system from potential threats, and the mandate to develop an agricultural system more conducive to nonhuman creation. While these three moral imperatives will figure prominently later in my critique of contemporary American agriculture, there is much more to be added to our moral understanding of agriculture as we discuss gratitude's second moment, the proper reception of the gift of good land.

The Recipient's Response to the Gift of Good Land

As stated earlier, a proper response to the gift of good land contains three aspects: a positive emotional response, a willingness to requite if the proper occasion arises, and grateful use of the gift consistent with the gift's nature or the benefactor's intentions. For the sake of convenience, I simply assume that nobody rejects the gift of good land and its fruits, food, since I have neither heard nor read about any American (or anyone else for that matter) protesting an adequate supply of food. Let us discuss these in order, beginning with the emotional response fitting to the gift of good land. Since the third aspect is far more pivotal in constructing a theological-moral position on agriculture, my comments on the first two will be relatively brief.

The phenomenon of feeling appreciation for a gift is about as diverse as there are individual persons. Nor is this variation anything to lament. Some act on these feelings of appreciation through personal prayers of thanksgiving. Others seize quiet, reflective moments and simply revel in the awareness of God and the blessings of living and being loved by God. Others feel compelled to share this sense of appreciation with their children and family members. Feelings of appreciation for the gift of good land and the food it provides also are expressed on a communal level through prayer and song at liturgies. While properly called expressions of emotions rather than emotions themselves, all these actions betoken a positive affective movement experienced by the beneficiaries of the gift of good land.

The major stumbling block to feeling appreciation for good land is the inability to train our emotions to respond appropriately. Everyone has probably experienced recalcitrant emotions that disallow one from reacting affectively in the right way to the reality of certain stimuli. The sight of a dead rattlesnake preserved in formaldehyde is likely to conjure up feelings of fear and dread, and in many instances is accompanied by frantic actions to place critical distance between the person and the snake, even though the rattlesnake poses no danger. On the other hand, almost nobody is frightened to jump in a car and drive to a favorite recreation spot, even though driving or riding in a car is one of the most dangerous activities almost all contemporary Americans engage in frequently. Emotions can be fickle, inaccurate indicators of reality; on the other hand, if properly trained to correspond to the correct meaning of stimuli, they help unify the moral agent and provide an affective boost, so to speak, in his or her pursuit of the good.

I mention this point only because our emotions are often askew, responding to the wrong things in the wrong way, and this need not be the case. A low interest rate on a home mortgage, a win by the home team, a higher-paying job, and a winning lotto ticket are often greeted with feelings of glee and joy. Yet these certainly pale in comparison to the gift of good land and the sustenance it provides, which make it possible to live and to enjoy these pleasurable moments. On the scale of the satisfaction of human needs, good land certainly ranks near the top, and accordingly it should engender deep-seated feelings of thankfulness and appreciation that are abiding, regularly acknowledged, and expressed in our spiritual lives. These considerations are reinforced by the theological belief that good land not only satisfies human needs, but represents God's love and compassion for us in a very practical, concrete manner.

The second aspect of a grateful response to the gift of good land, namely, a willingness to requite a gift of comparable value that meets the benefactor's needs if the occasion arises, is very difficult, if not impossible, to do. The value of the gift of good land is almost immeasurable in that it sustains our lives day after day, month after month, and year after year. How could we possibly return such a valuable gift to God? The fact is that we never can return something of comparable worth.

In a situation like this, where a recipient cannot requite a commensurate gift, a fitting alternative is to treat the gift as the benefactor wants it to be treated. Take, for instance, a benefactor paying the entire cost of a poor student's college education at a prestigious college or university, a student who would not have been able to attend college for financial reasons absent the benefactor's generosity and will most likely never be able to return a gift of comparable worth. The most ungrateful response to this gift would be to squander the education by drifting through college aimlessly, cutting classes, getting poor grades, and learning little or nothing in the process. It would be far more appropriate, and far more pleasing to the benefactor, if the student would apply himself or herself seriously, study diligently, get good grades, and acquire skills advantageous to his or her chosen career path. While there might be other viable options for satisfying this condition, the paramount concern around which all the possibilities revolve is to honor the benefactor's wishes by treating or using the gift in a manner consistent with the benefactor's intentions. To address this issue requires moving on to the final moment of gratitude, grateful use of the gift of good land.

Christians of all stripes might be surprised to learn that discerning God's intentions toward land use has quite a lengthy history. While various Christian denominations, especially the Catholic and Lutheran churches, have figured prominently in the national debate on agriculture in the United States during the past hundred years,[76] the ancient Hebrews were just as interested in understanding land use theologically; their agricultural ethic comprises a host of moral prescriptions and prohibitions that have found voice in contemporary denominational documents on agriculture. While some of the specific moral injunctions found in the Old Testament literature would be self-defeating and contrary to their original intention if transposed literally into our agricultural context, there are several discernible tendencies that shed light on a theological notion of land use.

The Sabbatical Year,[77] which required that agricultural land lie fallow every seventh year and that nothing be harvested from the fields that year, served several functions, one of which was religious:[78] just as God had rested on the seventh day of creation and the Hebrews rested on the Sabbath, the land, too, was to be given a respite from its work of producing food. Scholars suggest that letting the land lie fallow was an agricultural practice that augmented the soil's fertility; by allowing more plant matter that grew during the Sabbatical Year to be returned to the soil, whether seeds, fruits, vegetables, leaves, or stalks that normally would have been harvested, the increased organic matter helped rejuvenate the soil and allowed more nutrients to be replaced.[79]

Property owners were also required to give the landless poor unrestricted access to their farmland and the crops that grew during the fallow year.[80] Many vines and tree crops, such as grapes and olives, produce fruit every year. Yet even land devoted to grain production will produce during a fallow year, due to the fact that grain spilled during harvest lies dormant and then emerges and grows later. This was very advantageous to many poor people, since they lived in close proximity to agricultural areas. Unlike in the United States today, where most of the population resides in major metropolitan areas far away from agricultural areas, many people in ancient Israel were within walking distance of farms outside their villages.

Similar in intent to the Sabbatical Year, the practice of gleaning places strict restrictions on a farmer's agricultural practices to ensure that enough food is left in the fields to sustain the poor.[81] Farmers are exhorted not to harvest crops along the edges of their fields; not to pick up grain that spills on the ground during harvest; to harvest from their trees only once and to leave everything that grows subsequently undisturbed.[82] This food, as stated forcefully in Deuteronomy, belongs to the alien, orphan, and widow.[83]

The Jubilee Year was perhaps one of the most radical methods of social and economic transformation ever known.[84] In addition to freeing slaves, forgiving debts, and letting the land lie fallow, the Hebrews were commanded to return their property to the original civil owner every fifty years. This latter aspect combated intractable, long-term poverty by restoring property to former landowners who were dispossessed of their land because of natural disasters, personal misfortune, or mismanagement. This redistribution institutionalized the opportunity for the unfortunate to start anew and to reclaim a certain economic standing that broke their vicious cycle of poverty. In addition, the redistribution of land prevented expansionist tendencies and the "emergence of a landed aristocracy" that would horde land, which would either directly or indirectly cause hardship for the poor.[85] This issue of too few people having access to and control over the land seems to have been a pernicious problem for the ancient Hebrews, given the sharp warning directed to those who monopolize the land.[86]

As I stated above, these specific practices are ill-suited to attain their original objectives if institutionalized in our current Corn Belt agricultural system. Letting the land lie fallow every seventh year would result in fields chock full of weeds, which would drop their seeds and create monumental weed problems for farmers the following year. Soil fertility could be augmented much better by planting a cover crop that would prevent the emergence of weeds, add organic matter when tilled into the ground, and fix beneficial nutrients in the soil. Nor would the Sabbatical Year and gleaning benefit the poor much. Not only does a sizeable proportion of our poor people live far away from agricultural centers, but the regional specialization characteristic of contemporary American agriculture, in which the farmers in a certain geographical area grow only one or two crops, means that gleaning would hardly make a dent in the nutritional requirements of poor people taking food directly from the land. The rural poor in Iowa, for instance, would have only corn and soybeans available to them. To make matters worse, the vast majority of corn and soybeans grown in Iowa are considered "inedible" by humans (even though they can be consumed without any harm) since they are not designed for direct human consumption and are tasteless compared to the corn and soybeans bought in a grocery store. The Jubilee Year, too, and the practice of returning land to its original civil owner would have substantial deleterious effects on agriculture since it would return people to the land (assuming these people would actually farm the land instead of selling it, which is highly unlikely in contemporary America) who would probably have very little, if any, knowledge of agriculture and good farming practices due to the extended absence from the farm.

These reservations about specific practices, however, in no way diminish the meaning underlying the practices and the objectives they were intended to realize. One notable aspect to underscore is that land and agricultural production were not simply economic phenomena for the Hebrews, that is, a collection of objects, resources, and practices the purpose of which was to make money. Too often today agriculture is conceived as just another business, and the concepts, language, technologies, and self-conception presented to farmers reflect this understanding. Thus everything agricultural not only becomes couched in economic jargon such as "inputs," "outputs," "costs of production," and "operating expenses," among many others, but the structure and historical development of agricultural production has been dominated by profitability as the primary, and in many instances the exclusive, objective. The fact remains that agricultural production for the ancient Hebrews was inserted into a broader theological-moral order that specified certain ends and practices as mandatory for farmers, without any regard for their economic effects. As our brief survey above indicates, some of these even entailed substantial economic losses.

Phrased in contemporary terminology, agriculture and land use for the ancient Hebrews were subject to a "social mortgage," the primary purpose of which was to combat poverty through institutional measures designed in various ways to give the poor access to land and its fruits. As I have already indicated, we ought to resist attempting simply to resurrect these practices and to restructure our agricultural system accordingly. The positive effects would be minuscule, and I fear in the long run some of these practices might actually exacerbate the poverty of many. Instead, the spirit of the Hebrews' agricultural ethic could be honored better by, first, considering why poverty is so deleterious to the poor and, second, by examining moral responses that would be consistent with the Hebrews' moral vision, given our contemporary context.

While the phenomenon of poverty is certainly varied, let me offer a few generalizations. Poverty is morally problematic because it thwarts poor people's ability to secure the goods necessary for a decent life. While usually not as problematic if everyone shares the same standard of living, poverty becomes morally dubious, even pernicious, when certain people are denied access to the goods many enjoy. Some of the obvious areas where the poor suffer a comparative disadvantage are access to a sufficient amount of food; healthy food; adequate means of transportation; good health insurance, medical care, and dental services; professional psychological services; safe, affordable housing; adequate police protection; retirement plans; and others. Yet these only begin to scratch the surface of poverty's crippling effect. A quality education, which is probably the most valuable ingredient to ensure socioeconomic welfare in the United States, is frequently denied to the poor, even though poor people as a group spend a greater proportion of their annual income to educate their children. This, in turn, sharply limits job opportunities and has lifelong drawbacks that in many cases are insurmountable. Politically, the limited resource base of the poor often translates into lack of political clout, which means that their concerns and needs often go unnoticed in the public sphere. Socially, the poor are often stigmatized, forgotten, ignored, or blamed for their poverty. Psychologically, the poor often internalize the message implicitly conveyed by the more materially fortunate, namely, that they are not worthy of attention, care, and action, and this either becomes a self-fulfilling prophecy or an occasion for self-loathing, despair, or anger. Environmentally, the poor are subject to conditions that most people would find intolerable. In fact, poverty increases exponentially a person's likelihood that a garbage dump or toxic waste incinerator will be located in one's neighborhood.

While the goods denied to the poor are many and diffuse (and certainly many more could be added to the aforementioned list), this denial culminates in a class of people who are vulnerable, marginalized, and powerless: vulnerable because their lack of opportunity and access to goods make their lives more precarious and painful and fraught with danger, and also because their quality of life depends so greatly on the benevolence of other individuals, structures, and institutions; marginalized because they often live on the fringes of society, existing invisibly; and powerless because they are incapable of changing their lot in life. Phrased in this way, the parallels with the world of the ancient Hebrews become apparent. Were the poor who were the objects of the agricultural practices, land use policies, and periodic redistributions also appropriately characterized as vulnerable, marginalized, and powerless? Absolutely! And the Hebrews' response to these conditions, as we have seen, was to institutionalize measures, sometimes radical measures that would be highly unpopular today (land redistribution, for instance), that counteracted their poverty and allowed them more access to goods constitutive to their well-being.

This analysis suggests both a negative moral mandate and a positive heuristic moral principle. The moral mandate is that our agricultural system should not cause or exacerbate poverty and the vulnerability, marginalization, and powerlessness associated with it. This general mandate to give priority to the poor not only accords with the Hebrews' moral code, but has been reaffirmed subsequently by the early Christian community, notable Christian theologians, and various

Christian churches throughout history. Of course, while structuring our agricultural system in a particular way to avoid these conditions will not eliminate poverty, agriculture is part and parcel of the moral order and we should not be reluctant in the least to subject it to moral criteria that require structural adjustments, if necessary.

The positive heuristic moral principle is that agriculture and land use should actually promote a more enriching communal life, understood broadly. It is one thing to assert the minimalist criterion that agriculture not be a contributory factor in degrading the poor; it is another thing entirely to require that an agricultural system militate against vulnerability, marginalization, and powerlessness. This criterion, I think, is entirely consistent with the Hebrews' moral vision for agriculture. The goal of the prescriptions and prohibitions discussed earlier was not simply to guarantee that their agricultural system did not cause poverty or prevented a further downward spiral into poverty; the goal was to make poverty nonexistent, so that everyone could live the most decent life possible in the circumstances. The organizing *telos* behind the Hebrews' agricultural ethic was a social life that provided access to material goods, encouraged beneficial relationships, and distributed political power more uniformly.

This tendency to prescribe a certain kind of communal life has a strong parallel in Catholic social thought, which bases its normative moral statements on the inherent social nature of the human person.[87] As creatures with strong social inclinations, our well-being is inextricably intertwined with the quality of our social order. We naturally seek out others for play, amusement, learning, friendship, relaxation, competition, common projects, courtship, and marriage, to mention only a few of the many possible beneficial human interactions we value and try to protect. Stated in more technical terminology, social intercourse is inherently satisfying, or beneficial in its own right regardless of its instrumental value. In addition to its intrinsic rewards, it is a fact of human existence that we need others to survive and flourish through a coordinated, purposeful network of activities, relationships, and schemes of recurrence that ensure the availability of material goods. The interconnectedness and mutual dependency characterizing human life mean that others are needed to help build our houses; to heat our homes; to provide blankets, clothes, and cookware; to deliver water; to educate our young; to maintain recreational areas; and yes, to provide our food, among a host of others.

What this entails on a very practical, daily level is an extraordinary degree of cooperation on everyone's part, which is beneficial to the individual as well as to the larger community. The cooperation necessary for human flourishing, however, is undermined — and sometimes virtually impossible — if certain conditions exist. For instance, economic desperation, depression, lack of opportunities, anger, crime, alcoholism, and spousal abuse often grind people into the dirt, so to speak, and stifle any possibility of a flourishing communal life.[88] The list of conditions inimical to communal well-being could be expanded to cover incivility, political domination by elites, lack of public resources, fear of violence, and corrupt business leaders. The point here, however, is not to provide a catalog of ills related to communal decline, but only to indicate that social beings like humans need favorable conditions to thrive, and certain political, economic, and cultural conditions that effectively inhibit our social inclinations must be kept at bay.

I stated earlier that the normative prescription for agricultural and land use to contribute to communal life positively is "heuristic," which means that instead of providing a rather detailed program for ordering our agricultural system it is preferable to adopt a trial-and-error method whereby certain social ends are specified, our agriculture system is structured accordingly, and then we assess whether these policies, programs, or practices are actually achieving their desired objectives. This experimental method is advantageous for a number of reasons. First, social goods are only one aspect of a morally laudable agricultural system. We have already specified sustainability and a secure food production system as two other integral components (and more are discussed in the following pages), and the fact remains that social goals might conflict with these two objectives. Second, it is possible that conflict will exist between diverse social goals and that communities will have to select the particular social goals to be pursued, given their circumstances. Third, social goals take varying periods of time to come to fruition, which means that policies, programs, and practices designed to realize certain social goods need to be given time, sometimes years or decades, before their effectiveness can be assessed.

These considerations, however, should not blunt the force of the moral prescription that our agricultural system needs to be ordered to realize certain social goods and that as we consider the ongoing structural development of American agriculture we must continually return to questions integral to our Christian self-understanding: Does our agricultural system contribute to poverty? Does it make people vulnerable? Does it marginalize certain groups and make them passive, voiceless bystanders? Does it render them powerless by vitiating their ability to participate in public policy debates affecting them directly or indirectly?

Unintentional Side Effects

Another pertinent aspect of land use concerns harms resulting from the unintentional side effects of actions. This class of harms, in my opinion, will emerge this century as the most compelling topic for the Christian community to address, due primarily to its widespread, long-term, and rather pernicious effects on humans worldwide (and on many other creatures as well). Harms commonly grouped in this category include global warming, deforestation, species extinctions, depletion of fisheries, pollution, and the thinning of the ozone layer, among others.

American agriculture, as one might suspect, is no stranger to the issue of deleterious unintended side effects, and many agricultural practices have become notorious for the harms they cause. The popular media have warned Americans for decades about the health dangers posed by pesticides, and environmental groups are equally concerned about the many species of nontarget insects and animals killed by them. Ever since the Dust Bowl of the 1930s, soil erosion has become a focal point of agricultural policy, and many recognize this as a protracted, formidable threat to our food production capacity. Irrigation in the Great Plains has depleted the Ogallala Aquifer, the largest underground body of freshwater in the world, far beyond its ability to be replenished naturally, and in the process has caused thousands of acres of farmland to be contaminated and rendered unusable by salt, which is left on the surface when the water evaporates. Fertilizers have caused nitrate contamination in rural drinking water supplies; fertilizer runoff continues to degrade streams, ponds, lakes, and rivers and to kill aquatic life by the algae blooms and the oxygen deprivation they stimulate; and the economic fallout suffered by those downstream who depend on fish, clams, oysters, or other marine animals has been catastrophic.

Given the indignation often characterizing the public response to these problems, one might assume that Christian ethics possesses analytic devices clearly demonstrating why this indignation is warranted. On the contrary, in my estimation the dominant method of moral analysis is bedeviled by the issue of unintentional side effects, and when applied to these diverse problems would not only render highly counterintuitive moral judgments on the actions causing these problems, but would prove to be impotent to effect systemic, lasting change.

The method of moral analysis to which I am referring, which I will call "traditional act analysis," predominates in contemporary Catholic moral theology, although it also has a number of influential adherents in Protestant theological circles as well. This method of analysis judges the morality of every act according to three components: the object (what is done); the intention or end (the purpose for performing the action); and the circumstances (how the action was performed and relevant contextual factors). For an action to be morally right, every individual component of the action must be right, or the action as a whole is considered morally wrong. The important point to recognize about traditional act analysis is that any unintended consequence of an action is irrelevant in determining the morality of the action itself; only if the consequence was intended does it become morally relevant. Take, for instance, the mundane act of driving one's car to the grocery store. The object is driving a car; the intention is to get food; and assuming nothing unusual about this trip (speeding, driving dangerously or while intoxicated, etc.), there are no relevant circumstances worth mentioning. In no sense would any proponent of traditional act analysis find anything morally dubious about this act.

The fact remains, however, that this supposedly morally benign act of driving one's car causes a number of negative unintentional side effects by emitting pollutants into the atmosphere. The average car produces over one thousand pollutants, and while many of their effects are known, most are not. The main pollutants are benzene, one of the most highly toxic substances to humans for which there is no known safe threshold; carbon monoxide, which reduces the body's ability to carry blood to vital organs; nitrogen oxides, one of the leading causes of acid rain; hydrocarbons, which cause "drowsiness, eye irritation, and coughing" and frequently interact with other chemicals to form tropospheric ozone, a highly toxic substance to plant life; low-lying ozone, which "causes eye, nose, and throat irritation, headaches, coughing, and impaired lung function"; and diesel particulates, which are very fine particles that can penetrate deeply into the lungs and cause cancer, bronchitis, and asthma.[89] Of course, these are only the effects of a few well-understood pollutants, and it is probably safe to assume that a list of all negative consequences would be much longer.

According to traditional act analysis, these harmful consequences are irrelevant to the morality of the act of driving a car because the driver did not intend to bring them about. To be sure, if the purpose of a trip is to emit these pollutants into the atmosphere in order to cause harm, the act would be considered morally wrong. But this is almost never the case. Driving a car is simply a method to get from one location to another, and the pollutants emitted in the process are regrettable, accidental byproducts. This is also true of the issues mentioned above: nobody's action is intended to contribute to global warming, deforestation, species extinctions, depletion of fisheries, pollution, the thinning of the ozone layer, pesticide poisoning, nitrate contamination, aquifer depletion, or topsoil erosion or salinization; these are simply unfortunate unintended consequences.

Traditional act analysis leads to a host of incongruities. First, it creates the odd situation where these broad-scale, long-term threats to humans and others can be condemned unequivocally, but it disallows any condemnation of the individual actions that cause or contribute to them. In *The Ecological Crisis: A Common Responsibility*, for instance, Pope John Paul II remarks that global warming "has now reached crisis proportions," yet the pope's adherence to traditional act analysis[90] prohibits him from calling into question particular classes of actions that bring about global warming. Second, it disallows assigning moral responsibility for any of these problems. Although there has recently been a trend to extend responsibility to groups and corporations, the paradigm in Christian ethics for attributing responsibility is the individual moral agent and quality of his or her actions.[91] Yet moral responsibility in these cases is simply a phantom: none of the individual moral agent's actions causing these problems is wrong, so there is no negative moral responsibility to assign. Third, and related to the second point, this type of act analysis eviscerates the possibility of promoting positive change to counteract these problems by appealing to practical behavioral modifications. It makes no sense to me, for instance, to exhort people to drive less in order to reduce the emissions that cause global warming when each act of driving, assessed individually according to traditional act analysis, is morally right. How can one reasonably say that driving a car is morally right, yet we ought not to drive as much?

It is interesting to note that, in a few isolated instances, even adherents to traditional act analysis are disconcerted by the fact that negative unintended side effects are considered irrelevant to the morality of the act itself, and have tried to minimize the harms they cause by appealing to the principle of proportionality. The classic case is "collateral damage," or the unintentional deaths of innocent human beings while fighting a just war, which is usually considered in the context of bombing a military target located in a densely populated area that will kill hundreds of civilians. According to just war theory, if the harm unintentionally caused to innocent civilians is disproportionate to the good to be attained by the military strike, then the bombing is immoral.[92] In this instance, unintentional consequences not only are relevant to determining the morality of the action itself, but they might make an otherwise morally right action morally wrong. In two other areas, the principle of double effect and organ donation,[93] the principle of proportionality functions similarly.

These revisions of traditional act analysis validate inchoately the pervasive moral sentiment that the negative side effects of actions matter morally and that something is seriously askew when unintentional harms are blithely discounted from our moral radar screen. Even though all the broad-scale, long-term problems mentioned earlier are caused unintentionally, the predominant reaction to them is that many represent in some way moral failings of great magnitude. Yet are these sentiments correct? If so, what is the best way to understand these phenomena from a Christian moral perspective?

The first question should be answered affirmatively, and I will focus exclusively on physical harms in formulating an answer to the second question. The category of "harms," it seems to me, encompasses so many different types of injuries that any analysis of such a broad topic will tend to overgeneralize, not to make important, morally relevant distinctions between harms, and to make comments inapplicable to other forms of harm. Moreover, since many, if not most, of the negative side effects caused by agriculture involve physical harm in one way or another, this self-imposed restriction will not eliminate many pertinent issues from consideration.

A second caveat is that minor physical harms and major physical harms need to be distinguished. A shallow cut requiring a Band-Aid, a small bruise, or a bump on the head are qualitatively different, and should be treated as different morally, than harms that are life-altering and typically inflict a great deal of pain, suffering, and anguish, such as cancer, severed limbs, and severe burns. The latter require far weightier reasons to justify their infliction, and I am only interested in attending to these graver forms of harm.

It is axiomatic in Christian ethics that the infliction of physical harm needs to be justified morally; stated differently, there is a strong burden of proof placed on someone considering physically harming another to be able to offer specific, convincing reasons that the harm is warranted. This predisposition emerges from a number of elements commonly considered as valuable sources for Christian ethical deliberation. First, the life and behavior of Jesus as recorded in the Gospels give no indication that Jesus inflicted physical harm on anyone. When Jesus was within his legal rights to inflict physical harm, as with the adulterous woman about to be stoned, Jesus chose not to cast a stone.[94] When the observance of religious laws would have inflicted harm on others, Jesus subordinated these laws to the satisfaction of human need.[95] Portrayed as the compassionate one in the Synoptic Gospels who alleviates the suffering caused by a variety of harms (whether caused by humans or not), Jesus feeds the hungry, exorcises demons, cures the sick, and resuscitates the dead.[96] Jesus' teachings, furthermore, corroborate this trajectory. Jesus exhorts his followers to "turn the other cheek" and to love their enemies and to pray for their persecutors.[97] In one instance, the parable of Lazarus and the Rich Man, the rich man is apparently condemned not for the harms he inflicted on Lazarus, but for the harms to Lazarus he could have prevented.[98] Suffice it to say that Jesus had no reputation for inflicting physical harms and that his teachings indicate a strong predisposition to avoid harming others.

Second, an integral aspect of the Christian self-identity is generosity. While diverse theological bases have been adduced as the proper motivation for generosity, Christian generosity is characterized by a liberality and magnanimity that seeks to enrich the lives of others. A generous person gives regularly, freely, and with a certain degree of abandon simply because others have unmet needs. A frequent, although not necessary, component of Christian generosity is sacrifice, whether great or small. While I am aware of the checkered history behind the concept of sacrifice, which has sometimes been employed to subjugate, disempower, and dominate, we should not be reticent about asserting the importance of sacrificing in the right way at the right time so that others may live better lives. In fact, some of our loftiest moral ideals coalesce around practical instances of sacrifice embodied in the lives of our moral exemplars: Mother Teresa tending to the poorest of the poor in Calcutta, India; Maximilian Kolbe, the Polish priest and Nazi concentration camp prisoner, offering his life so another could live; Dorothy Day sharing almost everything she possessed with the homeless; and the list goes on and on.

It is difficult to see how this spirit of generosity could lead to the infliction of physical harm on others easily. If the goal of generosity is to help others live better lives, and ideally to enable others to have abundant lives, it seems that physical harm would be avoided assiduously since it rarely contributes to the betterment of the one on whom it is inflicted. Of course, certain physical harms might be advantageous to avoid even greater physical harms, but this reservation in no way undermines the contention that the Christian moral ideal of generosity militates powerfully against physically harming others. In fact, I think Christian generosity supports an even stronger conclusion: in some instances, it should inspire personal and communal sacrifices so that select individuals or groups can be benefited.

Third, theologians throughout history have acknowledged bodily integrity as one of the most valuable human goods, which is the reason that serious physical harms have consistently preoccupied the attention of Christian ethicists. Peruse the shelves of any university library and you will find the Christian ethics collection dominated by issues involving physical harm such as warfare, abortion, and euthanasia. While this preoccupation might emerge from a number of considerations, there is little doubt that there is a strong aversive guttural reaction to physical harms. Whenever we think about people being ravaged by cancer, harmed by violent criminal acts or debilitating diseases, or about people shot, burned, and blown apart during war, our reaction is a mixture of horror, dread, alarm, sympathy, and sorrow. We hope and pray that these harms never occur again and the images and feelings they frequently elicit are often emblazoned into our psyches permanently.

So many integral aspects of the Christian moral tradition coalesce around the position that we should be exceedingly squeamish about physically harming others and should strive valiantly to avoid situations where physical harms become likely. Moreover, these inclinations should obtain regardless of the harm's origin or the intentionality behind the harm (if any). Although a tautology, the phrase "harm is harm" captures well the fact that the effects of physical harms are no less crippling or devastating when intentionality or origin are known. A regimen of surgery, chemotherapy, and radiation for a cancer victim, for instance, will still have the same effects regardless of whether the cancer stems from a smoking habit, environmental pollution, a genetic flaw, or naturally aging cells. Likewise, a gunshot wound will cause the same damage regardless of whether or not it is inflicted intentionally.

What, then, do these considerations entail practically on the issue of physical harms resulting from negative side effects? First and foremost, it requires that the question, Is the harm necessary? needs to be raised, with the word "necessary" meaning no alternative ways exist to realize the good being pursued while avoiding the unintentional harm. Although this is a robust criterion, the idea that physical harm should be avoided if possible has a distinguished pedigree in Christian ethics. War, for instance, is permissible only if all other nonviolent alternatives have been exhausted (the "last resort" criterion). Inflicting physical injury on another in self-defense is justified only if there are no avenues of escape. If it is possible to escape, then one is morally obligated not to inflict physical violence on the attacker and simply to run away. The same obligation to avoid unnecessary physical harm obtains in cases of rape, kidnapping, or robbery. If one can avoid these criminal acts without physically harming the attacker, then one is obligated to do no harm.

Let me illustrate the criterion of necessity by discussing synthetic pesticide use in American agriculture. For the sake of simplicity I assume that the pesticide in question is carcinogenic, mutagenic, and causes a host of other unintentional serious physical harms, and that pesticide use actually does result in some harm being inflicted on someone. In my sense of the word, no pesticide use is necessary, and farmers throughout the course of human history have produced food without the use of pesticides by using a variety of natural methods to control bug populations. These natural methods are still available today and many scientists are continuing to develop new methods that achieve better results. To be sure, many might claim that pesticide use is "necessary" for a number of reasons, but their meaning of the word necessity is "A is necessary for B," not that no alternatives to pesticides exist. In this context, "necessity" means that pesticides must be used in order to avoid economic hardship, or to contribute to economic growth, or to provide chemists with jobs, or to provide stockholders with satisfactory returns on their investments, or to support a certain lifestyle for those in the agriculture industry, or to ensure the profitability of agribusinesses in the United States. These objections might be factually true, but they are morally irrelevant to the issue under consideration.

Abandoning the use of synthetic pesticides, as the criterion of necessity requires if alternatives exist, however, would probably be very costly for many farmers, and in some cases might cause severe economic hardship, maybe even bankruptcy. My response to this objection is quite simple: It betrays our Christian moral identity to inflict suffering, disease, and death on others when it is possible to produce food in other ways that do not produce these undesirable effects. Without wanting to sound callous about economic hardship and the many deprivations it causes, we should unflinchingly affirm the priority of bodily integrity and disallow economic considerations to undermine our resolve to protect this good for everyone.

But the more interesting issue raised by this objection is why synthetic pesticides, which are notorious for their manifold negative side effects, are cost-effective in the first place, to the extent that their use is an institutionalized, commonplace practice in American agriculture. Stated a little differently, why are farmers penalized economically for embracing practices that do not cause unintentional physical harms? With these questions the criterion of necessity becomes especially fruitful. Too often ethical analyses isolate one segment of dubious behavior without inquiring into the antecedent forces, policies, pressures, and limited choices that are part and parcel of that behavior's larger story, which help render intelligible the reasons for an action. It is these diverse components, I suggest, that are often most relevant to the criterion of necessity, since until they are changed farmers will still experience pressure to continue using pesticides and people will continue to suffer their unintended side effects. Without inquiring into the preconditions fostering pesticide use, not only will the problem continue unabated, but Christian ethicists will be involved in a largely irrelevant exercise of moral analysis that never really looks in the right places or asks the pertinent questions.

The criterion of necessity, then, leads directly to a moral assessment of our agricultural system's structural elements in an attempt to understand and rectify the problem of unintended harm caused by pesticide use. Although not exhaustive, such an account would certainly include scientific reductionism and the dismissal of complex relationships, which translates into a myopia concerned only about killing bugs; a childlike fascination with technology, which causes new technologies such as pesticides to be adopted widely without ever examining them critically; a robust individualism that precludes any meaningful communal control over pesticides; access to abundant supplies of fossil fuels, which make pesticides cheaper than alternative methods of bug control; the historically unprecedented growth of average farm size in the United States this past century, which practically eliminates the feasibility of natural methods of bug control; the "pesticide treadmill," as it is frequently called, which virtually guarantees significant bug problems if pesticide use were discontinued; consumers who demand unblemished food, which promotes pesticide use, even though cosmetic surface flaws are almost always benign; the cultural loss of knowledge of alternative methods of bug control due to disuse; and the comparative convenience of pesticides.

This formidable array of forces virtually guarantees that synthetic pesticide use will continue unabated in American agriculture — that is, unless the status quo is challenged and overcome. Yet this is precisely what the Christian moral vision as embodied in the criterion of necessity requires. Compassion, generosity, and a spirit of sacrifice are embodied in those who refuse to support the use of pesticides and try to create alternatives so that others do not have to suffer unnecessary physical harm: in the research scientist studying indigenous agricultural systems and their natural methods of bug control; in the banker who takes a chance, so to speak, and loans money to someone to start an organic farm; in the farmer who discontinues using pesticides; in the politician who supports legislation financially penalizing the pesticide industry; and in the consumer who spends extra money on groceries to support organic farmers.

To this point, my comments have been based on the assumption that pesticide use actually leads to physical harm. Before finishing this section on serious physical harms resulting from the unintentional negative side effects of actions, I want to reexamine this assumption and indicate a potentially problematic issue related to it, since it is confined not only to the specific topic of pesticide use, but is a common feature of many negative side effects caused by agricultural practices. The issue is that the physical harms caused by pesticides typically occur incrementally over long periods of time and probably from many different sources. For farm workers whose contact with pesticides is direct during application, there is probably one identifiable source. But even for these people, one dose most likely does not cause physical harm, but multiple contacts with pesticides over many years eventually causes some type of malady. For those with no direct contact with pesticides, such as citizens of a rural town whose public drinking water supply is tainted periodically by pesticides, the picture is even fuzzier: the pesticides probably come from a large number of sources and the harm, once again, occurs incrementally over years or decades.

The problem this poses is that a single pesticide application rarely causes any physical harm. If, for instance, cancer cells started growing in a person's body on the 2,000th episode of ingesting pesticides over a period of twenty years, does this mean that the prior 1,999 instances of pesticide ingestion were benign? In a factual sense, they did not cause any physical harm. They certainly created the conditions whereby more pesticide exposure would be physically harmful, but they were not actually harmful in themselves. This leads to the conclusion that it is difficult to designate pesticides as physically harmful when the vast majority of pesticide applications have no adverse health consequences. Moreover, even if pesticides could be designated as harmful, each farmer's contribution to a pesticide-related illness is probably so minuscule that it is difficult to affirm that any particular farmer's pesticide use caused the malady.

These problems can be successfully resolved in different ways. First, the last issue centers on the fact that taken individually, no farmer actually causes harm by applying pesticides. The side effects of an individual farmer's pesticide use are so diffuse and small that they do not cause any physical harm in a specific person, although they might contribute toward the person eventually getting sick; instead, the problem lies in the corporate, cumulative effects which taken together do cause physical harm. While this "contributor's dilemma," as it is often called, might seem formidable at first glance, the following hypothetical example helps illustrate some erroneous assumptions behind this reasoning:

Suppose a village contains 100 unarmed tribesmen eating their lunch. 100 hungry armed bandits descend on the village and each bandit at gunpoint takes one tribesman's lunch and eats it. The bandits then go off, each one having done a discriminable amount of harm to a single tribesman. Next week, the bandits are tempted to do the same thing again, but are troubled by new-found doubts about the morality of such a raid. Their doubts are put to rest by one of their number [who claims they can palliate their consciences by harming each person in a very small way]....They then raid the village, tie up the tribesmen, and look at their lunches. As expected, each bowl of food contains 100 baked beans.... Instead of each bandit eating a single plateful as last week, each [of the 100 bandits] takes one bean from each [of the 100] plate[s]. They leave after eating all the beans, pleased to have done no harm, as each has done no more than subthreshold harm to each person.[99]

Why is this scenario so disturbing? Because it assumes that if the total amount of harm can be spread among more people and in smaller increments, then one is effectively absolved of moral responsibility. This, in turn, is supported by another assumption: moral judgments must be based on the actual harm done. The second assumption, however, is false. In fact, no actual harm is necessary to render a negative moral judgment in many cases. Throwing a rock at someone out of anger is morally wrong regardless of whether blood is drawn or not. Driving while intoxicated is morally wrong regardless of whether anyone is injured in the process or not. Discharging a gun in celebration into the air in a crowded urban neighborhood is morally wrong even if the bullet falls harmlessly to the ground. While there frequently appears to be a tight link between moral judgments and actual harm because many classes of actions evaluated negatively morally are typically accompanied by serious injuries, the moral sphere should not be conflated with the factual sphere, nor should moral judgments be based exclusively on actual harms. Merely placing another in a situation where physical harm is more likely to occur is in many cases sufficient to warrant a negative moral judgment.

From a moral perspective, it seems more fitting to describe each bandit as stealing a bowl of food, even though this is not factually correct. This description is accurate because in some instances it is not the discrete, individual action that specifies the appropriate moral description, but a pattern of actions, the cumulative effects of which produce a distinctive type of harm. For instance, if I lose my temper on one occasion and yell at my children, they might temporarily experience hurt feelings. If, on the other hand, I lose my temper many times a day for years on end, the harm caused to my children transcends temporarily hurt feelings and will probably culminate in long-term psychological problems. This dichotomy between individual acts and the distinctive harms brought about by patterns of action is apparent in a number of cases: eating one cheeseburger versus being on a first-name basis with the staff at the local McDonald's; smoking one cigarette versus being a two-pack-a-day smoker for thirty years; or abstaining from one meal per week during Lent versus abstaining from seventeen meals every week throughout the entirety of one's adult life. While all the aforementioned individual actions might produce some harms, understood very broadly (raising your cholesterol level by .000001 percent, a dry throat and maybe coughing or sneezing, and hunger pangs), the harms caused by the patterns of action (heart disease, emphysema, and anorexia and its many physical effects) are different and much more morally relevant insofar as they exercise a far greater influence on our ability to pursue human goods. If this is correct, patterns of actions possess a life of their own and must be evaluated morally apart from the individual acts comprised in them.

Patterns of action, however, also need to be contextualized in relationship to others' actions to be made morally meaningful. While there is a strong tendency in Christian ethics to consider actions in the abstract, denuded of the details and circumstances that situate them and make them intelligible in our lives,[100] this tendency should be resisted. To render a moral evaluation about a farmer's pattern of applying pesticides annually for a period of thirty years, for instance, it must be known whether the people affected by the farmer's pesticide use also were exposed to pesticides from other sources. Consider two different scenarios. One, the residents of a rural town were exposed to pesticide runoff from only one source, a farmer who applied pesticides an average of twice per year over two hundred acres. Two, in addition to the aforementioned farmer, the residents were also exposed to pesticide runoff from a hundred other comparably sized farms at the same application rate for the past thirty years, which greatly increases their cumulative exposure to pesticides. These contextual differences lead to different moral assessments of the farmer's pattern of action, and I suspect almost everyone would agree that the farmer's pattern of action in the second scenario is far more reproachable, even though the farmer is acting identically in both scenarios. The morally relevant difference here is that the residents in the second scenario are already far more contaminated by pesticides and their bodies far less resistant to pesticide-related illnesses due to the cumulative, corporate effects of pesticide exposure. Thus, the farmer's pattern of action in the latter scenario is much likelier to result in serious physical harm to someone (or perhaps to multiple persons), or at the very least, it paves the way for another farmer's pesticide use to have adverse effects. Either way, the identical pattern of action becomes more injurious and deadlier when placed in the larger context of other people's actions.

This analysis suggests that the appropriate moral framework for assessing pesticide use is not individual instances of pesticide application and the harms they cause. Instead, a farmer must consider the total effects of his or her pattern of pesticide use; the number of people affected negatively by incidents of pesticide ingestion and the number, type, and severity of maladies caused; and the same for farmers whose pesticide use affects the same people. So, for instance, if the pesticide applications of a hundred farmers during their thirty years of farming result in the deaths of a hundred residents of a Midwestern town (assuming similar pesticides and rates and areas of application), then it is appropriate to say that each farmer is morally responsible for the death of one person. This does not mean that each farmer's pesticide use actually results in the death of one person, no more and no less. On a factual basis, some farmers might have caused multiple deaths and other farmers none at all. But as I showed above, factual matters and moral matters are distinct, and actual harm is not necessary to make a pattern of action morally reproachable.

While this method of assessing the morality of pesticide use better captures our settled moral convictions regarding unintentional side effects resulting in serious physical harm, its main weakness is the extraordinary amount of empirical data necessary to render accurate moral judgments. Needless to say, gathering this data is never easy, and sometimes downright impossible. The range of impediments is expansive: scientists do not know the full physical effects of pesticide exposure, especially the effects of multiple combinations of pesticides in the human body; pesticides affect people differently depending on age, susceptibility to different diseases, and an individual immune system's strength; farmers use different pesticides for different insect problems, which vary in toxicity and effect; new pesticides are being created and used every year, which might bring about different effects or exacerbate already existing physical maladies, and the effects of these new pesticides might take years, if not decades, to uncover; other environmental factors operate in tandem with pesticides to produce certain effects, making it difficult to determine precise cause-effect relationships; exposure rates vary from year to year depending on rainfall, the frequency of high winds, or evaporation rates; and it is always difficult to determine, even under the best conditions, where pesticides eventually migrate and who ingests them in what quantity.

In my opinion, these are not fatal flaws; they simply necessitate the use of hypotheses, generalizations, inferences, and other devices commonly employed to make sense of partial, fragmentary factual knowledge. My concern is that the all-too-human tendencies to rationalize and trivialize will seize on these uncertainties to create moral paralysis and inaction. This has become a common feature especially in contemporary politics, where any degree of ambiguity is consistently met by calls for further study before any judgments can be made or new policies implemented. Nor is this phenomenon confined to the political realm; individuals in all walks of life rely on uncertainty to justify dubious behavior or to protect their self-interest. In reality, all this amounts to placing an impossible burden of proof on nonomniscient human beings to demonstrate an airtight cause-effect relationship; a burden of proof almost never gets turned back upon its advocates in the form of an equally legitimate question, Can you disprove it?

Even granting the factual ambiguities surrounding pesticide use and the specific harms they cause, it is indisputable that pesticides increase the risk of serious physical harm to many, especially in rural areas where exposure to pesticides is more frequent and the levels of ingestion higher. If this rather thin claim is valid, does it permit some type of moral judgment to be rendered about pesticide use, a judgment that can avoid the tangles involved in determining actual, specific physical harm? Yes it does. Pesticide use manifests a disordered moral personality, insofar as the requisite character traits that we should be striving to inculcate in ourselves on a daily basis are inconsistent with increasing the possibility of others suffering unnecessary physical harm as a result of our actions.

As I have argued elsewhere,[101] moral goodness consists in a consistent pattern of striving to form ourselves to embody certain characteristics, which include compassion, generosity, and a spirit of sacrifice at the right times and in the right ways. It is difficult, if not impossible, to reconcile striving to become compassionate, generous, and sacrificial with pesticide use. If compassion involves alleviating others' suffering, how does one become compassionate by increasing the risk that others will experience substantial physical injury by the unintended side effects of one's actions? If generosity involves freely offering beneficial gifts to others, how does one become generous by creating, or better yet imposing, added risk to another's physical health? If a spirit of sacrifice is especially warranted to help others avoid physical harm, how does one become sacrificial by releasing toxins into the environment?

The answer to these questions is, One does not! For character development, what matters is not whether anyone actually suffers physical harm from one's actions; prior to external actions is the acting subject, the Christian who is called to strive to become a certain person embodying certain traits, and these traits are morally praise-worthy or condemnable regardless of the actions they engender. To be sure, in practice it is often difficult to separate trait from action, since a charitable person, for example, will usually act charitably, and an indolent person will usually act lazily. Yet it is important to recognize that characteristics and actions are separate objects of moral evaluation. If a charitable person who gives frequently to the poor is actually fostering a servile dependency, then his or her actions might be morally wrong. But this hardly justifies a similar negative moral evaluation of the person's charitable disposition. On the contrary, we should wholeheartedly applaud the person's charity, yet insist that there are better ways morally to translate this cultivated disposition into action.

It should be noted that this critique extends far beyond the issue of farmers applying pesticides on their fields. A number of support personnel willingly cooperate at various stages to make pesticides available to farmers: chemists, research scientists, manufacturers, advertisers, and transportation providers; millions more should be added who support the pesticide industry indirectly through their purchases. If character is also formed by free choices to support, encourage, tolerate, or conveniently ignore, and I believe a strong case can be made to affirm this position, then the question becomes equally pertinent to these people whether their participation in the pesticide industry in some form embodies compassion, generosity, and a spirit of sacrifice.

In the final analysis, unintended side effects resulting in physical harm turn out to be far more relevant to the Christian moral life than previously thought. By choosing actions that physically harm others indirectly, not only do we fail to conform our actions to the moral order God intended, but we also stifle the growth of valuable character traits that are central to our Christian self-identity. As I said earlier, my analysis of unintended side effects was limited exclusively to serious physical harms, and the normative criteria discussed were not intended to be applied to issues not involving serious physical harms. These issues, in my opinion, should be evaluated according to different moral criteria, and the sheer number of variables, goods, and effects usually involved necessitate a case-by-case analysis.

Sustainability Revisited

I want to return briefly to the issue of sustainability, which was mentioned in passing earlier. Suffice it to say that sustainability has entered the domain of political correctness, and nearly everyone involved in agriculture, from spokespersons for the petrochemical industry to advocates of organic farming, wants to have his or her preferred set of agricultural practices regarded as sustainable.[102] Given the diverse interests and agendas operative in American agriculture today, the term "sustainability" has acquired considerable elasticity due to the various ways it is used.[103] In a very practical way, this evacuates any intelligible fixed meaning to the word and often causes a considerable degree of confusion among readers of agricultural literature because the term describes anything and everything — which means in reality nothing at all. So, it behooves us to state precisely a working notion of sustainability. Before proffering my working definition, however, a few preliminary remarks about sustainability are in order.

It is absolutely vital to recognize sustainability not as a set of specific practices, but as a concept.[104] The concept specifies an end goal — the indefinite persistence of the conditions necessary to produce food — but does not mandate any methods, technologies, or practices to attain this end. The most obvious reason for this flexibility is that sustainability might be attained in a wide variety of ways,[105] from the traditional Amish method of a three- to five-year rotation of corn, oats, hay, and winter wheat, to fruit farming, to flower farming, to tree farming, to a combination grain-animal operation.

Yet another reason is the need to allow for new discoveries to be implemented that better approximate the ideals of sustainability. It would be highly counterproductive to disallow in principle any new technologies, scientific discoveries, management techniques, or farming methods that make an agricultural system more sustainable simply because they do not conform to a preconceived model or package. In fact, farmers historically have been some of the most creative and insightful inventors, and their uncanny knack of problem solving and innovating should be given free reign, even strongly encouraged, to make American agriculture more sustainable.

Another consideration is the need to adapt to changing conditions. The increasing scarcity of fossil fuels, the creation of new pests, dwindling fertility stemming from topsoil erosion, new climatic patterns, water shortages, topsoil compaction, and a host of other variables change the equation, so to speak, and require a certain degree of adaptability in the agricultural sector to attain sustainability in new and different contexts.

Please do not mistake this considerable flexibility in the possible means to attain sustainability as an indication that all means are equal, or that the concept of sustainability is vacuous on the practical level. While open to multifarious forms of agricultural production, the various components making up the concept of sustainability will eliminate certain forms in principle and create a strong predisposition either for or against other forms. In other words, not all types of farming are equally sustainable.

What, then, is my working notion of sustainability? A sustainable agriculture system is one that is "relatively free from internal threats,"[106] relies on dependable inputs to maintain vital processes, and given these inputs will keep key indicators of system health within a specified range[107] indefinitely, barring any unforeseen events. This definition is trying to capture five essential ideas. First, it is important to understand agricultural production as a *system* that reaches far beyond the farm and is made possible by a number of external, off-farm factors. A common mistake when considering agricultural sustainability is to ignore the complex web of dependencies, relationships, and support systems that affect a farm's ability to function properly. To give but one example, corn production in the United States relies heavily on synthetic nitrogen, the production of which is heavily dependent on fossil fuels. In this way, fossil fuels become part and parcel of the agricultural system, as well as the entire array of coordinated activities that make fossil fuels available, including extraction, refining, bulk delivery to points of sale, and the host of support personnel needed directly and indirectly at every stage of this process. Thus things not commonly associated with "the farm" are integral aspects of an agricultural system's health, which means that the task of erecting a sustainable food production system must consider these aspects too.

Second, the phrase "internal threats" means that anything external to the system that can or sometimes does interfere with an agricultural system negatively, or possibly destroy it altogether, does not mean that the system is unsustainable. Nuclear contamination, fallout from an asteroid impacting earth, or protracted warfare might render an agricultural system unproductive or its products unfit for human consumption. Sustainability requires only that an agricultural system's internal mechanisms and conditions not be the cause of its decline.

While external threats pose a small degree of risk, internal threats have proven to be far greater problems for agricultural production in the Corn Belt. Topsoil erosion, nutrient depletion, soil compaction, and pesticide resistance in bugs have emerged this past century as the most widespread, protracted, and formidable obstacles to overcome. Each, in its own way, degrades the system's health, and in many instances this degradation will be accompanied by other secondary effects that either further exacerbate already existing problems or cause new types of threats inimical to the system's smooth functioning. Consistent with the already stated predisposition to ensure a wide margin for error in our agricultural system that is forgiving of human folly and other factors negatively affecting the system as a whole, the appropriate moral reaction to these internal threats is to prefer technologies, policies, farming practices, and relationships that effectively keep these problems at bay. Ideally, however, we should strive to ensure these problems become nothing more than topics in history books by creating conditions in which topsoil accumulates, nutrient content and soil structure are favorable for growing a wide variety of crops, and pesticide-resistant bugs are nonexistent.

Third, inputs essential for maintaining an agricultural system's vital processes should be abundant, able to be acquired easily and consistently, and available for the foreseeable future. The reason for this criterion is that choosing inputs with these characteristics militates against structural fragility and risk. Any time a crucial input becomes an integral feature for the system to function well, the probability increases that at some point the system will suffer a serious breakdown, if that input is or could become scarce, erratic, or unpredictable in its availability; entirely depleted; or subject to price fluctuations that make it cost prohibitive.

As a general rule, this criterion gives strong preference to solar-based agricultural systems and to resources that can be generated on the farm. Why? There is no better energy supply than the sun: it shares its bounty with the earth every day, it is perpetually free for the taking, and it is renewable for billions of years. Organizing an agricultural system around solar energy is perhaps the best way to eliminate system-wide unpredictability and risk. Fossil fuels, in contrast, the dominant energy forms in contemporary American agriculture, are subject to the vicissitudes of geopolitics and global economics, which sometimes make prices fluctuate wildly, and their supplies are dwindling world-wide and will eventually be depleted in the not-too-distant future (not to mention the numerous negative effects stemming from pollution). Long before this occurs, however, diminishing supplies will make them cost prohibitive for all but the wealthiest farmers. Constructing an agricultural system on a foundation of fossil fuels is comparable to the proverbial house built on sand: given sufficient time, the precariousness of the structure will eventually result in something undesirable, maybe even disastrous, occurring. And at the very least, it creates an unnecessary level of risk and unpredictability.

The strength of relying on resources that can be generated on the farm itself is that it reduces the scope of vicissitudes and contingencies that can make inputs undependable in various ways. For instance, the production of synthetic nitrogen, the most widely used fertilizer in the Corn Belt, makes a farmer (and on a larger scale the entire system) susceptible to the vulnerabilities associated with fossil fuel use. These vulnerabilities are far less conspicuous in Amish agriculture, since Amish farmers obtain a great deal of nitrogen through their standard three- to five-year crop rotation program, which includes nitrogen fixers such as alfalfa or clover.[108] Neither political conflict in the Middle East, nor reduced oil production by OPEC, nor the dwindling fossil fuel supplies and their eventual exhaustion will affect as greatly the ability of Amish farmers to supply their fields with nitrogen.

As I stated above, the preferences given to solar-based agricultural systems and on-site resources obtain generally. There will probably never be an agricultural system based exclusively on solar power or capable of producing all inputs on the farm itself. Some deviations from this preference also do not pose much risk to the continued smooth functioning of the system. This being said, I think it indisputable that preferring inputs that are abundant, readily accessible, renewable, and available locally will, on the whole, strengthen our agricultural system and insulate it from a number of potentially disruptive, negative contingencies.

Fourth, sustainability requires predictability and consistency in key criteria of systemwide health, given the presence of sufficient inputs. Similar to the self-regulating process of homeostasis in humans, in which the human body and its component parts operate within specified ranges if humans receive certain amounts of oxygen, hydration, food, and nutrients, a sustainable agricultural system should function in a relatively predictable manner in terms of the major benchmarks commonly employed to assess the system's vitality.

The most important criterion of systemwide health is the quality and quantity of topsoil. Topsoil is the "mother-lode of terrestrial life"[109] and the lifeblood of any type of agriculture. Without this vital medium, large-scale agriculture becomes an exercise in futility. It is obvious that we need topsoil in sufficient quantities, since productivity diminishes with each inch of topsoil lost. Yet the health of an agricultural system is as equally dependent on the topsoil's fertility, which is connected to organic matter content, soil composition, nutrient content, porosity, texture, and microbial decomposers. Each of these aspects, in their different ways, provides a beneficial service by making topsoil a more hospitable environment for crop production.

In my estimation, impact on topsoil quantity and quality should be one of the paramount indices for evaluating policies, technologies, and practices in the agricultural sphere. Due to the long periods of time required to create topsoil, which range from thirty to a thousand years for one inch of topsoil to accumulate, topsoil should be treated as if it were a nonrenewable resource. The fact is that creating the right type and quantity of topsoil in which to grow crops is not simply a matter of wedding American scientific ingenuity, political determination, and hard-working farmers across the Corn Belt to rectify a technical problem. No, creating the right type and quantity of topsoil is a long-term affair that took millions of years to achieve before European immigrants sank plows into the native tallgrass prairie, and will assuredly require centuries-long effort and attention on our part to ensure that the natural bounty we inherited continues to succor God's creation indefinitely.

An agricultural system ordered to ensure that topsoil accumulates and remains fertile for growing a wide variety of plants is the best way to create a wide margin for error and to allow topsoil to withstand mismanagement, abuse, and pernicious governmental policies without substantially jeopardizing its ability to produce food. Allowing our topsoil to degrade, on the other hand, is comparable to playing Russian roulette: while we might find some way to compensate for infertile land, the specter of topsoil incrementally degraded and lost over long periods of time signals substantial tribulation for future generations and the agricultural system they inherit from us.

Fifth, sustainability refers to an agricultural system's long-term capacity for consistent performance, because God intended good land to provide sustenance for people as long as we exist. Commentators have noted that the phrase "long-term" is rather vague and nonspecific.[110] Does it refer to twenty years in the future, fifty, a hundred, five hundred, a thousand, or perhaps more? The point is well taken, but somewhat finicky. I am not convinced there is a substantial difference between a five-hundred- and one-thousand-year agricultural development plan. Perhaps there is, but my interest lies more in shifting our frame of reference from the immediacy frequently characterizing discussions in agricultural circles to a thought process that includes future generations and the vitality of the agricultural system they inherit from us.

Conspicuously absent from my working notion of sustainability is any reference to maintaining current production levels, or perhaps incrementally increasing production levels every year. While it can be safely assumed that a sustainable agricultural system, according to my definition, will most likely be able to maintain consistent production levels, the fear that reduced productivity presents a threat to food security or human welfare is misplaced. This might sound like heresy in agricultural circles, but the truth is that productivity is a highly relative term, and very inconsequential in itself. In fact, corn and soybean productivity could decrease in the Corn Belt without any inimical consequences for Americans. Why?

Seventy percent of the corn and soybeans grown in the Corn Belt, which are virtually the only major cash crops grown there anymore, are fed to livestock; the remaining 30 percent is either converted into ethanol, consumed directly by humans, or used in various food products (vegetable oil, corn syrup, additives, cereal, chips, pet food, etc.) or industrial manufacturing processes, among the most popular. This habit of feeding grain to livestock, however, represents a very inefficient and wasteful use of farmland. Consider, for instance, the grain-to-meat ratios among common types of livestock. Cattle are the most inefficient converters of grain into meat, requiring sixteen pounds of grain to produce one pound of beef (a ratio of 16:1); pigs fare better at a grain-to-meat ratio of 6:1; turkeys, 4:1; chickens, 3:1; and catfish, 1:1.[111] These grain-to-meat ratios alone would lead one to suspect that cattle are by far the largest consumers of the Corn Belt's corn and soybeans, since it takes disproportionately more grain to produce beef than any other meat; this suspicion is confirmed by a rather shocking statistic on Americans' proclivity for beef: While the U.S. population composes approximately 4 percent of the world's population, we consume 23 percent of the beef produced worldwide![112]

Now imagine a different scenario. Instead of using this farmland to grow corn and soybeans for animals to eat, what if we were to grow food that is consumed directly by humans: edible corn and soybeans, broccoli, cauliflower, eggplant, asparagus, carrots, onions, raspberries, blackberries, and many others? The loss incurred by the inefficient conversion of grain to meat simply evaporates, and it is now possible either to feed as many people as before on far fewer acres of farmland, or to feed many more people if the total amount of acres is kept in agricultural production.

"Productivity," then, is a highly fluid and abstract term that is virtually meaningless by itself. The more important criterion is whether an agricultural system is capable of producing enough safe, nutritious food to satisfy our daily caloric needs. In this context productivity becomes relevant because we require a certain amount of calories to function well and our agricultural system must produce a specific quantity of foodstuffs to meet these needs. Yet, as I have indicated, there are many ways to produce these goods, and it is not necessary to continue producing as much corn and soybeans in the Corn Belt to ensure the caloric and nutritional needs of Americans.

Another notable absence from my notion of sustainability is profitability. This term, too, is very relative in practice. An indisputable fact about American agriculture is that it is one of the most heavily subsidized industries in the United States. Deficiency payments, low-interest loans, favorable depreciation rates on buildings and machinery, tax deductions for business losses, the ability to pass along various costs or harms to others (commonly called "externalities") which artificially deflates operating expenses, and federally subsidized fossil fuels are a few of the devices our government employs to make farming profitable. While at one time in the history of the United

States, profitability hinged upon good farming practices, personal ingenuity and self-discipline, and more than a fair share of luck from the weather gods, the most crucial determinant of profitability today is the federal government. For the better part of a century, the federal government has ensured that farming is profitable for those willing to mold their farms in a particular way to take advantage of federal financial incentives. By and large, this has meant that capital-intensive, highly mechanized, specialized, and large farms have been the most profitable. Remove these artificial supports, however, and the profitability of these farms pales in comparison to other types of farms.

The fact remains that the United States has consistently mustered the political will and the financial wherewithal to make virtually any type of farming profitable we desire, and our widespread desire for "cheap food" guarantees extensive government involvement in American agriculture for the foreseeable future. Thus, in my opinion profitability is a moot issue since there is little doubt that American agriculture will continue to be profitable for many farmers, and downright lucrative for a select few who are in a good position to take advantage of federal programs.

The more relevant question is, Who should profit? While a definitive answer to this question is premature due to the fact that much relevant information in chapter 2 has not yet been addressed, the short answer is that farms realizing the objectives consistent with a Christian ethic of gratitude should be given preferential treatment by government policies and programs. There are clearly winners and losers under my proposal, and the determinant of financial success in farming, in my opinion, should depend upon the degree to which a farmer realizes these objectives.

Indigenous Agricultural Systems

While the definitional elements of the term "sustainability" indicate, in varying degrees of specificity, the structural characteristics of agricultural systems that promote their ability to persist for long periods of time, it is important not to overlook actual historical examples of agricultural systems that have existed for millennia and are almost universally acknowledged as sustainable. Indigenous agricultural systems have flourished on every continent since the beginning of human history, and many have weathered the processes of colonization, environmental degradation, reduction of living space, the introduction of exotic species, and other factors while remaining intact and productive. As embodiments of sustainability, indigenous agricultural systems can offer valuable clues to determine the type of characteristics most conducive to the long-term viability of American agriculture.

"Clues" is the operative word in the preceding sentence. The major limitation in determining whether indigenous agricultural systems are relevant to attaining agricultural sustainability today is the extraordinary degree of contextual differences which might undermine the assumption that the greater the structural and functional similarities between Corn Belt agriculture and indigenous agriculture, the greater the chance that our food production system will be sustainable. The following, for instance, represent some of these differences: many indigenous peoples did not rely exclusively on settled agriculture for their food needs, but practiced a seminomadic, hunter-gatherer lifestyle; many were not incorporated into and pressured by a market economy; many operated under strict social and cultural constraints; most practiced subsistence agriculture; many had access to large tracts of nonagricultural lands (forests, marshes, meadows) from which to glean inputs and resources; and many had the option of locating farmland on prime agricultural sites.

Nor is it always easy to determine the relationship of certain structural features of indigenous agricultural practices to sustainability. Relative to contemporary American agriculture, for instance, indigenous agricultural systems relied exclusively on simple technologies. Yet it might not be clear whether these technologies actually fostered the sustainability of their agricultural systems, or whether these technologies were adopted simply because they were the only tools available at this time and actually had little connection to sustainability.

In my opinion, while these hermeneutical issues might entail more investigative work to determine precisely why indigenous agriculture was sustainable, we should be exceedingly reluctant to dismiss indigenous agricultural systems as being too primitive, unsophisticated, or unproductive to offer any relevant insights for contemporary American agriculture. Many who voice these types of criticisms are nothing more than ideologues trying to protect vested interests by maintaining the status quo in American agriculture. Moreover, in many instances this dismissive attitude is simply a disdain for anything different than our preferred method of food production. Given the facts that indigenous agricultural systems have proven to be sustainable for millennia and that American agriculture in its present form (capital intensive, fossil fuel dependent, chemical intensive, large-scale, mechanized, industrialized, and specialized) is a marked historical deviation from time-tested practices that is truly an experiment in progress due to its infancy and novelty, it seems appropriate to place the burden of proof on contemporary American agriculture to show that its preferred type of food production is sustainable. Thus instead of rejecting indigenous agricultural systems because they do not fit a preconceived model and the host of presuppositions and implicit value judgments upon which it is based,[113] we should be open to the possibility that our model of agricultural production is flawed and the indigenous agricultural systems might provide beneficial correctives to current unsustainable practices. Many contemporary scholars are convinced that the sustainability of indigenous agricultural systems is no mistake and that an analysis of these food production systems reveals a recurrent pattern of similar structural characteristics, each of which contributes vitally to the system's sustainability. Let me discuss these features briefly.

Indigenous agriculture is knowledge intensive. The sophistication, breadth, and level of detail of an indigenous farmer's knowledge about local soils, climate, plants, animals, craft skills, natural processes, and the relationships between these variables is unparalleled in contemporary American agriculture. Lacking external support systems such as extension offices and educational centers to train specialists, an indigenous farmer had to master all facets of his or her respective agricultural system in order to make it function effectively. The principal source of knowledge was local agricultural traditions handed down orally from generation to generation, which in turn was based on firsthand experiments by farmers that occurred over hundreds, if not thousands, of years. The knowledge generated by this tradition tended toward holism insofar as a premium is placed on understanding the interrelationships between various aspects of the system.[114]

Indigenous agricultural systems relied on crop diversity for the following reasons:[115] to promote a better diet by making available a wide range of crops that better fulfilled nutritional requirements; to exploit beneficial relationships between different plants; to extend the growing season; to minimize crop damage due to pest infestations, disease, or pathogens; to help control weed problems; and to take advantage of the full range of local resources. Contemporary Americans are likely to think that "crop diversity" means three or four types of crops grown on the same farm. To capture the diversity of indigenous agriculture, however, we need to think on a scale of hundreds of varieties of crops. In the Peruvian highlands, for instance, natives cultivate between four hundred and two thousand different varieties of potato![116]

In turn, this degree of crop diversity allows indigenous farmers to exploit the full range of microenvironments effectively.[117] Since patches of farmland might differ in terms of soil type and composition, water absorption and retention, temperature, altitude, slope, sunlight, and physical proximity to pests, each piece of ground presents manifold restrictions and possibilities which permit the farmer with the greatest degree of crop diversity to take fullest advantage of each site's particular growing conditions.

Indigenous agricultural systems do not require massive alteration of or control over the physical environment, and indigenous farmers are much more tolerant of things commonly considered to be "problems" by contemporary American farmers. Fewer plants and bugs are classified as "weeds" and "pests," respectively, because indigenous farmers use these for human or animal food, medicines, fertilizers, fuels, or religious ceremonies. Crop diversity also contributes to this lack of need for extensive environmental alteration because the greater the range of available crops, the better the chance of having a plant that can thrive under unique conditions without having to alter its physical environment. While it might be convenient to explain this lack of need to control or alter environmental conditions as stemming from technological limitations that precluded substantial environmental modifications (i.e., no heavy machinery), this phenomenon is better explained by the fact that indigenous agricultural systems have been adapted to local conditions and therefore do not need to change environmental conditions greatly to produce sufficiently. In this context, it might even be highly disadvantageous to alter the physical environment to a greater degree in some instances, since this might jeopardize processes or relationships that are beneficial to the system's smooth functioning.

Multiple, complex recycling processes help maintain soil fertility by ensuring a regular infusion of nutrients and organic matter. Animal manure, crop residues, leaves, ashes, household garbage, and a host of other "wastes" are deposited on the fields. Topsoil erosion is minimized by terracing, fallowing, tilling only during dry periods, weeding only after the root systems of crops are well developed, and planting seeds directly into sod whenever possible, without breaking the soil.[118] Indigenous farmers recognize the necessity of fertile topsoil in sufficient quantities and have developed multiple site-specific strategies to create and retain topsoil.

The technologies used in indigenous agricultural systems tend to be simple by today's standards. Of course, most indigenous peoples did not have the physical infrastructure or specialized scientific knowledge necessary to produce "complex" technologies. Yet there is probably a more compelling explanation for this preference for simple technologies, and given the option to adopt supposedly complex technologies modeled on the implements used in contemporary American agriculture, I suspect that many indigenous peoples would decline. Why?

Complex technologies such as heavy machinery (tractors and combines) and implements (plows, planters, sprayers, cultivators, etc.) cannot be used effectively in small-scale, diversified agricultural systems. These technologies need large, uniform environments in which to operate, and each is designed to perform a limited number of tasks. On a small, one-acre patch of cultivated land containing twenty to fifty different types of plants spaced apart unevenly and intercropped, a multifunctional tool capable of maneuvering in a variety of ways is not only highly desirable, but absolutely necessary. A hoe, for instance, can accommodate a variety of needs: it can be used to drill holes in sod, in which seeds can be planted directly to avoid soil disturbance; it can create a wide range of soil structure, ranging from large clumps of soil turned over once to soil of a finer texture; it can cultivate weeds between wide or narrow rows, and also remove weeds from between plants in the same row; it can dig deep or shallow holes for root crops; it can move topsoil into large or small mounds; it can dig trenches for row crops; it can extract root crops from underground; it can work fertilizers and manure into the soil; it can spread mulch over the soil and between plants; it can extract unwanted rocks and tree roots; and it can dig canals to channel rainwater to a cultivated area. Given the environmental conditions, scale of operation, and the tasks necessary in indigenous agricultural systems, there is no question that simple technologies like the multifunctional hoe represent the best tools for the job.

Indigenous agricultural systems rely on local, renewable inputs. To a certain extent, these features are simply a result of mobility constraints and the fact that many of the available inputs happened to be renewable. But the benefit of this arrangement is that these inputs were readily accessible and regularly available, which provided a great deal of security for indigenous agricultural systems.

Food production was oriented toward the local community, although some indigenous peoples occasionally used surplus crops to sell or barter at regional markets. While this characteristic can also be attributed to mobility constraints, an obvious advantage of producing food primarily for local consumption is superior nutritional content. It is something of a truism that the fresher the food, the healthier it will be, and recent studies confirm this claim's veracity. Food today travels farther and is stored for longer periods of time than ever before, which allows more time for decomposition that reduces nutritional quality.[119] Compared to fifty years ago, our major foodstuffs pale in comparison. Potatoes have lost 100 percent of their vitamin A, 57 percent of their vitamin C and iron, 28 percent of their calcium, 50 percent of their riboflavin, and 18 percent of their thiamine. Calcium in broccoli, a vegetable that epitomizes healthy food, has dropped by 63 percent, and iron by 34 percent. A person would have to eat eight oranges today to get the same amount of vitamin A as from a single orange grown fifty years ago.[120] As a general rule, by producing and consuming food locally, indigenous peoples avoid many of these nutritional losses and thus eat healthier foods.

While this cursory presentation obviously leaves many issues unaddressed, let me hazard a few comments about the relevance of indigenous agricultural systems for understanding sustainability better. The attractiveness of indigenous agricultural systems as a model for agricultural development is not only their sustainability, but also their consistency with the robust precautionary attitude articulated earlier: to minimize structural risk by insulating food production systems from various vicissitudes. Of course, one way to minimize risk is to gather data, to determine cause-effect relationships, and to infer and make predictions based on this knowledge; in other words, to make a well-informed, well-educated guess. To a great extent, however, indigenous agricultural systems eliminate this epistemological uncertainty; these systems have been tested by a host of vicissitudes over long periods of time, and have proven capable of maintaining their structural integrity. While indigenous agricultural systems are probably as context sensitive as any other type of agricultural system, they certainly enjoy a lengthy track record of success and provide a basis for moving beyond what we *think* constitutes sustainability to what *actually has been* sustainable. This critical difference, in my opinion, makes indigenous agricultural systems an indispensable resource for considering agricultural development today.

Second, indigenous agricultural systems provide a general recipe for sustainability that could be implemented today: knowledge-intensive agriculture; local food production and consumption; fertile topsoil in sufficient quantities; low technology; crop diversity; small scale; use of renewable resources for inputs; nutrient recycling processes that create fertility from waste; and adapting to local environmental conditions. To be sure, over the past century American agriculture has moved away from most of these characteristics, and it would take a long period of time to remake American agriculture in a different image and likeness. But there is nothing in principle that precludes American agriculture from eventually embodying these characteristics.

Third, the sustainability of indigenous agricultural systems does not lie in one practice or structural feature, but emerges from a network of interrelated, mutually conditioned parts that together form a sustainable system. In other words, sustainability is a product of a holism capable of understanding the multiple relationships, components, and dynamics necessary to make an agricultural system persist indefinitely. There is a tendency today in the agricultural sector to attach the sustainable label to particular technologies or practices (three decades ago it was chisel plows; today no-till production methods, Bt corn,[121] and genetic engineering are favorites). In their day, all these were hailed for their ability to promote sustainability. If the lesson gathered from indigenous agricultural systems is correct, however, we should be very wary about such claims, since they often divert attention from other equally relevant — and unsustainable — components of a system and presuppose the contemporary reductionist inclination to consider aspects in isolation from one another. These typically culminate in a predisposition to tinker on the periphery of American agriculture by implementing policies or practices designed to improve one aspect of our food production system, while other structural aspects are left untouched. In the long run, however, if the various components of an agricultural system are not revamped to support and maintain one another, then sustainability will be unattainable.

Finally, there seems to be a strong correlation between sustainability and restraint (whether natural or self-imposed). The success of indigenous farmers has hinged as much on what they have *not* done as on what they have done. Increasing farm size, producing for the open market rather than local communities, specializing in one or two crops, purchasing expensive technologies or inputs — all these differences would have introduced new dynamics and pressures into indigenous agricultural systems, and each probably would have engendered compromises that would have diminished the system's sustainability. While this assertion is somewhat speculative, the ability to resist conditions that would have undermined the aforementioned characteristics and the multiple systemwide relationships they engendered seems to be the sine qua non for sustainability. If this is correct, sustainable agriculture will best be encouraged through a culture of restraint, a culture that produces farmers, policymakers, rural communities, and consumers who are capable of exercising the self-control necessary to ensure that the conditions required for sustainable agriculture are supported and implemented.

Conclusion

I have argued that the best theological context in which to understand the gift of good land is an ethic of gratitude. In addition to an emotional response of thankfulness that gets expressed in our spiritual lives through prayer and worship, an ethic of gratitude generates a series of normative moral positions that should be employed to assess the moral palatability of agriculture in the Corn Belt, including the following:

1. A robust precautionary predisposition to insulate and protect our agricultural system from various vicissitudes, due to the fact that it supplies a basic good necessary for life.

2. The need to fashion an agricultural system more conducive to the flourishing of animals, because God intended good land to benefit them too.

3. Creating a sustainable agricultural system that can persist indefinitely and provide food for future generations.

4. Ensuring at a minimum that our agricultural system does not cause or contribute to poverty and the marginalization, vulnerability, and powerlessness of certain groups; ideally, however, it would strongly counteract these tendencies.

5. The absence of practices that unintentionally cause serious physical harms.

While I will be proposing other minor moral benchmarks to assess agriculture in the Corn Belt, these positions represent the heart of a Christian agricultural ethic and will dominate my analysis in chapter 2.

The next step is to examine agriculture in the Corn Belt to determine in what ways and to what degree it coheres with these moral criteria. The object is not simply to make moral judgments about the current suitability of American agriculture, but also to assess the manifold policies, practices, values, and technologies that have exercised a formative influence on its development. The catalysts behind the historical development of American agriculture are essential structural features that make our food production system unique. They also continue to exercise enormous influence on the developmental trajectory of American agriculture and need to be brought to explicit awareness and evaluated morally if our food production system is to be shaped according to a Christian ethic of gratitude. To this end, let us turn to significant trends in American agriculture and begin piecing together this story.

Chapter Two

Trends in American Agriculture

Introduction

The structural and conceptual shifts in American agriculture during the past three centuries have been breathtaking. Thomas Jefferson's vision of our newly founded republic as an agrarian society, with the countryside teeming with small-scale farmers,[1] was based on his belief that farmers served a unique, and irreplaceable, political function.[2] Farmers, unlike any other class of people in early America, possessed the requisite virtues[3] — a spirit of independence and self-reliance — to counteract totalitarian political tendencies and to make our fledgling democracy a truly participatory government responsive to the will of the people and free from domination by a small group of political elites.[4] Whether their stubborn independence was a preexistent character trait that made the farming lifestyle attractive, or whether the demands of farm life necessarily inculcated the independence Jefferson observed in American farmers, farmers as a group were mavericks who preferred to make decisions for themselves and staunchly resisted any paternalistic, external imposition of ideas, values, or political programs.[5] Their self-reliance, especially during this era, was legendary. A farm's success depended largely on a farmer's ability to perform a wide range of tasks either by himself or herself, or with the help of a spouse and their able-bodied children: anticipating problems with animals or crops and taking preemptive action, working long hours during planting and harvesting seasons, finding creative solutions to problems with limited resources, performing daily chores and routine maintenance, and cultivating the self-discipline to rise early in the

78

day and to withstand the rigors of frequent, physically demanding, manual labor.

Farmers, according to Jefferson, were the most dependable and capable front-line defense against the totalitarian pressures from which Americans had been recently liberated.[6] Their capacity for free thinking and their repugnance for anything curtailing their autonomy were necessary to counteract the ideological and behavioral hegemony that the political elites needed to exert their self-interest effectively. Their self-reliance, initiative, and ingenuity made farmers the most effective and formidable force against pernicious political programs. Their extensive involvement in local politics ensured a vibrant, grassroots network of active resistors to measures intended to benefit a few elites at the expense of farming communities nationwide. Farmers, in other words, were the vital ingredient in maintaining a flourishing, participatory democracy capable of representing the will of the people.

Jefferson's dream of an agrarian society, of course, is virtually dead in contemporary America — and along with it any consideration that farmers play an important political role in preserving a genuine democracy. Imagine lamenting the decline of participatory democracy in contemporary America and attributing this directly to the historically unprecedented small number of farmers today. The audience, I strongly suspect, would probably frown politely or openly question your sanity. Farmers, for contemporary Americans, play no grand political role at the national level; their political involvement is restricted to self-interested lobbying for larger grain subsidies, better access to foreign markets, property tax relief, or more emergency relief aid — a far cry from the substantive political contribution Jefferson envisioned.

The shift in Americans' conception of farmers can be attributed to a number of causes. Political liberalism, which dominates academic discourse in contemporary America and provides much of the vocabulary and many of the concepts operative in the mass media, virtually ignores Jefferson's message that a democracy's success hinges on the virtues of its citizenry (or at least on virtues other than those not directly connected with or promoting "freedom" — tolerance, respect, and noninterference, for example). In this climate of opinion, Jefferson's idea that people need to have a certain type of character or habits for democracy to survive seems a little outlandish — and along with it the notion that farmers might have something unique and substantive to offer America politically.

Sociocultural causes, I suspect, are also partly responsible for the shift in Americans' conception of farmers. While mention of the "family farm" typically evokes highly positive emotions, and while most Americans believe that farmers are hard-working, industrious, decent folks who make an honest living and who inculcate the same laudable values in their children, there is, strangely enough, a strong, albeit sometimes unspoken, prejudice against farmers.[7] Disparaging words or phrases such as "local yokel," "country bumpkin," and "hick" are all characterizations of farmers.[8] Sometimes not-so-subtle innuendo conveys the impression that farmers are simpletons who are somewhat naïve, provincial, earthy, dirty, and smelly, and who earn their money by the sweat of their brow because they are too unskilled to secure a more preferable white-collar job. Although most Americans appreciate farmers' work ethic and the food they provide, farming is not a lifestyle parents readily promote to their children, nor does it entail the social and economic prestige of other occupations (imagine a parent telling his or her child to be not a doctor, lawyer, teacher, or scientist, but a farmer). Once again, the contrast between Jefferson's vision of farmers — and the virtues they incarnate — as the backbone for our fledgling participatory democracy's success, and the contemporary attitude of thankfulness for farmers and the food they provide coupled with a tongue-in-cheek assessment of farmers' native skills, aptitude, and social standing, is stark.

Another cause in the shift of Americans' conception of farmers is the almost total dominance of economic jargon in the agricultural sector, which not only has affected the terms and concepts most Americans use to conceptualize farmers and their function, but also has altered the way farmers understand themselves. Especially in popular agricultural magazines, farmers are no longer farmers; they are business managers, or production overseers, or chief executive officers. Pigs, cows, and chickens have become units of production. Building repairs, machinery maintenance, dead animals, and gasoline use are labeled as costs of production. From beginning to end, from the farmer and the various tasks he or she performs, to the animals tended, to the crops grown, to the mechanical and chemical devices used, everything about farming is couched in economic terms, and everything is ultimately reducible to its effect on the bottom line, the profit margin. While many issues could be raised about the traditional cost/benefit analysis that dominates contemporary American agriculture, the only point I wish to make is that the infiltration of economic terms and concepts represents a significant historical shift in the way farmers conceive of themselves, what values enter their moral radar screen, and what values are dismissed as morally irrelevant.

My purpose in presenting this limited, albeit highly notable, shift in the way American farmers are perceived is to illustrate that American agriculture has undergone something of a revolution the past three centuries, a revolution so thorough and far reaching that even farmers, a group renowned for its traditionalism and conservatism, have essentially redefined themselves according to its tenets. As one might suspect, other sectors of American society less resistant to winds of change have wholeheartedly embraced this revolution and have internalized the messages frequently mouthed to legitimize the ongoing structural renovation of American agriculture. Slogans such as America being "the breadbasket to the world" and the constant litany of praises emanating from the popular media about American agriculture's enormous productivity and technological progress have engendered a considerable degree of enthusiasm among most Americans that our agricultural system should be a beacon of light to the world, especially to Third and Fourth World countries.

It is unquestionably true that through the combined efforts of research universities, heavy industry, the U.S. Department of Agriculture, mechanical engineers, botanists, geneticists, and scores of hard-working, determined farmers across the United States, American agriculture has become the most productive agricultural system the world has ever known (measured strictly by output),[9] and to this extent American agriculture succeeds in fulfilling one moral criterion of an ethic of gratitude, namely, that it provide a sufficient amount of food for people to survive and flourish. Yet this is only one relevant moral component, and a growing chorus of contemporary critics[10] contend that the values impelling the ongoing structural renovation of American agriculture are shortsighted, environmentally damaging, inimical to the vitality of rural communities, and ultimately self-destructive. Moreover, they assert, the longer business as usual in the agricultural sector is tolerated by Americans, the more the natural capital upon which agriculture depends is undermined and the more probable it becomes that eventually transitioning to a more morally palatable agricultural system will be difficult and painful, and maybe impossible. In other words, when our moral analysis extends beyond the criterion of providing a sufficient amount of food and begins assessing American agriculture according to the other components of a Christian ethic of gratitude, American agriculture has "been weighed on the scales and found wanting."[11]

As will become apparent, I believe most of the charges leveled against American agriculture by contemporary critics are right on target, which creates a considerable climate of urgency for structural reform. The large-scale nature of American agriculture, which comprises hundreds of millions of acres,[12] poses a distinct — and very daunting — challenge. Despite our supposed technological and scientific prowess, the sheer magnitude of degradation to our land might permanently thwart even the most brilliant scientific proposals and concerted political programs to restore the productivity of American farmland, or at the very least would require many centuries to reverse the damage already done. Quick fixes in the agricultural sector are well-nigh impossible, and American ingenuity might prove to be practically impotent when faced with such formidable tasks.

So how exactly does American agriculture fall short of the vision provided by a Christian ethic of gratitude? What forces, policies, and practices have impelled this structural renovation? What practical effects have these produced? To answer these questions, let us examine various trends in American agriculture and assess the formative influences that have shaped Corn Belt agriculture into the food production system it is today.

Major Trends in American Agriculture

Increasing Average Farm Size and Decreasing Total Farm Population

Inspired both by Thomas Jefferson's vision of America as an agrarian society and by a desire to reap substantial economic benefits through westward expansion, the federal government in the 1800s passed a series of bills — Land Law (1820), Preemption Act (1841), Graduation Act (1854), and Homestead Act (1862) — intended to entice adventurous spirits into establishing farms either by giving away farmland for free or by making it available at nominal cost. Furthermore, in this legislation the federal government showed a decided preference for small-scale operations; strict limits were placed on the acres an individual or organization could own, which counteracted concentration of land ownership.[13]

This federal legislation proved to be remarkably successful; scores of people migrated westward, claimed farmland, and began breaking and working the soil. Jefferson's dream was at least partially realized. While the countryside was not teeming with farmers, the farms that existed were small by today's standards (under the Homestead Act, the largest tract of land for which a farmer was eligible was 160 acres), and there were no evident signals that eastern industrialists or speculators had been very successful in circumventing federal law and acquiring large tracts of land, even though they were actively engaged in various enterprises to obtain land for resale.[14]

As one would expect, by the late 1800s a large proportion of Americans — about two-thirds — lived on farms. Farm size, by today's standards, was relatively small, usually between 40 and 160 acres. Beginning in the 1900s, however, the farm population has experienced steady, but enormous, reductions, and the average farm size has grown remarkably. Farm population decreased from 30 million in 1940, to 22 million in 1955, to 20 million in the mid-1960s, to 5.4 million in 1985, to just over 2 million in 2002. In terms of percentages, people living on farms constituted approximately 66 percent of the total American population in the mid-1800s; today, only about 2 percent live on farms.[15]

Average farm size increased similarly during the 1900s. The most significant trend, however, has been the emergence of "megafarms," or farms averaging $250,000–$500,000 in gross sales per year. In 1990, almost 50 percent of all food grown in the United States was produced by the largest 4.1 percent of farms, and 33 percent was produced on the largest 1.2 percent of farms. If this trend continues, the United States Department of Agriculture (USDA) projects that 50 percent of all farm products will come from the largest 1 percent of farms in the near future.[16]

Proponents of industrialized agriculture frequently cite such statistics to demonstrate the efficiency of American agriculture: not only are farmers today able to farm much more land per capita than farmers of a hundred years ago, but the sharply declining farm population (which has not negatively affected production; in fact, production has consistently increased throughout the twentieth century) has essentially freed many farmers for other types of employment.[17]

Statistics on the declining farm population, however, are deceptive. While it is true that the farm population has experienced a precipitous decline in the twentieth century, there has been no significant reduction in the total amount of people involved in American agriculture. The reason is the increasing number of people indirectly involved in agriculture. A farmer in the mid-1800s, for example, would use a team of draft horses for plowing, planting, and cultivating, and most of the horses' needs (feed, water, shelter, etc.) were supplied by the farmer himself or herself with very few external, off-farm inputs. Traction power for a contemporary farmer — a tractor — in contrast requires a bevy of external inputs and a vast array of indirect support. The diesel fuel alone powering the tractor requires (1) an oil drilling operation, either domestic or foreign, and the engineers, managers, and production workers necessary to bring the oil to the surface; (2) ship or rail transport from the point of extraction to the refinery (which also involves a host of support personnel); (3) the refining process and everyone employed by the refinery; (4) ship, rail, or tractor-trailer transport to the point of sale; and (5) a retail operation and its support staff and bulk transport to the farm itself. Considered by itself, the diesel fuel powering the tractor involves an almost baffling array of highly coordinated efforts and scores of people to get the fuel from deep underground to the farmer. This is only one vital component for ensuring the tractor's smooth functioning. Also needed would be an assessment of the direct and indirect support required for producing and maintaining the tractor's tires; oil filter; gas filter; the steel making up its frame, body, and engine; electronic circuitry; computers; lights; glass windshield; plastic steering wheel and seat; paint; and lubricating oil, among many others. To give an accurate estimation of the amount of indirect, external input required by the average contemporary American farmer, it would be necessary to calculate all those involved in the production and distribution of pesticides, fertilizers, herbicides, plows, cultivators, planters, sprayers, grain dryers, storage buildings for machinery or grain, seeds, and tools.

The claim, then, often made with a great deal of pride by proponents of industrialized agriculture that fewer and fewer farmers are needed to provide Americans with a sufficient amount of food, which implicitly contains a highly positive assessment that former farmers are now available for other types of employment, turns out to be more an interpretive sleight-of-hand than anything else. Yes, fewer farmers are needed today than a hundred years ago. No, this does not entail any significant reduction in the total number of people engaged in agriculture since contemporary industrial farming requires so many more indirect, external inputs than before. Of course, the proponent of industrialized agriculture should be asked why it is more beneficial to have fewer farmers and more manufacturing workers producing diesel fuel, pesticides, spark plugs, headlights, and steel for tractors. But I do not want to pursue this issue here.

The major issues surrounding the trend of declining farm population and increasing farm size are the heavy economic and social costs incurred by rural communities. As early as the 1940s, rural sociologists began establishing empirically that as farm size increases, rural communities dependent on the surrounding farms deteriorate in various ways. The first extensive survey, Walter Goldschmidt's comparison of two California farming towns, was something of a bombshell in the agricultural sector,[18] and his findings have been corroborated by sociologists ever since. Goldschmidt studied two towns in close physical proximity in California's San Joaquin Valley, Dinuba and Arvin, the only significant difference between them being the size of surrounding farms: the average farm around Dinuba comprised 57 acres, and that around Arvin 497 acres.[19] From a strictly economic perspective, Dinuba enjoyed a host of advantages: its merchants did two-thirds more retail trade; it had more than twice as many businesses, and the variety of businesses was greater; there were more restaurants, clothing shops, and home furnishing stores in Dinuba; it had almost twice the number of agricultural equipment and supply stores. The social consequences of farm size were equally stark: Dinuba had four elementary schools and a high school while Arvin had one elementary school; Dinuba had three parks and two newspapers compared with one playground and one newspaper in Arvin; Dinuba enjoyed twice the number of civic organizations, churches, and churchgoers; Dinuba had more paved streets, sidewalks, garbage disposal equipment, and sewage disposal conduits; and Dinuba had appreciably less social stratification and less economic disparity between rich and poor.[20]

The tale told by these statistics is one known experientially across rural America: as farm size increases, quality of life in farming communities is affected negatively and systemically. The reasons for the positive correlation between increasing farm size and the overall decline of farming-dependent communities are varied. While large farms tend to generate more profits (despite their inefficiency compared to small and medium-sized farms), those profiting from large farms tend not to spend their disposable income in their local communities. Because wholesalers of farm supplies offer discounts to their high-volume customers, owners of large farms frequently bypass local businesses when purchasing farm-related equipment or supplies in favor of lower prices elsewhere. Even when owners of large farms patronize local businesses, their disproportionate economic power (and often the desperation of local businesses) allows them to negotiate lower prices compared to owners of smaller farms.[21] Furthermore, owners of large farms tend to travel greater distances to purchase non-farm-related, high-ticket items from businesses that offer more product diversity and lower retail prices. In each instance, the result is the same: a comparatively smaller amount of money circulating in local farm communities dominated by large farms, which imposes hardships on local businesses most directly, and indirectly affects all the public services dependent on the local tax base.

Another reason for the diminishment of quality of life is the level of tenancy associated with large farms. As a general rule, the larger the farm, the more land will be rented to nonowners or farmed by others for wages. In Arvin, for example, tenants composed 42 percent of farm workers, yet in Dinuba only 14 percent. As Goldschmidt's study showed, farm tenants as a group tend to be less active in local politics, with the consequence that their concerns and interests often go unnoticed in local decision making. Thomas Jefferson identified the cause of this phenomenon over two hundred years ago: when intergenerational transmission of farmland is the norm, farmers have a vested interest in local politics since their children and grandchildren will most likely be affected by the political decisions made in their communities; permanency for tenants, on the other hand, is a rarity, and thus they have little incentive to be active policy makers at the local level since their longevity in any community is usually uncertain. This leads, as it did in Arvin, to highly unequal representation by and participation in influential political groups. Phrased in Jeffersonian terms, this is the reality of the politically elite, in this instance large farm owners, who exercise a disproportionate influence on local decision making.

In addition, Goldschmidt's study identified another reason for the correlation between large farm size and declining quality of life in farming communities: greater concentration of economic power. Widespread farm ownership characteristic of towns like Dinuba surrounded by small family farms resulted in a more equitable distribution of wealth, as evidenced by a higher median income per family, as well as fewer people at the extremes of the economic scale.

Subsequent empirical studies on farm sizes in California, Kansas,[22] and Nebraska[23] have verified Goldschmidt's main contention that quality of life in farming communities depends most not on the volume of farm goods sold or the total income generated by farmers, but on the number and size of farms in the immediate vicinity.[24] As one sociologist writes, "Everyone who has done careful research on farm size, residency of agricultural owners and social conditions in the rural community finds the same relationship: as farm size and absentee ownership increase, social conditions in the local community deteriorate."[25]

The increasing average farm size and accompanying depopulation of the American countryside fly in the face of a Christian ethic of gratitude. They virtually guarantee that intractable, long-term poverty will be a regular feature of life in rural America. They marginalize groups politically, create formidable class divisions, and render scores of people relatively powerless to change their lot in life. For rural Americans, these abstractions become tangible aspects of daily life in the form of consolidated schools, lack of hospitals or medical clinics, dilapidated buildings, unkempt houses, closed businesses, farm foreclosures, predatory behavior among existing farmers, and an aura of despair and desperation in the residents of dying rural communities. As one commentator writes, many rural Americans have psychologically adapted to these conditions by embracing a no-frills stoic survivor mentality that functions as an effective coping mechanism in this situation:

> Long-term residents run a gauntlet of ghosts whenever they drive down familiar county roads. Every few miles or so, at every wind break or cluster of trees where a farm house has vanished or fallen to ruin, there is the memory of a neighbor who is no longer there. And as the distance opens up in the space between one farm site and the next, an anxious foreboding settles in, as each farmer wonders who will be the next to go. Although we rarely think of the economic disorder stalking the American countryside as a form of terror, there are profound parallels in the traumatic social isolation that attends the state-sanctioned loss of community.[26]

The effects of increasing farm size and dwindling rural population, however, are not confined to the social and economic arenas. The ability to construct a sustainable agricultural system is also affected by these trends. Making our food production system sustainable will most likely require a rather substantial shift to a knowledge-based agriculture, and in this different context a premium is placed on people who are willing and able to seek out appropriate knowledge, both local and scientific; to accept conditions of restraint imposed by local biotic communities and available resources; and to experiment, reflect, and adapt to function more effectively. While many current farmers certainly fit this bill, I suspect that the construction of sustainable agricultural systems will be greatly enhanced by an infusion of new blood. Especially as sustainable agriculture programs at land grant universities become more prominent, there exists more valuable human capital in the form of young people whose habits of mind, pre-dispositions, values, and accumulated knowledge will serve well the objectives of sustainable agriculture.

The major problem is that the deteriorating social, economic, and political conditions of rural America create little incentive for aspiring farmers to take up residence and begin plying their trade. Nobody wants to have his or her children bussed for hours each day to attend school. Nobody wants to live at great distances from doctors and hospitals or grocery stores. Nobody wants to live in a town with poor public services, inadequate police protection, shoddy playgrounds, and few recreation areas. Nobody wants to live in a community plagued by a sizeable proportion of its population living in poverty. While these considerations might not affect those inclined to regard sustainable farming as a noble religious calling, it cannot but act as a powerful deterrent to many considering a long-term commitment to a particular place.

Another pertinent issue concerning farm size is the amount of debt incurred by large farms. Farm debt in general has increased enormously the past sixty years. In 1940, the total farm debt in the United States totaled a little over $10 billion; by the mid-1980s it had risen to $216 billion. The average debt-to-asset ratio[27] has escalated similarly, from 9.3 percent in 1950 to 20.6 percent in the mid-1980s.[28] Although the growing debt-to-asset ratio is troubling, it is highly alarming when applied to different-sized farms. The smallest farms with an average of $5,000 in sales per year enjoyed the best debt-to-asset ratio, 11 percent. As farms get larger and average sales increase, so too does the amount of debt: farms averaging $20,000–40,000 in sales per year had a debt-to-asset ratio of 16.7 percent; the debt-to-asset ratio on the largest farms, or those averaging $50,000+ in sales per year, was 38.1 percent.[29]

The comparatively high amount of debt on large farms has important consequences. Large farms usually are far more financially vulnerable than their smaller counterparts. While a high debt-to-asset ratio does not necessarily doom a large farm to eventual financial difficulty or failure if its cash flow is sufficient,[30] it does significantly reduce the margin for error and greatly diminishes the ability to tolerate negative economic disruptions.[31] Because of their sheer scale, even the smallest price fluctuations in either inputs or commodity prices could cost the owner of a large farm thousands, if not tens of thousands, of dollars. Given the vicissitudes of farming and the many relatively unpredictable variables — droughts decreasing production; a large grain surplus suppressing grain prices; increased costs of fertilizers, pesticides, or herbicides; rising interest rates; mechanical failures necessitating the purchase of new machinery; rising costs of crop insurance, etc. — sooner or later the large farm will experience some economic disruption that will cause a substantial decrease in profits, or even a financial deficit, which frequently necessitates more credit to meet expenses and places the large farm in even further debt. In contrast, the same economic disruptions typically have a less negative effect on the owner of a small farm. Since the small farm loses less money during bad years, personal frugality and family savings are often sufficient to meet expenses and to avoid further indebtedness.

A significant consequence of the economic vulnerability of large farms is the need for substantial government intervention to prevent widespread bankruptcy during difficult economic periods. Although federal government intervention in agriculture has always occurred in some form in the United States, especially after the farm crisis of the 1980s which was caused by overproduction, dwindling demand overseas, and falling grain prices, the federal government has increasingly been called upon to insulate farmers, especially large farms, against economic adversity. Today, the array of government programs designed to protect farmers is staggering, ranging from low-interest loans to price and income supports, deficiency payments, and set-aside programs that compensate farmers for not producing grain. The cost of these programs is astronomical: between 1986 and 1990, price and income supports alone cost the federal government almost $70 billion.[32]

Despite these expensive programs, their practical effects have promoted precisely the conditions leading to economic vulnerability; not only have they generally promoted overproduction that lowers commodity prices, the programs also give a financial advantage to large farms, which creates a strong incentive for farms to get even larger.[33]

Another disadvantage of large farms is their relative rigidity and fewer production options compared to small farms. Although replacement of human labor with capital is perhaps the defining characteristic of Western agriculture as a whole, it is especially evident on large American farms.[34] Large farms "tend to have more long-term investments in land, buildings, and equipment,"[35] and there is practically no alternative for costs associated with necessary inputs such as seeds, fertilizers, pesticides, herbicides, gasoline, and energy used for drying grain. In consequence, operation and production patterns on large farms tend to be more invariable, and most costs are fixed. Take, for example, the ability to reduce costs by applying animal manure over farmland in order to reduce the quantity of nitrogen needed for corn production. The owner of a small farm is much more likely to have access to sufficient quantities of manure, since he or she needs a smaller amount to achieve a comparable result than the owner of a large farm, and the time needed to spread the manure over the small farm is much less than for the large farm. As a result, when prices for nitrogen fertilizer rise, the owner of a small farm is typically in a much better position to implement cost-cutting alternatives. In a similar way, owners of small farms are better able to cut herbicide costs by using human labor to remove weeds from their fields. On a larger farm, where a virtual army of workers would be required to control weed populations sufficiently, it becomes practically impossible to reduce herbicide use. More examples could be adduced, but the point would be essentially the same: smaller farms are able to be more innovative, flexible, and adaptable as conditions change and different forms of production are needed to be economically viable.

All these aspects related to growing farm size in the United States bode ill for attaining sustainability in American agriculture. In fact, in many ways large farms epitomize unsustainability. Their almost complete reliance on fossil fuels takes them as far away from a solar-based agriculture system as one can imagine. Their sheer size forces them to rely on external inputs due to insufficient quantities of local resources. Their rigidity and lack of production options and alternatives greatly diminish their ability to deal effectively with internal threats. Their level of debt virtually ensures that cost-cutting methods or increased productivity will be given priority, even if this means poorer topsoil management, environmental damage, or harm to the community in the form of synthetic chemical contamination. Their margin for error is minuscule, which makes them more susceptible to a wide variety of untimely negative vicissitudes. The almost insatiable desire for more land and the predatory behavior it encourages wreak havoc on local relationships and on a community's cohesiveness. While some notable exceptions to these statements certainly exist, large farms as a group (and the ongoing trend toward even larger farms) represent one of the greatest threats to sustainability and the long-term vitality of our food production system in the Corn Belt today.

Increasing Use of Synthetic Fertilizers and Pesticides

Before the fossil fuel revolution, which made available a wide array of synthetic pesticides, herbicides, and fertilizers, farmers were limited to natural means to fertilize crops and manage pests. Soil fertility was usually enhanced in two ways.[36] First, animal manure was applied to the fields, either by letting animals graze in the fields or by physically hauling manure from a barn or confinement area and spreading it over the fields.[37] Second, farmers practiced crop rotations to maximize soil fertility. The general idea behind crop rotations is that every type of crop affects the soil in different ways and needs different nutrients to grow best. Corn, for example, needs comparatively large quantities of nitrogen to flourish. A hay crop such as alfalfa or clover, on the other hand, fixes nitrogen in the soil and thus leaves an excess of nitrogen behind when harvested. Planting corn in the same field where alfalfa or clover was grown the previous season thus allows a farmer to reduce his or her nitrogen fertilizer applications, or perhaps even eliminate them altogether. By knowing precisely how certain types of crops affected the soil, a farmer was able to maximize production by employing a particular crop rotation sequence.

The major economic drawback to practicing extensive crop rotations is the necessity of growing low-profit crops to augment fertility. As a general rule, many of the crops which traditionally have been part of a farmer's rotation program are not as profitable to grow as corn and soybeans; today they are principally used as animal feed. Especially after the large-scale commercial introduction of synthetic fertilizers into American agriculture after World War II, extensive crop rotations virtually disappeared.[38] Farmers were now able to grow one or two of the most profitable crops continuously.

As one would expect, the amount of synthetic fertilizers applied to farmland has grown steadily throughout the twentieth century. The use of synthetic nitrogen, for example, the most frequently used fertilizer in the Corn Belt, has increased enormously. Shortly after World War II, farmers in Illinois applied 10,000 tons of synthetic nitrogen to their fields, with an average harvest of 50 bushels of corn per acre. Twenty years later, they applied 400,000 tons of synthetic nitrogen and averaged 95 bushels of corn per acre.[39] Today approximately "forty million tons of [synthetic] fertilizers are applied to America's fields each year — approximately 330 pounds for each person in the country."[40]

Although synthetic fertilizers are not the exclusive reason for the dramatic, consistent increases in productivity in the latter half of the twentieth century,[41] they undeniably play a large part. The major issue, however, is the negative unintended side effects of synthetic fertilizer use. As the statistics above on nitrogen use in Illinois indicate, the near doubling of corn production required a fortyfold increase in nitrogen use. At first glance, this statistic is confusing: Why would a fortyfold increase in fertilizer applications only result in a doubling of production? The answer is that synthetic nitrogen only supplements nitrogen already present in the soil. During its active growing and flowering periods, corn absorbs synthetic nitrogen as well as nitrogen naturally present in the soil, and studies indicate that approximately 50 percent of synthetic nitrogen applied to fields never gets absorbed by corn.[42] Poorly timed applications, overapplications, and rainstorms that wash away the synthetic fertilizer are the principal culprits, but the effect is the same: a corn plant still needs nitrogen to grow and flourish, so it absorbs whatever is left, mostly naturally occurring nitrogen. Over time, this depletes the soil's natural fertility, sometimes severely, which makes it necessary to apply increasing amounts of synthetic nitrogen to keep production levels the same.

The problem with this scenario is not simply the law of diminishing returns obviously operative with synthetic nitrogen application. Psychologically, synthetic nitrogen effectively conceals degradation to the soil's natural fertility, since it is possible to maintain comparable yields while simultaneously rendering the soil virtually unfit for corn production, absent synthetic nitrogen. Thus, the shocking incongruity of synthetic nitrogen use is that it allows American farmers to produce record-breaking corn crops nearly every year, while concealing the fact that the topsoil is being rendered more and more naturally unfit for corn production.

One of the insidious effects of synthetic nitrogen use is the almost necessary dependency it creates. Once a farmer chooses to apply synthetic nitrogen instead of resorting to manure applications or crop rotations to augment nitrogen in the soil, the incremental degradation of the topsoil's naturally occurring nitrogen begins, typically resulting in the necessity of applying more and more synthetic nitrogen to maintain production levels, and effectively locking the farmer into a cycle of chemical dependency.

While this dependency on synthetic nitrogen is problematic, the more pressing long-term problem raised by synthetic nitrogen use is the virtual inability of farmers to transition to alternative — and more sustainable — methods of agriculture. It would probably take years for an organic farmer to increase nitrogen content to a suitable level for corn production on farmland previously treated with synthetic nitrogen annually, because the natural nitrogen would have been so depleted that the corn would produce comparatively much smaller yields. At best, synthetic nitrogen use has sharply curtailed future possibilities of a large-scale adoption of less chemically intensive forms of agriculture; and at worst, it has virtually assured that any transition to a more chemical-free agricultural system will be well-nigh impossible absent a considerable infusion of government monies in the agricultural sector to offset decreasing yields that would almost inevitably occur in the short run.

Another problem raised by synthetic nitrogen use is surface and groundwater contamination. The 50 percent of synthetic nitrogen applied to farm fields that never gets absorbed by corn invariably finds its way to streams, rivers, lakes, or oceans, or it leaches below the ground and eventually settles in the water table or an underground aquifer.[43] In terms of surface water contamination, the increased nutrient levels caused by synthetic nitrogen stimulate algae growth, which eventually depletes oxygen in water bodies and often reduces (and sometimes eliminates) aquatic life.[44] Groundwater contamination resulting from synthetic nitrogen use has a more direct impact on humans, especially farmers and nonfarmers living in agricultural areas. Nitrogen pollution has been linked to cancer, especially in the young or aged who are also exposed to pesticides, and to an increased incidence of birth defects when pregnant women ingest nitrates in doses as low as five to fifteen parts per million.[45] The most alarming problem is the accumulation of nitrates in underground water supplies, which when ingested in sufficient quantities can significantly retard a child's brain development. Studies throughout the 1970s and 1980s show an alarming incidence of farm well contamination by nitrates: in Washington County, Illinois, 73 percent of farm wells were contaminated; in Merrick County, Nebraska, 70 percent; in fourteen Iowa counties, 40 percent; in 47 other Iowa counties, 20 percent; and nationwide in the United States, 20 percent.[46]

The fossil fuel revolution also inaugurated a period of increasing synthetic pesticide[47] use in American agriculture. Prior to the invention of synthetic pesticides, American farmers relied on a variety of natural methods to control detrimental insect populations. One method involved creating a receptive environment for a pest's natural enemies such as predators, parasites, pathogens, and nematodes by creating and maintaining an abundant food supply and/or appropriate shelter for them. In this way, a farmer could be assured of a fairly constant population of beneficial organisms in his or her fields that acted as a natural check on undesirable insects.[48]

Another method of natural pest control was to diversify the genotypes of crops in a particular field as much as possible either by extensive intercropping (planting two or more crops in close physical proximity) or by planting different genetic strains of the same crop in the same field. As a general rule, the more genetic diversity existing in a field, the higher the probability that crop damage due to insects will be minimized, since crops with different genotypes exhibit varying degrees of resistance to particular types of predation. While intercropping never completely eliminated some crop losses due to detrimental insects, it functioned reliably in reducing predation, especially large-scale losses due to insects.

The chief problem with natural pest control methods is the amount of knowledge and work necessary to make them effective. To control the population of any particular undesirable insect, a farmer needs to be able to identify its natural enemies, common ports of entry, whether natural enemies are present locally in sufficient numbers, how they can be attracted into his or her fields, how they can be enticed into staying there, and how they can be protected from their natural enemies, if any. The acquisition of this knowledge depends not only on extensive, firsthand, local knowledge of crops and natural enemies, but it also requires a significant cultural transmission of knowledge from farmer to farmer that conveys specific strategies, gained through experience, which have proven effective.

The work involved in natural biological methods might also be formidable. If a farmer is lucky and lives in a geographical area where undesirable insects are sparse, he or she might be able to implement a satisfactory plan of insect control through intercropping alone. On the other hand, the farmer might have to monitor insect populations daily by walking through his or her fields, to grow flowers or other plants to attract beneficial insects, to build roofs or arbors to provide shelter for wasps, assiduously to avoid destroying ant nests during field work, to supplement topsoil with various additives to encourage the growth of pathogens, and to undertake various environmental improvements in areas surrounding the fields to ensure sufficient populations of beneficial insects.

In short, natural biological control of destructive insects requires vigilance, dedication, time, and sometimes a significant amount of physical labor to be successful. Little wonder, then, that natural biological methods of insect control have been virtually abandoned in contemporary industrialized American agriculture in favor of synthetic pesticides, which have greatly simplified the process of insect control. A farmer today needs only to determine the types and number of undesirable insects present, purchase the correct pesticide(s), and apply it to his or her field.

While synthetic pesticides might appear to be something of a technological marvel, saving farmers time and labor, the astonishing fact is that they have proven to be no more successful than natural biological methods in controlling undesirable insects. Studies indicate that either form of insect control results in a comparable degree of crop loss.[49] The reason average crop losses have remained fairly constant both before and after the introduction of synthetic chemicals is widespread resistance to a large number of pesticides. Pesticides are highly effective and usually have a very high kill rate when applied in the field. There is, however, almost always a handful of targeted insects that survive a pesticide application, due to a genetic variation that makes them resistant to the specific pesticide. Due to reduced competition for food from the insects killed by the pesticide application, the surviving bugs now have a veritable feast before them. Eventually, these pesticide-resistant bugs will reproduce and become the dominant population in a field.

At this point, a farmer has three options: increase the toxicity of the pesticide used previously by diluting it with less water, apply a different pesticide, or mix together and apply a combination of pesticides (sometimes called a pesticide cocktail). Regardless of the strategy employed, the result is the same: a small population of resistant bugs remains alive and eventually repopulates the field.

Pesticide resistance has currently become a major problem in the agricultural sector, and the continued use of pesticides only promises to exacerbate the problem. It is estimated that between 264 and 440 insect species are resistant to commonly used pesticides today.[50] Furthermore, pesticide applications have created so-called superpests, which have become resistant to multiple pesticides, and in some cases to all known pesticides.

Similar to the dependence created by synthetic nitrogen use, a farmer switching from biological insect controls to synthetic pesticides almost necessarily gets enslaved to newer and better pesticides to control pest populations.[51] While a boon for entomologists, chemists, and corporations manufacturing pesticides,[52] since farmers need — and are usually willing to purchase — the latest pesticide available to control undesirable insect populations, it makes farmers economically vulnerable: they must either purchase the latest, and perhaps the only effective, pesticide or face the possibility of significant crop losses.

Other problems directly associated with pesticide use are pest resurgence and the creation of new pests.[53] Pesticides kill indiscriminately, both those bugs intentionally targeted as well as nontargeted beneficial predators and competitors. When a pesticide wears off, the resulting environment is usually far more favorable to insect populations than before, often resulting in higher pest populations (and the further, more desperate, need to control undesirable bugs). In addition, bugs that were not categorized as pests since their populations were sufficiently low due to predation and competition often become pests after pesticide applications kill their competitors and natural enemies.[54]

The danger pesticides pose to humans is also considerable. Especially in Third and Fourth World countries, where there is an urgent need to increase agricultural production to feed burgeoning populations, pesticide-related injuries, diseases, and deaths are high. "Worldwide, 49,000 people are killed annually by [pesticides], and in third world countries, one person suffers pesticide poisoning every minute."[55] The reasons that residents of Third and Fourth World countries suffer disproportionately from pesticide use are manifold. Most governments in these "underdeveloped" countries do not have the resources necessary to educate farmers on a large scale about the proper handling and application of pesticides. Second, most pesticides are manufactured in Western industrialized countries and often have instruction and warning labels printed in a language unintelligible to farmers in Third or Fourth World countries. Third, safety equipment designed to minimize or eliminate a farmer's contact with pesticides is often too expensive for poor farmers to purchase.

In our contemporary era of globalization and free trade in which many of our agricultural products are imported from Third and Fourth World countries, however, the impact of pesticide use in foreign countries affects the health of Americans. Although the U.S. Food and Drug Administration (FDA) monitors imported agricultural products, the practical reality is that the FDA is capable of inspecting only a small fraction of these products for pesticide residues or contamination. For example, the FDA inspects approximately two thousand food shipments yearly at the U.S.-Mexican border, while during the peak shipping season from January through April an average of nine hundred truckloads of produce per day cross the border into the United States. In 1986, less than 1 percent of the produce entering the United States from Mexico was tested by the FDA for pesticide residues. When illegal levels of pesticide residues are detected, it is often too late to prevent Americans from consuming the contaminated produce, since it takes an average of eighteen days to acquire test results, and by the time the FDA is notified the contaminated produce has usually already entered the United States and found its way to grocery store shelves.[56]

While it is uncertain how many foodstuffs with dangerous levels of pesticide residues make their way to Americans' dinner tables, there is a growing body of evidence linking pesticide exposure with a number of serious ailments. Studies conducted in the Corn Belt show increased incidences of leukemia, non-Hodgkin's lymphoma, stomach cancer, and multiple myeloma in persons consuming water contaminated by pesticides.[57] Other studies have linked pesticide exposure to "brain cancer, neuroblastoma, neurological disorders, immune system dysfunction, asthma, breast, ovarian, and testicular cancers, and lowered sperm counts" and to "early-onset Parkinson's disease, decreased physical stamina, short-term memory impairment, a doubling of stillbirths due to congenital abnormalities, and a host of birth defects."[58] The most severe degree of damage due to pesticide exposure, of course, is suffered by farmers, their families, and farm workers (particularly migrant workers who harvest crops by hand) whose direct contact with pesticides is regular and frequent. Statistics from California, the state with the strictest reporting law on pesticide-related harms in the United States, are disturbing:

> Agricultural workers reported fifteen times more doctor visits for symptoms that were potentially pesticide related[59] than a control group of the same ethnic and socioeconomic background. In 1982, 235 cases of pesticide-related illness were reported in California. If the estimated reporting rate of 1 percent is correct, this represents 23,500 cases among about 300,000 farm workers. That is about an 8 percent illness rate. Applied nation-wide to seasonal farm workers, assuming this is the most vulnerable group, this means a conservative estimate of some 156,000 cases of pesticide-related illness per year.[60]

Other studies show that in some California counties one-half of farm children exhibit one or more signs of pesticide poisoning annually.[61]

On so many counts, pesticides represent an abject failure. Compared to traditional biological controls, pesticides do not result in average lower crop losses. Some scholars have suggested that pesticide use has actually resulted in greater crop losses.[62] Pesticides contaminate water supplies, leading to higher incidences of cancer and other serious illnesses. The negative health effects of pesticides are borne unequally, affecting farmers and their families, people living in rural areas, and migrant workers most severely. Through the creation of "superpests" resistant to every toxin known to the scientific community, pesticide use increases the probability of large-scale, regional crop losses due to bugs being immune to any killing method that modern science and industry can formulate. The indiscriminate killing power of pesticides also destroys beneficial pests, birds, and animals, and in some instances disrupts feeding cycles in ways that lead to extensive, unforeseen environmental damage.[63] As one commentator writes, "Quite frankly, pest control is in a state of chaos, and the associated problems have placed a staggering impost on society and the environment."[64]

Since I have already discussed the morality of pesticide use in chapter 1, I will not belabor the reader with more arguments on this subject. Instead, I want to pose a simple question: Why do farmers still use pesticides today? After the publication of Rachel Carson's seminal *Silent Spring*, the American public has regarded pesticides with an admixture of fear, anger, and sometimes outright hostility. Nor are pesticides embraced with enthusiasm by farmers. I have never personally encountered a farmer who was not reticent about using pesticides, and most only resort to pesticides when "necessary" (which almost always means an undesirable financial loss would occur if they were not used). Probably the principal reason pesticides continue to be used is the large size of Corn Belt farms today. Biological methods of pest control require a certain economy of scale, a scale best suited to smaller farms. Monitoring fields frequently, cultivating local sources of predators and competitors, and keeping them in close proximity to pests require that a farmer actually can visually and/or manually inspect his or her fields and that sufficient local sources exist and can take up residence near the source of the problem. None of these conditions can be realized, however, in the context of large fields, large farms, and monocultures of corn and soybeans filling the countryside. Large farms are simply locked into a harmful, unsustainable practice that will not abate until farms in the Corn Belt become smaller.

Increasing Specialization

Diversity of crops and animals was a hallmark of farming in early America, for two reasons. First, subsistence farming was predominant at this time, and farmers grew crops and raised animals principally to feed their families. Surplus grain and animals, if there were any, were sold in nearby towns and villages. Although some farmers fortunate enough to live near large population centers sold proportionately more of their farm products on the market, farming was typically envisioned as a way to provide one's family with the basic necessities of life. In this context, it is understandable why diversity of crops and animals was widespread: consumption of a wide variety of foods provided the healthiest diet possible for farm families.

Second, crop and animal diversity protected farmers against natural vicissitudes that could have devastating results. Droughts, excessive rainfall, cold weather, late snows, early frosts, pest infestations, and a multitude of diseases and viruses could result in widespread crop losses and the death of scores of farm animals. Unlike contemporary American farmers whose state and federal governments are responsive during times of crisis and can mobilize large amounts of aid resources, farmers in early America had nobody but neighbors and nearby friends to help them in times of need. As such, hunger and starvation were possible threats during bad years.[65] The best way to minimize harm from natural occurrences was diversification, in the hope that what would damage or destroy one crop or animal species would have a less deleterious effect on another.

The typical farm in early America, then, contained a wide variety of plants in the standard three- to four-year crop rotation, with wheat, rye, barley, oats, corn, turnips, clover, beets, and potatoes being the most common. Farmers also raised an assortment of animals (chickens, cows, pigs, horses, sheep, goats), which not only provided a steady supply of nutrient-rich manure, but also supplied the farmer and his or her family with eggs, milk, lard, and meat.[66]

The diversification characteristic of farms in early America has gradually given way to increasing specialization in contemporary American agriculture. Specialization occurs along two lines: first, a farmer typically either raises animals or grows cash crops; second, a farmer specializes further by focusing on one particular animal or growing one or two cash crops. While exceptions to these generalizations can be found, especially among smaller family farms, there is little dispute that as a whole, farms today exhibit a degree of specialization unprecedented in American agriculture.

Specialization has affected not only individual farms, so that farmers identify themselves as hog farmers, or cattle farmers, or cotton farmers, etc.; specialization also occurs along geographical lines, with corn and soybean production dominant in the Corn Belt, cotton production in the Deep South, fruit in California and Florida, cattle in the Southwest, potatoes in Maine and Idaho, and wheat in the Great Plains, to mention only a few.

Specialization is both a blessing and a curse. On the positive side, it allows farmers to grow crops or raise animals in areas most conducive to high production. Engaging in large-scale citrus fruit production in the Corn Belt, for example, is impossible, given the shorter growing season, extreme temperature fluctuations and lower average annual temperatures, and threat of unpredictable early frosts. In a similar vein, farmers in the Corn Belt would scoff at the idea of growing potatoes in their deep black, fertile soil. Since potatoes can be grown in rocky, marginal land, whereas corn and soybeans — the Corn Belt's staple cash crops — would whither and probably die in such an environment, it would be grossly inefficient and wasteful to attempt to grow these crops in areas ill-suited for their production.

In terms of gross production, then, regional specialization has been a boon to American agriculture. It has allowed farmers to match growing conditions with particular crops, thereby enabling them to be as productive as possible in their respective region. As one informed, well-educated farmer once told me, the Corn Belt is unquestionably the "best place" in the United States to grow corn and soybeans.[67] While it is true that some crops cannot be grown in certain geographical areas of the United States, and to this extent some degree of regional specialization is necessary to produce these crops commercially at all, it is important to take claims like this with a grain of salt. What, exactly, does it mean to say that the Corn Belt is the "best place" to grow corn and soybeans? Usually it means that the Corn Belt can produce more corn and soybeans than any other region in the United States. While true, it presupposes that maximum production is beneficial (which usually translates into a moral imperative to grow only corn and soybeans in the Corn Belt), and this presupposition is dubious at best. As I discussed earlier, the criterion of production is relative to and gets its moral meaning from the more foundational moral benchmark of providing safe, nutritious food in sufficient quantities for people. If the meaning of the word "best" is given content by this standard, then the Corn Belt might be considered the best place to grow a number of other crops. Midwesterners, for instance, might be better served if Corn Belt farmers would commercially produce broccoli, asparagus, tomatoes, and apples since these products lose a great deal of their nutritional value during transport from other regions of the United States. Defining the "best" in relationship to productivity is exceedingly slippery, to say the least, because the fact remains that even if Corn Belt farmers could double, triple, or quadruple their annual harvest of corn and soybeans, this does not mean that Corn Belt agriculture is producing the safe, nutritious food that people need. (At most, it means cheaper meat, and more likely it means gargantuan mounds of grain sitting adjacent to grain elevators in the Midwest every fall, with no plan for how to use all this grain.)

The drawbacks of specialization are legion. The regional specialization I mentioned above, in which agricultural products tend to be grown or raised in specific areas of the United States, is wasteful. Regional specialization places large distances between producer and consumer, which raises transportation costs enormously and is environmentally damaging due to the burning of fossil fuels during transportation. It is estimated that every agricultural product travels an average of thirteen hundred miles from farm to consumer.[68] Especially now, when a strong consensus exists within the international scientific community that global warming is a legitimate long-term problem[69] and that the United States is disproportionately responsible for this predicament affecting everyone globally,[70] it seems problematic to create an agricultural system that unnecessarily creates great distance between producer and consumer and thereby causes more carbon dioxide, the principal greenhouse gas, to be emitted into the atmosphere.

Although it has become something of a truism that specialization increases efficiency (which in turn enhances productivity and profitability), this is not necessarily true in the agricultural sector. The unique quality about agriculture, which often limits the efficiency gained through specialization, is its seasonal nature. A Midwestern farmer specializing in corn and soybean production, for instance, has two intensive work periods during the year, spring and fall. During spring, a farmer's major tasks are planting seeds, cultivating the soil to remove weeds,[71] and applying fertilizers and herbicides, and maybe pesticides. By early summer, most of these tasks will have been completed. The next intensive work period begins in the fall, when the grain needs to be harvested. As a rule of thumb, this process is usually finished by the first snowfall.

Overall, a corn and soybean farmer works diligently for one-half to two-thirds of the year. During the summer and winter months, there is little field work for a farmer, although routine maintenance on machinery, implements, buildings, and other odd jobs often occupy a farmer's time. While I am reluctant to give the impression that farmers enjoy unlimited free time during the off-season, the fact is that outside of the planting and harvesting seasons, most farmers specializing in corn and soybean production are not engaged in time-sensitive labor, where tasks must be performed quickly or money will be lost, and most are far less busy during the off-season.

As commentators have noted, farmers specializing in corn and soybean production often underutilize their own labor, due principally to the fact that field work for these farmers is seasonal. The scenario is much different, however, on a more diversified farm. If, in addition to growing corn and soybeans, a farmer also raises cows and grows hay to feed the cows, he or she is able to use his or her labor during the winter calving season, and during the summer to cut, bale, and store the hay. A farmer can also spend time during the winter months spreading manure across fields (which also saves money in fertilizer costs). Further examples could be adduced, but they would only reinforce the fact about diversification: it is the best way for a farmer to use his or her own labor.[72]

Another benefit of diversification is the symbiotic relationship between animals and plants that is ecologically and economically advantageous. On a farm with a wide variety of animals, crops, and grasses, a farmer is more protected from the vagaries of the market and fluctuating prices that might cut deep into his or her profit margin. With grains and grasses, a farmer is able to feed a wide variety of animals (cows, pigs, horses, sheep, chickens, goats, turkeys, etc.), thus decreasing, or perhaps even eliminating, the need to buy animal feed on the open market. Furthermore, after the harvest, animals can be turned loose in the fields to eat the stalks, husks, and spilled grain (in most cases, these remnants are left in the field to decay).

For their part, animals contribute to the health of the farmer's fields by providing a steady supply of manure. This regular incorporation of animal manure into the soil contributes substantially to topsoil quantity and health, which in turn promotes sustainability. When manure is incorporated into the topsoil, it adds valuable organic matter, which supports greater populations of earthworms and microbial decomposers; it provides valuable nutrients, especially nitrogen; it helps loosen dirt particles and creates spaces for moisture and oxygen to penetrate; and it allows the topsoil to capture and retain a greater degree of moisture. In consequence, plants growing in soil regularly enriched with animal manure become stronger and healthier, and less susceptible to common viruses, bacteria, fungi, and other pests.

Another drawback of specialization is that it usually requires farmers to use single-purpose equipment and buildings that cannot be modified for other types of farming without exorbitant renovation costs, which severely limits a farmer's options in times of economic stress. Marty Strange writes:

> The "best" technology available for producing hogs is a system of very specialized buildings and equipment that, when fully used, produces hogs in conveyor-belt fashion. But the buildings are designed to do just that and only that. If hog prices were sharply reduced and the hog farmers who own these facilities tried to produce other crops for awhile, they would find themselves with an expensive, empty building. The building won't do for cattle, sheep, or chickens without substantial remodeling. In fact, the buildings are so specialized that one designed to fatten adult hogs isn't suitable to nurse young pigs, and still another can be used effectively only to handle pregnant sows.[73]

Given the practical inability of specialized farmers to grow different crops or raise different animals, they are highly vulnerable even to slight price fluctuations, either in the form of lower market prices for farm products or higher prices for inputs required to grow crops or raise animals. A hog farmer, for example, selling twenty-five thousand hogs annually might see his or her profit margin vanish if the market price dips a mere one dollar and the price of inputs remains unchanged.

In the twentieth century, the economic vulnerability resulting from the increasing degree of specialization in American agriculture gave rise to the federal government's enormously expensive price-support programs, which cost taxpayers billions of dollars per year. Specialization has, in effect, created a precarious dilemma: either the federal government supplements farmers' incomes, or a multitude of farmers will go bankrupt during difficult economic times, causing a great deal of hardship in rural areas and most likely concentrating farmland in even fewer hands.

Increasing Use of Fossil Fuels

The historian Clive Ponting calls the transition from renewable energy sources to our almost complete reliance on nonrenewable fossil fuels the "second great transition in human history"[74] (the rise of settled agriculture was the first transition) that thoroughly transformed human society. Prior to the fossil-fuel era, farmers were limited by the available energy sources: the sun, wood, water, and wind. Compared to the forms of energy used widely today, these forms of energy provided meager sources of power for many farm-related tasks. Humans and animals, which get their energy indirectly from the sun by consuming plants and other animals, were the principal sources of power on the farm. Animals provided traction power for plowing, cultivating, tilling, and crushing grain; humans supplied the power for tending the animals, harvesting grain, cutting grass, baling hay, and a host of other activities.

By the twentieth century, fossil fuels had supplanted human and animal power as the principal source of energy on American farms. The practical advantages of fossil fuels are manifold. Compared to humans and animals, fossil fuels provide much more power: a tractor can plow many times more ground per hour than a team of draft horses. Fossil fuels also provide the intense heat needed for industrial manufacturing, which makes possible the mass production of tractors, combines, plows, and cultivators. Compared to most other energy sources, there really is no question about the advantages of fossil fuels: they make it possible to produce bigger, faster machines that can perform tasks quicker; the mass production processes they make possible can produce a wider variety of farm implements that allow the farmer to perform highly specialized tasks; they allow farmers to avoid strenuous physical labor that was once a necessity for farming; they allow grain to be dried quickly; they provide enough power to suck water from aquifers deep underground to irrigate crops; and they have given rise to the wide range of petroleum-based products such as pesticides, fertilizers, and herbicides that farmers use extensively to boost production levels. With the exception of Amish farmers, who consciously limit their use of fossil fuels,[75] almost every phase of agricultural production in America today depends directly or indirectly on fossil fuels.[76] Indeed, fossil fuels have become so essential to our brand of mechanized, industrial farming that agricultural production in the United States is virtually unthinkable without them: "Within the context of modern agriculture, nearly all operations are energy-intensive. From traction to shape and move the soil, to fertilizer and pesticides, harvest, threshing and drying — all operations are based on fuels or electricity."[77]

To illustrate American agriculture's degree of dependency on fossil fuels, consider statistics on agricultural production expenses between 1940 and the early 1980s. While total production expenses increased twentyfold, costs associated with energy inputs rose even faster: "nearly thirty times for fertilizer, twenty-five times for petroleum fuels, eighty-three times for pesticides, and seventy-five times for electricity."[78] American corn production between 1945 and 1970, while increasing average yields per acre by 135 percent, also greatly increased various energy inputs: electricity consumption rose 870 percent; energy for drying, 1,100 percent; gasoline, 47 percent; pesticides, 1,000 percent; machinery, 133 percent; nitrogen, 1,500 percent; and potassium, 1,100 percent.[79] Although these increases in energy use are striking, if a broader historical perspective on corn production in the United States is taken, similar energy consumption patterns are detectable. From 1700 to the 1980s, for example, energy inputs in American corn production increased fifteenfold, while yields rose a mere 3.5-fold.[80]

While statistics on American agriculture indicate increasing dependence on and use of fossil fuels, a comparative analysis reveals striking contrasts between the agricultural production systems in the United States and in "underdeveloped" countries in terms of total energy use, as Judith Soule and Jon Piper write:

Developed countries consume five times the commercial energy for agricultural production as do developing nations. North America alone uses 28 percent of the worldwide agricultural energy budget. Because the developing countries account for the majority of the world's population, the difference in per capita annual energy use is even greater. Developed countries use sixteen times the energy per person-year for agricultural production as do the developing countries. In the United States, the per capita energy use in agriculture is nearly twice that of the other industrialized nations as a whole. Clearly, such inequality cannot be sustained indefinitely. Nor can the rest of the world afford to be as extravagant as the United States is. In their chapter in *Agroecology*, David Pimentel and Wen Dazhong put U.S. energy use into stark perspective when they pointed out that if the world per capita agricultural energy use were equalized in 1984 at the U.S. level, agriculture alone would have used up the world's fossil fuel supply by 1996.[81]

While American agriculture is the most productive agricultural system the world has ever known (measured strictly by output), the primary reason for such unprecedented production levels is access to and extensive use of inexpensive fossil fuels. The most obvious negative costs associated with American agriculture's level of energy use, however, are troubling: growing disparity between energy inputs and production levels, indicating that the law of diminishing returns is operative (and there is no reason to suspect this disparity will diminish); energy inefficiency compared to agricultural systems in developing countries, which use less energy — and far less amounts of fossil fuels — to grow a comparable amount of crops; and a growing net loss between calories required for food production and calories consumed by humans.[82]

The fundamental problem with transitioning to renewable energy sources in American agriculture, however, is the profitability of using fossil fuels. Despite the diminishing returns and inefficiency of fossil fuel use in American agriculture, it would be more expensive to use other forms of energy to grow crops. It has been shown, for example, that hand labor with simple tools is a far more energy-efficient method of growing corn than our current mechanized, fossil-fuel-intensive form of corn production. Labor costs associated with this method of corn production, however, are expensive.[83] A more economically viable proposal is the substitution of animal power for fossil-fuel power whenever possible.[84]

Although criticizing our use of fossil fuels is likely to raise charges of being a Luddite or a lunatic, such criticism needs to be undertaken. Exorbitant fossil-fuel consumption has become something of a national addiction in America,[85] and our almost insatiable desire for fossil-fuels functions as the implicit, and often unquestioned, operative assumption underlying our *Weltanschauung*, or comprehensive worldview, which typically equates progress with sophisticated technology, speed, complex machines, and physical power — all of which are made possible by fossil fuels. The reasons a critique of fossil fuel use in American agriculture is needed are twofold. First and most obviously, fossil fuels are a nonrenewable resource, and at some point supplies will simply vanish, or their scarcity will make them very expensive and uneconomical for agricultural production. For over a hundred years Americans have enjoyed an abundant, cheap form of energy in fossil fuels, and almost all aspects of American agriculture, especially agricultural technology, have been developed around this abundance. While scientists continue to debate whether it will take decades or perhaps centuries for fossil fuels to become scarce, and American oil companies continue to search farther, dig deeper, and deploy new technologies to detect and extract oil, the fact remains that fossil fuels are a short-term energy supply, and at some point American agriculture will have to be weaned off the fossil-fuel teat. Fossil fuels, in other words, have little or no discernible future in the long-term development of American agriculture.

Second, since agriculture provides a necessary human good we should be exceedingly cautious about allowing our food production system to be so thoroughly dependent on a nonrenewable energy source. As I argued earlier, due to its unique status as a supplier of a product necessary for human existence, agriculture, more than almost any other industry, should be insulated from various vicissitudes that could cause short- or long-term disruptions in agricultural production or could result in rapid, substantial price fluctuations in commodity prices, which would eventually make food more expensive and impose a disproportionate hardship on the poor. By allowing agricultural production to become so dependent on fossil fuels, we have greatly increased the probability that at some point war, political conflict, economic embargoes, legal impediments to oil exploration, dwindling supplies, disruption of supply lines, or some other occurrence will cause the price of oil to increase, which will escalate food prices. While no agricultural system can be insulated entirely from random or improbable circumstances affecting production, it certainly is possible to enact structural changes that minimize the negative consequences if such circumstances are realized. Our fossil-fuel dependence does just the opposite; it makes our agricultural system more vulnerable, fragile, and susceptible to conditions largely beyond our ability to control.

From a long-term perspective, sooner or later we will have to transition to an agricultural system based on readily accessible, dependable, renewable energy forms, and the sooner we make this transition the better, since the switch to alternative energy might involve a lengthy, substantial structural overhaul of American agriculture. Agricultural production, from heavy machinery to farm implements; to synthetic fertilizers, herbicides, and pesticides; to drying and storage methods; to the particular crops grown has been developed around our access to cheap, abundant supplies of fossil fuels. Given the enormity of American agriculture, the process of being weaned from fossil fuels will involve Herculean effort, extensive cooperation between government and private industry, substantial capital inputs, new research agendas at our land-grant universities, technological innovations, and massive social and cultural shifts to implement changes efficiently and successfully. While speculation about structural change in something as complex and large as American agriculture is bound to be somewhat fanciful and hypothetical, it does not seem unrealistic to suspect that the eventual transition to alternative energy forms will take decades, if not the better part of a century, to accomplish. Thus it behooves us soon to begin cultivating the willpower, political resolve, and cooperation necessary to embark on the long, arduous, yet highly rewarding task awaiting us.

Fanciers of technological solutions to agricultural problems might respond that abundant alternatives to fossil fuels exist (hydrogen, propane, fuel cells, etc.) that have already proven successful in other settings, which means that any foreboding about the eventual transition of American agriculture from the fossil-fuel teat is unwarranted. While these technophiles might be correct, there is something disturbing about the willingness to gamble on something as integral to our well-being as our agricultural system, a gamble that amounts to a substantial leap of faith in our scientific ingenuity to devise a feasible alternative to fossil fuels. While some might claim that this faith is well-founded, given past successes at finding technological solutions to a diverse array of problems, some might point out that the scientific community has proven impotent on a number of other important issues: we are still searching for a cure for cancer and for various other diseases, a technological solution to global warming, and a fix for aging, among many others. The reality is that neither I nor the technophile knows for sure how American agriculture will fare during the inevitable period of fossil-fuel scarcity. But when faced with this epistemological uncertainty, it seems best not simply to hope that we can find a solution, but to extricate ourselves from this dependency as soon as possible.

Decreasing Genetic Diversity of Crops

The hallmark of traditional agricultural systems is substantial genetic diversity of crops, not only in terms of high species numbers, but also in terms of widespread diversity of crops within fields (sometimes called intercropping).[86] Before the advent of gene recombination technology, farmers had to grow crops that were capable of flourishing in an almost unimaginable array of local environments that differed according to annual average temperature, length of growing season, amounts of rainfall and sunlight, elevation, insects, pathogens, soil microorganisms, as well as a host of other variables. Over decades, even centuries, farmers selectively bred crops uniquely suited to their specific growing conditions, which resulted in a staggering array of genetically different crops as diverse as the local environments in which they were grown. Genetic diversity was also enhanced through the common practice of saving seeds from each year's harvest and replanting them in succeeding years, which allowed farmers gradually to improve seed stock by selecting certain characteristics in their crops advantageous to specific conditions on their particular farms. As a result, it was not uncommon for farm families to have developed over time a score of genetically unique crops found nowhere else. Although the advantages of this extraordinary genetic diversity of crops were many, the cumulative effect was to insulate the farmer against natural vicissitudes such as drought, pest infestations, viruses, temperature fluctuations, or something else, which decreased the probability of widespread crop loss. The governing principle underlying the link between genetic diversity and crop survival is that the more varied the genetic base of one's crops, the more likely a significant percentage of one's crops will be resistant to specific types of adversity and will thus be able to weather predictable as well as unpredictable threats. In addition, genetic diversification also contributed to a regular food supply for the farmer throughout the year, since by planting crops with different maturation rates a farmer was able to ensure that crops — sometimes members of the same crop species — would ripen and be edible at different times during the growing season.[87]

The commercialization of the hybridization process in the 1930s inaugurated a precipitous decline in the genetic diversity of crops worldwide. With hybrid crops, it is not practically feasible for farmers to save their seeds and plant them year after year. While hybridization produces astonishing uniformity in first-generation crops, it interjects a great deal of unpredictability in subsequent generations, which means that farmers using hybrid seeds must buy new seeds every year from seed companies. While this dependency on seed companies is a decided disadvantage for farmers, insofar as they now have to pay money for seeds that were once free, the boost in productivity gained by hybrid crops was an irresistible temptation for farmers worldwide. When coupled with high chemical inputs such as fertilizers, pesticides, and herbicides, hybrid crops yielded at least several times more grain than their nonhybrid counterparts. Especially with abundant, cheap supplies of fossil fuels making chemical inputs relatively inexpensive, the productivity increases made possible by hybrid crops became financially lucrative, and profits were greatly increased by transitioning to hybrid crops.

The subsequent narrowing of the genetic base of major cash crops was astonishing as new hybrid seeds were disseminated and grown by farmers, and traditional landraces, or locally adapted crops, were displaced, and in some cases, became extinct:

> Genetic erosion is already substantial: the US soy crop, which accounts for 75 percent of the world's soy, is a monoculture that can be traced back to only six plants brought over from China.... [O]f the seventy-five kinds of vegetables grown in the United States, 97 percent of all the varieties have become extinct in less than eighty years.... In the United States just ten varieties of wheat account for most of the domestic harvest, while only six varieties of corn make up more than 71 percent of the yearly crop. In India, farmers grew more than thirty thousand traditional varieties of rice just fifty years ago. Now, ten modern varieties account for more than 75 percent of the rice grown in that country.[88]

This narrowing of crop species grown commercially stems principally from the overarching objective of the hybridization process, to increase grain yields. Although other traits indirectly related to increased production were bred into various strains of crops, the catalyst behind commercial hybridization processes was a desire for more grain. The widespread implementation of this goal, however, had momentous, unintended side effects on the genetic diversity of popular cash crops. From the rather sizeable gene pool available in each plant species, scientists focused on and incorporated into their breeding programs those maximizing yields. Thus out of the possible hundreds or thousands of genetically different lines of crops available to scientists, only a handful became foundational stocks in commercial breeding programs. The ensuing widespread genetic uniformity of many major cash crops proved to be a double-edged sword: while boosting production levels, it also greatly increased the probability of widespread crop loss. Genetic diversity militates against significant crop loss by increasing the odds that a large proportion of crops will be resistant to certain threats; genetic uniformity does the opposite by making entire populations of crops vulnerable in identical ways to specific threats.[89]

The principal method for overcoming narrowing genetic bases and the increased risk of substantial crop loss is to infuse new genes into established lines to enhance certain characteristics that render crops less vulnerable to pests, pathogens, viruses, or other stresses that have emerged and proven to be detrimental to production levels. Crop stressors, however, are moving targets, so to speak; they mutate, exhibit different tactics, attack different vulnerabilities, display resistance to old forms of control. In consequence, new genetic strains of crops are continually needed to combat new and sometimes entirely unpredictable threats. As one would expect, the life of the average crop line is exceedingly short, approximately seven years. By this time, something has usually emerged that substantially jeopardizes crop production. Farmers are thus caught on another dependency treadmill: the need to buy the newest seeds designed to thwart the most recent crop threat, regardless of the cost. If they do not, farmers face the possibility of substantial crop loss.

The difficulty with interjecting new genes into established crop lines to achieve better resistance to stresses is the scarcity of new genes.

Scientists cannot create genes; they can only insert and manipulate genes already in existence, and the only place to find new, beneficial genes is landraces, or indigenous, locally adapted crops that have hitherto been neglected for large-scale crop production. Ironically, the success of our high-tech, scientifically complex, supposedly "advanced" plant breeding program is intimately dependent on Third and Fourth World agriculture and subsistence farmers who have cultivated genetic diversity in their crops.[90] Thus far, the savior of American agriculture's crop breeding program has been those isolated, remote, and often overlooked crop varieties tucked away on mountainsides and in valleys and small fields that contain sufficient genetic diversity to provide resistance to threats experienced in our own agricultural system. Landraces, however, are vanishing quickly.[91] Given the economic benefits of planting hybrid crops instead of indigenous, locally adapted crops, most Third and Fourth World farmers have abandoned the latter, causing a notable decline in the stock of beneficial genes available, and in some cases resulting in the extinction of certain strains of crops and the genes they could have provided.

While the declining numbers of landraces worldwide seems to portend an ominous future for our commercial crop breeding program, the recent major scientific breakthrough of transspecies genetic engineering has opened new vistas for transferring genes and at least potentially offered a solution to the worldwide dwindling genetic base of cash crops. Prior to the invention of transspecies genetic engineering, genetic manipulation was limited to closely related species. To insert a new gene into an established corn line, for example, a gene would be needed from another strain of corn, or perhaps even a plant closely related to corn. Transspecies genetic engineering, on the other hand, does not suffer a comparable limitation; for the first time, it is possible to cross the species barrier and to commingle genes from wholly unrelated organisms. Theoretically at least, it would be possible to insert genes from a bacterium, soybean, squash, oak tree, rabbit, horse, fish, human, or any other organism into a corn plant to create or enhance desired characteristics. While this might seem like implausible science fiction, the gene transfers from different species already successfully undertaken in commercial plant breeding programs is quite expansive: genes extracted from chickens, moths, viruses, bacteria, fireflies, flounders, hamsters, and petunias have been inserted into major cash crops,[92] and companies are busy exploring a wide variety of other genes from different organisms for their potential beneficial effects.

The applications of transspecies genetic engineering are truly breathtaking; with the large reservoir of new genes available for manipulation, the number of traits that can be enhanced has skyrocketed. The following is only a small sampling: herbicide tolerance, which could decrease herbicide use; virus resistance; toxicity to insects, which could lessen the need for pesticides; altered ripening schedules; altered composition of seeds positively affecting nutritional quality;[93] altered metabolism; resistance to environmental stresses; increased yield; production of industrial enzymes; and production of polymers.[94] It should be noted that this list only includes characteristics in seeds already marketed or currently being developed and tested. It is hard to imagine the types of genetic manipulation possible in the next several decades as scientists refine their techniques.

Opponents of biotechnology, and transspecies genetic engineering in particular, have vociferously objected to these new forms of manipulation and the risks they raise. Genetically manipulated crops, critics claim, will "create superweeds, alter our genetic legacy, create resistant agricultural pests, kill unintended targets,"[95] transmit their genes to wild plant populations with unknown effects, affect ecosystems in ways difficult to estimate, facilitate the creation of new viruses, threaten crop diversity on a global scale, and cause entirely unpredictable and unforeseeable negative ecological consequences.[96] Although the specter of potential disasters associated with genetic engineering has not led to any legislative action in the United States, the European Union recently instituted a moratorium on planting genetically modified crops.

The sustained, comprehensive ethical analysis the use of biotechnology in American agriculture deserves is simply beyond the scope of this book. What I want to do instead is raise a few salient points about the morality of biotechnology that I think will be pertinent as ethicists consider whether or in what forms biotechnology is morally appropriate. First, biotechnology has the potential to make many beneficial contributions to developing a sustainable agricultural system in America. The wide degree of applications likely to emerge as scientists continue to explore this technology could serve unique, valuable objectives that could improve American agriculture environmentally and socially.[97] The major issue is whether biotechnology will actually lead to a more sustainable agricultural system. My answer: highly, highly unlikely. Why?

Biotechnology is the offspring of large agribusinesses that have invested enormous sums of money to develop technologies that can be successfully applied commercially. These technologies are highly capital intensive;[98] they require state-of-the-art equipment, some of the best scientists our universities are capable of producing, scores of support personnel, and extensive commitments to research and development. These enormous investments must eventually reap financial benefits. Biotechnology, in other words, is not only the invention of large agribusinesses, but its development and specific applications are also controlled by large agribusinesses and will almost assuredly serve their financial interests.[99] This would be unproblematic if the objectives of American agribusinesses promoted the objectives of a Christian ethic of gratitude — but they rarely do. The high-tech, industrialized, mechanized, chemical-, and energy-intensive form of agriculture promoted by agribusiness does little, if anything, to promote sustainability, a solar-based agricultural system, an agriculture system friendlier to nonhuman creation, reduced use of synthetic chemicals, or other aspects consistent with a Christian ethic of gratitude. In fact, many of the long-term, systemic problems of American agriculture can be traced directly to the unwitting acceptance of agribusiness's particular vision for American agriculture.

Agribusinesses developing biotechnologies tend to be heavily involved in manufacturing agricultural chemicals, and it is in their self-interest to develop biotechnologies that create short- and long-term profits by increasing chemical sales. Not surprisingly, agribusinesses have done just that by using biotechnology to create ongoing dependence on their chemical products. Take, for example, Roundup Ready soybeans, which have been genetically modified to be resistant to Roundup, a popular broad spectrum, postemergent herbicide. The chief advantage of Roundup Ready soybeans is a farmer's ability to employ "over the top" herbicide applications. After both the soybeans and weeds have emerged, a farmer sprays Roundup over his or her entire field, killing the weeds but leaving the soybeans unharmed. In this instance, profit seems to be the motivation for using biotechnology. (This strategy was quite effective: A mere three years after their introduction commercially, Roundup Ready soybeans had captured over one-half of the soybean market in the United States.)[100] Several other major agribusinesses are using biotechnology for the same purpose, to create resistant crop varieties that must be used in conjunction with the herbicides they manufacture.[101]

Another example of biotechnology being deployed to increase profits is Delta and Pine Land's development of a "terminator gene," which renders genetically modified seeds infertile in subsequent generations, thereby making it necessary for farmers to buy new seeds every year instead of saving seeds and planting them the next growing season. While terminator technology caused a public relations nightmare for Delta and Pine Land and for Monsanto, a potential buyer of the technology, and was never marketed commercially due to staunch political pressure, this is another glaring instance of agribusiness using biotechnology not to promote sustainable agriculture, but to make farmers more dependent on their products in order to increase profits.[102]

If biotechnology were being developed by independent companies with no vested interest in promoting and selling their other agricultural products, the possibility of biotechnology contributing positively to creating a food production system more consistent with a Christian ethic of gratitude would increase. At this time, however, the enormous expenses associated with biotechnology mean that only a select few, large agribusinesses are capable of generating the economic wherewithal to begin biotechnological research programs and to make them successful on the commercial level. As long as this situation obtains — and it most assuredly will for the foreseeable future — biotechnology will simply continue to reinforce business as usual in the agricultural sector.

For several reasons, our general attitude toward biotechnology should be strongly precautionary.[103] While an outright rejection of biotechnology is not warranted, we should approach biotechnology with a healthy skepticism and erect strict safeguards to ensure the safety of genetically modified crops. Safety, of course, is a minimalist criterion that does not begin to address the larger, and much more pertinent, issue of biotechnology's role in constructing a sustainable agricultural system. But given the nascent state of biotechnology, especially transspecies genetic engineering, and the unprecedented and rather spectacular modifications envisioned by scientists and biotechnology companies, it behooves us to be cautious and extremely judicious about the types of genetically modified crops allowed to be marketed commercially.

One reason favoring a robust precautionary attitude toward biotechnology is the inability of scientists to predict the manifold consequences of specific genetic manipulations in crops. Although field tests provide valuable empirical data revealing statistical probabilities of certain events occurring as a result of growing genetically modified crops, scientists argue that such field tests cannot adequately predict risk on a commercial scale.[104] Unlike controlled field tests, in which variables are known and intentionally minimized as far as possible, the number of variables potentially affecting commercial crop production is vastly greater. The almost unlimited variety of particular ecosystems in which crops are grown in the United States means that in practice, the interaction between genetically modified crops and environmental conditions will be far more complex and unpredictable than in controlled field tests. Thus despite the most rigorous, scientifically sophisticated testing program we can implement, the transition from field testing to commercial use involves an intractable element of ignorance that could lead to a variety of harms, great or small. Of course, a certain degree of unpredictability attends even traditional crop breeding programs in the movement from testing to commercial production. The genetic modifications occurring in traditional crop breeding programs, however, tend not to involve such dramatic or qualitatively different alterations of crops; since plants are bred to members of the same species or in some instances to closely related species, the gene pool is relatively limited and thus the plant characteristics that can be enhanced are limited too. The gene pool that transspecies genetic engineering makes available is vaster and presents the possibility of inducing a far greater number of substantial alterations in crops. But most importantly, transspecies genetic engineering can introduce completely foreign genes into a crop line, and with absolutely no precedent to help understand the implications of such a transfer, the potential for significant negative consequences skyrockets.

To give some indication about the pervasive unpredictability currently besetting transspecies genetic engineering, perhaps it would be helpful to articulate some questions scientists have posed that indicate its potential risks. Can transgenic crops become weeds? Can they transfer pollen to wild relatives, which then become weeds? Can herbicide resistance be transferred to wild relatives, which would make them immune to current herbicides? Will crops genetically altered to manufacture pesticides or drugs harm beneficial, nontargeted insects or fungi? What are the effects on animals that consume crops genetically altered to produce drugs, hormones, or vaccines? Will this also have some affect on humans who consume these animals? Will crops manipulated to produce plantwide toxins to kill insects accelerate the resistance process in bug species? Will other nonbeneficial fungi, bacteria, or viruses also develop resistance to genetically altered crops?

Will unintended gene transfers to landraces threaten important centers of gene diversity? Will genetic manipulation cause new types of viruses to emerge?[105]

While some of these questions have been answered partially, none has been answered completely, and the relative youth of transspecies genetic engineering makes it impossible to forecast with any degree of certainty its long-term implications. One need not be a reactionary Luddite to be troubled by the cloud of unknowing surrounding transspecies genetic engineering technology and the commercialization of transgenic crops. If there is one aspect characterizing the current debate on genetically modified crops, it is a pervasive ignorance about the long-term effects of certain genetically modified crops. In one sense, this unknowing is perfectly understandable; the technology was invented recently, and with any new, significant technological advance it takes time to detect its manifold effects. Yet in another sense, this unknowing is profoundly disturbing since transspecies genetic engineering involves such a qualitative leap that is literally unprecedented in the agricultural sector.

At the very least, such extensive gaps in our predictive capabilities coupled with the unprecedented novelty of transspecies genetic engineering should make caution the order of the day and culminate in a robust burden of proof being placed on biotechnology companies and regulatory agencies to demonstrate that transgenic crops pose no threats to human health and cause no additional, undesirable environmental side effects. Ideally, however, we should muster the political willpower to mandate a long-term, well-organized, and extensive testing program that would carefully monitor transgenic crops and the ecosystems and organisms they affect, which would allow us not only to understand better the full import of the technology we have created, but also to take preemptive action if any serious negative effects of transgenic crops become apparent.

Transspecies genetic engineering has brought American agriculture to a new threshold. Now, more than ever before, we can tinker with nature and modify our major cash crops to attain certain desired ends.

The novelty and lack of knowledge surrounding transspecies genetic engineering, however, should engender a cautious attitude about its commercialization. At the very least, we should be extremely skeptical about grandiose statements emanating from biotechnology industries, whose spokespersons often invoke humanitarian reasons such as feeding the world's hungry to promote transspecies genetic engineering. As commentators have shown, such claims are misleading and baseless.[106] Ideally, however, we should engage in a lengthy, well-informed public discussion that identifies the long-term effects of transspecies genetic engineering, and considers precisely how it promotes or undermines a Christian ethic of gratitude.

Increasing Technological Sophistication

Contemporary Americans are heirs to a technological revolution that has substantially renovated our daily existence and made highly complex technologies available to and usable by the common person. Sophisticated technologies are so commonplace today that they are a normal part of our landscape, drawing little attention to themselves even while being used. A culture so accommodating to technology, of course, is no accident, and the dynamics creating a group of people so receptive to — even desirous of — technology continue today. Our national pride is connected to masters of technology — astronauts, scientists, inventors, and doctors — and invoking the names of these heroes evokes a sense of awe and respect. Our children, who represent the future of technology, are introduced to sophisticated technologies at a young age, and their formal education process is designed to adapt them to and to make them comfortable with an increasingly technological world. The popular media consistently sound ominous warnings about technological deficiencies, the failure of American educational institutions in the areas of math and science, and America's growing inability to compete in a global marketplace due to comparative disadvantages in our technical skills. The strong liberal arts focus of our early colleges and universities has given way to our institutions of higher education functioning as centers of technical learning.[107]

The effect of these various messages is the creation of a psychological climate highly favorable to technology. As a people, Americans tend to embrace with gusto new forms of technology. We are captivated by any gadget that can perform tasks quicker, process information more rapidly, move faster, dig deeper, fly higher, reach farther, etc. Our embrace of technology often resembles that of a little child enthralled with a new toy: a naïve, unquestioning enthusiasm that revels in the joy of something different, something that grabs the attention, stimulates the senses, and offers a new kind of satisfaction.

Our fascination with technology and our all-too-easy acquiescence to new technologies, however, breed a cultural milieu that reinforces, perhaps even institutionalizes, a myopia severely limiting our ability to grasp a specific technology's full import, especially that of highly sophisticated technologies. While this lack of knowledge might be relatively inconsequential when considering technologies connected to the production of trinkets and gadgets, it becomes highly problematic when considering American agriculture and the necessary good it provides: food. Agriculture, perhaps more than any other industry, needs to be built on a solid foundation, and the technologies that become part and parcel of its routine operations need to be understood well and appropriate to the goals of a Christian ethic of gratitude.

To illustrate the manifold implications of complex technologies, let me offer a few generalizations and then analyze one highly popular piece of technology in American agriculture, the tractor, to show precisely how it either realizes or frustrates the moral agenda for American agriculture outlined earlier. While tractors might be a very commonplace sight in the Corn Belt today, from a historical perspective they are a relatively recent phenomenon. From time immemorial, humans have relied principally on animals (horses, mules, and oxen) for traction power, and it was only in the early 1900s that a majority of Corn Belt farmers abandoned their draft horses in favor of tractors. Since then tractors have become much bigger, faster, and more powerful,[108] and virtually every farmer, with the exception of the Amish, relies on a tractor for fieldwork. In this sense, tractors represent a large-scale experiment in American agriculture, an experiment still under way as tractor use continues to exert influence on the contours of our food production system.

Compared to the simpler technologies they replace, complex technologies today tend to exhibit the following characteristics:

1. capital intensiveness;

2. the necessity of technically trained people;

3. a specialized division of labor;

4. a large, diffuse, worldwide mass of means necessary to create and support the technology;

5. a highly developed and coordinated organizational structure;

6. dependency;

7. unintentional side effects; and

8. uncertainty.[109]

Tractor use, in varying degrees, realizes all these characteristics.

Tractors are certainly capital intensive. A new four-wheel-drive tractor with a three-hundred- to five-hundred-horsepower engine will cost upward of two hundred thousand dollars. Even a smaller, used row crop tractor with less horsepower can cost seventy-five thousand dollars or more. For most farmers, purchasing a tractor involves credit, monthly payments, a sizeable cash flow, and expensive buildings to house tractors. Draft horses, in contrast, usually require far less capital investment. Although the price of a draft horse will depend on its size, level of training, and temperament, the average cost of a working horse in the United States today is around three thousand dollars.[110]

The mass of technically trained people required to produce, transport, and maintain tractors is mind-boggling. Scores of civil engineers, chemical engineers, mechanical engineers, geologists, metallurgists, electricians, transportation experts, computer scientists and repair personnel, welders, die casters, and many others are necessary components in a process that probably begins in the Australian outback at an iron ore mine and ends with a tractor rumbling across farm fields in the Midwest. Perhaps the defining hallmark of complex technologies today is the level and extent of technical expertise involved in every stage of its creation. At the opposite end of the spectrum is the draft horse, which requires very little technical training. Beyond the occasional need for a veterinarian, no formal schooling or technical expertise is needed to keep a draft horse satisfied and functioning well, and for centuries farmers have relied on a cultural transmission of knowledge to gather important information on raising and caring for their work horses.

Almost every facet of tractor production requires a sharp division of labor. Experts supply the necessary knowledge, production managers coordinate patterns of actions, smelters separate and reshape the metals, workers on the assembly line fit parts together, accountants keep track of revenues and expenses, human resources personnel attend to hiring, firing, and the payroll, etc. Every person is responsible for one specific component of the overall operation, and usually their respective component is essential for the smooth functioning of the production system. While many reasons might exist for this division of labor, the complexity and size of the operations necessary to produce a tractor far surpass the ability of a few people to accomplish successfully. In contrast, a farmer, who is the principal and sometimes the exclusive caretaker for a draft horse, is the consummate generalist and can successfully care for the horse by himself or herself. All the knowledge, human labor, skills, and time needed to perform necessary tasks are supplied by the farmer.

The means necessary to create a tractor involve a worldwide, coordinated network of relationships and arrangements designed to guarantee a consistent supply of resources. Although fictional, it would not be surprising to learn the origins of the following tractor components (and in the context of contemporary global free trade, this is hardly wild speculation): the metals come from Australia, the electronic circuitry from Japan, the computers from California, the plastics from Mexico, the glass from South Africa, the tires from Brazil, the oil from the Middle East via a diesel fuel refinement facility in Texas, the lubricants from Germany, the filters from China, and the nuts and bolts from Ohio. Needless to say, such a widespread system of inputs requires a considerable amount of planning, cooperation, resources, and effort. The means necessary to maintain a draft horse are relatively few in comparison, and the network of relationships needed to acquire necessary off-farm inputs (horseshoes, halter, bridle, medicines, etc.) can usually be obtained locally.

The dependency associated with tractor use occurs in two ways. Most obviously, the tractor makes agricultural production dependent on a wide array of people, resources, and relationships worldwide, and as currently constituted our agricultural system could not function without these elements in place. The other type of dependency occurs when tractors become institutionalized in American agriculture and cause structural changes that in turn limit options. Tractors (along with combines) made possible the growth of farm size in the Corn Belt, along with the subsequent depopulation of the countryside. The bigger, faster, and more powerful tractors became, the more work a farmer could do by himself or herself. With the large increase of the average farm size in the Corn Belt in the twentieth century, however, farms became too big to return to animal traction. On a small farm of eighty acres, a team of draft horses can perform all the necessary field operations in a timely manner; on an eight-hundred-acre farm, the same team of draft horses would be clearly insufficient. As a result, at this point in American history most farmers have no viable alternatives to tractors (short of reducing the size of their farms).

Commentators have noted that unintentional side effects are an unavoidable aspect of complex technologies.[111] This is probably true of any technology, complex or simple. The difference with complex technologies is that their side effects tend to be less foreseeable, and it is often decades before a cause-effect relationship between a specific technology and certain conditions are discovered. Even a brief perusal of formerly popular, widely used technologies shows a rather remarkable inability to foresee the full scope of their effects: the Dalkon

Shield, asbestos, PCBs, DDT, radiation, chlorofluorocarbons, estrogen supplements for postmenopausal women, Agent Orange, lead paint, and mercury in dental fillings.[112] When first introduced, all these technologies were regarded as safe and widely used; over time, however, unforeseen side effects were detected, which caused many of these technologies to be withdrawn from the marketplace.

The tractor is no exception to the rule of unintentional side effects. We have already seen how tractor use engendered the growth of average farm size in the Corn Belt. While a side effect, this was probably very foreseeable. Less foreseeable was the chain of events set into motion by the increasing size of farms. As we discussed earlier in this chapter, Walter Goldschmidt and subsequent rural sociologists have established a strong correlation between growing farm size and poverty, political disenfranchisement, and social stratification.

Large farms also encourage pesticide use. Natural, biological control of insects requires rather intensive monitoring of crops to detect pest infestations and outbreaks. Practically, this means that a farmer employing biological controls must be very familiar with conditions in his or her fields, which requires physically examining fields and determining the type of bugs present, their numbers, and crop damage being caused. Prior to the widespread use of tractors, when farms were typically much smaller, it was easier for farmers to walk through their fields and examine enough territory to ensure that pest problems were detected. After tractor use became predominant in the twentieth century and farms became larger and larger, the sheer size of most farms precluded farmers from being able to give a firsthand, thorough examination of their fields since it would take hours, if not days, for most farmers to inspect their crops sufficiently. In this context, it becomes practically necessary to abandon biological controls and opt for pesticides that do not require such extensive human input and monitoring.

The same line of thought pertains to herbicide use. On a small farm, weed control can be achieved by people walking through fields and cutting or pulling weeds, effectively substituting human labor for herbicides. While it is certainly possible to substitute human labor for herbicides on large farms as well, the sheer numbers of people required to control weed populations sufficiently represents a daunting logistical task. Contacting, hiring, training, equipping, transporting, feeding, and supervising a few people is one thing; doing the same for a small army requires extensive time, energy, coordination, oversight, and skill.

Tractors also have a tendency to change the physical layout of fields, which has environmental implications. The ideal scenario for farming with a tractor is large, square fields with no impediments such as rocks, trees, ponds, creeks, wetlands, or gullies that would interrupt or slow a tractor's progress. Absent these obstacles, a farmer is able to maximize his or her tractor's efficiency by keeping it moving as fast as possible, which allows the tractor to perform its task as quickly as possible. Any type of maneuvering usually requires slower speeds or maybe even frequent stops, which means delays and longer time periods required to perform the task at hand. Tractor use, in consequence, breeds straight lines; the fewer the turns, diversions, obstacles, and curved routes, the quicker and easier a tractor can move through a field. This leads to important environmental consequences. Scores of wetlands, for instance, were drained and brought into cultivation in the twentieth century.[113] Although historically regarded by many farmers as nothing more than a nuisance, our attitude toward wetlands has changed dramatically thanks to ecologists and environmentalists. Wetlands serve as valuable filtration systems that capture chemical runoff from agricultural fields and purify it before it seeps downward into the water table or escapes into creeks or rivers. In addition, wetlands are renowned for supporting an extraordinarily diverse array of animal life. Indirectly then, tractor use and the desire to remove impediments from fields have contributed to poorer water quality.

Tractor use also affects soil erosion rates. When faced with inclines or declines in fields, a farmer using a tractor often goes straight up the hill or straight down the valley. From a soil conservation perspective, however, this is precisely what should not be done. During a rainstorm, water gathers in the small trenches between each row of crops and begins rushing downward.[114] It continues to pick up speed — and more topsoil — as it rushes to the bottom of the hill. The preferable method is contour farming, where the trenches cut across inclines and make it necessary for water to fill a trench, gently spill over into the next trench downhill, and so on until the water reaches the bottom of the hill. By creating a continuous series of obstacles that rainwater must surmount as it progresses downhill, contour farming greatly slows the speed of water as it moves downward and thus reduces its destructive ability to erode the topsoil. The problem, of course, is that the curved, meandering, sometimes circular routes required by contour farming mean more maneuvering, more frequent stops, and more time required than the preferable method of farming in straight lines.

The last characteristic is the experimental nature of complex technologies. The outcome of any experiment is to some degree uncertain. We might be able to make educated guesses based on past experiences and legitimate inferences about what might occur, but the reason that something is called an "experiment" is the opacity of our knowledge: We simply do not know for sure how a trial or test will turn out.[115] This feature is certainly true of tractor use in the Corn Belt. As tractor use became more widespread in American agriculture, a series of direct and indirect effects emerged that affected the topsoil, the economic vitality of rural communities, political participation, social arrangements and relationships, and habitat for certain animal species. Of course, these are only the most pronounced effects of tractor use. If we also include the extensive worldwide network of relationships, arrangements, and resources necessary to produce and maintain tractors, the scope of effects would assuredly be more widespread.

There are several points to these considerations about complex technologies. First, when draft horses and tractors are analyzed comparatively according to the moral criteria outlined in chapter 1, the use of draft horses as traction power offers several moral advantages. The energy source powering horses — the sun via plant photosynthesis — is free, dependable, renewable for billions of years, and available to everyone. Most of the resources necessary to maintain horses can be supplied by the farmer himself or herself, and this would probably result in greater dependability and security. The use of draft horses limits farm size, and if tractors had not replaced draft horses in American agriculture, it is much likelier that the average farm size in the Corn Belt would be much smaller today, which in turn would mean that many of the negative effects experienced by rural communities would have been less pronounced, or perhaps avoided entirely. The smaller farm size consistent with the use of draft horses also would have made it easier to implement biological pest control methods instead of pesticides, which probably would have resulted in fewer people suffering serious physical harm. While a complete comparative evaluation of draft horses versus tractors is admittedly more complex than the brief analysis I have presented,[116] the evidence is strong that widespread adoption of draft horses for traction power would help realize more of the moral criteria outlined earlier.

This claim, of course, is likely to be greeted with suspicion, skepticism, and even downright disdain by many in the agricultural community, and the practical difficulties involved in making this transition to animal traction would be legion:

1. Farmland now producing cash crops would have to be converted to different crops in order to feed the animals, and very few farmers are willing to undergo this conversion for financial reasons.

2. Farmers would have to learn to care for the animals and perform daily chores to maintain their health and strength.

3. Human labor would increase, and the labor would sometimes involve strenuous physical activity (at least more strenuous than sitting atop a tractor or combine).

4. Farming with draft horses would not be considered glamorous, progressive, or rewarding, and most farmers would have to

contend with social stereotypes labeling this type of farming primitive and outdated.

5. Farming with draft animals would curtail the acres a farmer could physically work, which would mean that large farms would be unable to substitute animals for traction power without a great deal of additional human labor or a reduction of farm size.

The message I want to drive home, however, is that appropriate agricultural technology, by which I mean technology that helps realize the moral objectives of a Christian ethic of gratitude, is not always the fastest, most powerful, most expensive, most glamorous, or most socially prestigious tool. While the ideology of progress dominant in contemporary America typically makes onlookers react with awe, excitement, and pride when watching a behemoth five-hundred-horsepower, four-wheel-drive tractor speed across a swath of the American heartland, we must not let this childlike fascination dictate our technological preferences. Instead, technology must be chosen on the basis of its compatibility with legitimate moral objectives, and when these criteria are fulfilled by a technology more "primitive" or "unsophisticated," then we should strive to ensure that this becomes a reality.

Leaving aside for a moment the specific issue of tractor use in American agriculture, the second point to emphasize is the need to reject the common view that technologies are neutral in themselves and moral issues arise only in relation to their use and the consequences they cause. This "instrumentalist view of technology,"[117] as it is often called, became very popular in the United States in the mid-1900s when a number of influential scientists sought to deflect criticism of themselves and their inventions (the atom bomb, chemical and biological weapons) by insisting that their technologies could be used for either good or ill, thereby denying technology any moral meaning prior to its use. While never influential in academic circles, the instrumentalist view of technology finds considerable voice in the popular media and exercises a strong influence on Americans today. The view is flawed insofar as it fails to recognize that technologies, especially the complex technologies of today that demand a worldwide support system of resources and personnel, rearrange familial, cultural, social, economic, political, and environmental structures in order to be created. This is neither inherently good nor bad since there is no moral mandate to preserve and protect existing structures. But this recognition requires that technologies be assessed not only in reference to effects stemming from their use, but also for the many ways our world is refashioned to create and maintain them.

Third, it behooves us to deliberate very carefully about new technologies before they are adopted in the agricultural sector. Once introduced, new technologies tend to proliferate rapidly due to the considerable financial pressure placed upon other farmers to embrace them, and once they become a common feature of American agriculture around which other technologies, practices, and systems are adapted, our dependency on them increases and it becomes very difficult to chart a different course. As one commentator writes,

> The paradox of the 'technological treadmill' has long been evident in agriculture. When innovative farmers adopt new technologies that increase output or reduce costs, total farm production goes up as more farmers adopt the technology, causing prices to fall, which, in turn, forces more farmers to adopt the technology, even as the added benefits of adoption are eliminated.[118]

In my opinion, the Amish represent the best alternative to the technological treadmill. Before any new technology is allowed to be adopted in a particular Amish community, the Amish engage in an extensive dialogue about the ways the new technology will affect core values and goods. This process encourages a wide degree of participation, draws information from a number of people who have firsthand experience with different technologies and their effects, and raises critical questions about a technology's place within the broader horizon of Amish life: How does it affect families and interaction between parents and children? How does it affect the ability to attend religious services and to fulfill religious obligations? Will it eventually lead to compromises in personal integrity? How does it affect topsoil fertility? How does it affect relations with neighbors? After these questions are posed and answered to the best of their ability, the community as a whole decides whether or not to adopt a technology, and the decision is binding upon all members of the community.

This deliberative process and communal control over technological proliferation are important facets militating against the technological treadmill and the strong pressure on individual farmers to adopt new technologies it commonly engenders. But this is only part of the story. The Amish, too, are affected by the technological treadmill operative outside their communities, which results in low commodity prices stemming from new technologies that increase production levels. The main reason that the Amish feel less pressure from the technological treadmill is the diversification of their farms. For the typical specialized Corn Belt farmer whose sole source of income is the sale of corn and soybeans, there is no way to compensate for low grain prices; the only option is to cut production costs (most of which are fixed) or to produce more corn and soybeans, which means adopting the new technology. The diversification of Amish farms, in contrast, means that low commodity prices can usually be offset or minimized by the sale of other agricultural products. As a result, an Amish farmer is more sheltered from economic vicissitudes, far less susceptible to the coercive force of the technological treadmill, and in consequence enjoys a greater degree of freedom over the technologies adopted on the farm. As one Amish farmer writes, "The Amish are not necessarily against modern technology. We have simply chosen not to be controlled by it."[119]

There is an exceedingly important lesson to be learned here. If sustainability entails something other than the current direction toward which Corn Belt agriculture is heading (and it most assuredly does!), it is imperative that farmers have the freedom to adopt certain technologies and practices and the freedom to say "no" to others, which entails a strong preference for diversity on farms and the economic insulation it affords. To be sure, genuine freedom does not guarantee that our agricultural system will become more consistent with a Christian ethic of gratitude. But without this freedom through diversity, the technological treadmill will continue unabated, leading us further and further away from certain moral objectives.

Conclusion

Nobody can deny that Corn Belt agriculture produces an almost mind-boggling amount of corn and soybeans every year. Yet one also cannot deny that our high-tech, chemically intensive, capital-intensive, specialized, large-economy-of-scale, fossil-fuel-dependent agricultural system in the Corn Belt strays far and wide from the moral vision of a Christian ethic of gratitude. Indeed, one cannot but feel a strong sense of embarrassment and disappointment at the missed opportunities and lamentable state of affairs brought about by Corn Belt agriculture. Farms continue to get bigger, and with the growing farm size come the inevitable economic strangulation of small farming communities and the demise of public services dependent on the local tax base. Corporate ownership continues to grow, and with it tenancy and an extremely high rate of soil erosion.[120] Pesticide use continues unabated, despite growing pesticide resistance, increased dependency, no better control of bugs compared to biological methods, and serious harm being caused. Herbicide use is still commonplace, even growing in some sectors due to the advent of "no-till" farming, despite growing concerns about the safety of the best-selling herbicides and herbicide resistance in weeds.[121] Synthetic fertilizer use, too, shows no signs of dissipation, while the natural fertility of farmland continues to be degraded, herbicide runoff continues to pollute groundwater drinking supplies, and the health of our aquatic ecosystems and the industries dependent on them continues to be undermined. Despite recent advances in soil management techniques and government policies designed to retain topsoil, soil erosion levels continue to be higher than the soil replenishment rates in many areas, which gradually decreases the land's fertility and productivity.[122] American agriculture continues to rely principally on nonrenewable fossil fuels and to develop technologies around these fuels, especially oil, despite the near certainty that affordable oil will become nonexistent within the next century.[123] The capital intensiveness of contemporary American agriculture coupled with the high cost of farmland fueled principally by land speculation that artificially inflates land prices prohibit many of the younger generation from entering farming, foster a robust expansionist mentality among farmers to acquire more land, and decrease a farmer's economic margin for error. The high degree of specialization in American agriculture has made farmers, more than ever, economically vulnerable, which has created the need for significant federal government intervention in the form of subsidies to prevent widespread bankruptcy of farmers, given rise to a technological treadmill that curtails options, and prohibited farmers from adopting technologies more conducive to sustainability. The monocultures characteristic of American agriculture have truncated genetic diversity, made our major cash crops more vulnerable to widespread loss, and created inhospitable environments for a wide variety of animals. The commercialization of transspecies genetic engineering is already well underway, an experiment in technology so novel and unpredictable that we have virtually no idea how it will turn out.

Healthy, vibrant rural communities; fertile topsoil in sufficient quantities; an agricultural system safe and secure from vicissitudes; necessary inputs supplied locally; the use of renewable energy sources, especially solar power; appropriate agricultural technologies; the physical health of people in rural communities; an agricultural system more generous to nonhuman creation; an agricultural system that sustains future generations — all these components of a Christian ethic of gratitude are either unrealized or directly or indirectly undermined by the predominant method of agricultural production in the Corn Belt.

Is this the best we can do? Is Corn Belt agriculture simply the best compromise possible, even though it deviates widely from a Christian ethic of gratitude? The answer to both these questions is a resounding "No!" There is nothing inevitable about the historical development or future trajectory of Corn Belt agriculture, and an agricultural system consistent with a Christian ethic of gratitude is entirely possible, although it will certainly take a great deal of time, political willpower and cooperation, resources, and energy to steer our agricultural system in a different direction. What direction, then, should we take? To this question we now turn.

Chapter Three

An Alternative Vision for American Agriculture: Incarnating a Christian Ethic of Gratitude

Introduction: Necessary Structural Adjustments

The transition to a morally palatable agricultural system in the Corn Belt will require substantial structural adjustments. While it is tempting to regard the current state of American agriculture as an inevitable consequence of fundamental realities that have functioned in a highly deterministic manner and produced a predictable outcome in the agricultural sector, especially economic realities and dynamics consistent with postindustrial capitalism, nothing could be further from the truth.[1] Our current Corn Belt agricultural system is the product of individual choices, policies, technologies, research agendas, corporate interests, and government preferences that have directed its development. There is nothing inevitable about American agriculture; like our cities, our transportation system, our parks and museums, and our educational institutions, our food production system is equally the product of human agency, formed by our choices and capable of being reshaped and reconstituted in a manner consistent with a different moral vision.

The recognition that American agriculture is an extension of human agency, however, offers little solace to farmers who are often in no position to implement anything but a short-term economic perspective. Financial considerations frequently prevent farmers from focusing on anything but making enough money to feed their families, to avoid further indebtedness, and maybe even to avoid bankruptcy, which practically entails adopting the most cost-efficient means of production regardless of whether they are consistent with a Christian ethic of gratitude or not. Since the mid-1980s, farmers have been financially pinched by a number of intermediaries: while the real price of food has risen about 3 percent, the farm value of that food has decreased by more than 35 percent.[2] Policymakers and legislators, understandably sensitive to the lamentable financial predicaments of many farmers, likewise get preoccupied with instituting measures designed to increase short-term profitability while usually ignoring larger, more substantive issues about the future of American agriculture. In turn, public policy debates typically revolve around ensuring the financial viability of American farmers, which usually gets translated into calls for opening new foreign markets to dump our grain surpluses, higher subsidies, tax relief, or more low-interest loans to farmers.

This near-obsession with short-term economic considerations at all levels of the national debate on American agriculture effectively diverts our attention not only from the underlying structural conditions fostering such dire economic constraints for residents of rural America, but also from assessing the moral vision underlying the critical elements responsible for shaping American agriculture into its present form. So, the largely ineffectual yearly cycle of enacting legislative measures designed to alleviate the financial crunch experienced by certain sectors of American agriculture continues, while the forces precipitating the perpetual problems in American agriculture are left intact. Needless to say, this epitomizes an exercise in futility. Until the structure of American agriculture is changed substantially, there is every reason to believe that current trends in American agriculture, inimical in so many ways to a Christian ethic of gratitude, will only be exacerbated over time, leading us further away from the moral vision articulated earlier.

Given the fact that various forms of agriculture are consistent with a Christian ethic of gratitude, it is important in considering structural adjustments not to succumb to the strong contemporary inclination for homogeneity that prescribes one agricultural system and results in sameness and uniformity throughout certain geographical areas. In fact, it is highly desirable to create space for many different types of farming, which allows farmers to match local environments and growing conditions to specific forms of agricultural production in order to promote the ends of a Christian ethic of gratitude. Sustainability, for instance, might be attained very differently in the relatively sandy, hilly areas of eastern Iowa compared to the loamy, flat fields of central Iowa. While we are conditioned to regard one particular type of agricultural production in the Corn Belt as being the "best," we ought to accept the fact that agriculture is embedded in countless local contexts and that these unique contexts dictate different forms of production.

Consistent with these considerations, let me propose two structural adjustments that are essential for creating a morally palatable agricultural system. I use the word "essential" intentionally to indicate that certain features of our agricultural system function as linchpins supporting, preserving, and protecting various subsidiary elements of the system. Changing these features almost necessarily causes a ratchet effect that places pressure on almost every facet of the system and allows for new possibilities to emerge in response; leaving these features intact, on the other hand, virtually guarantees that agricultural development will continue along the same trajectory for the foreseeable future. Thus my recommendations are not intended as a detailed blueprint for agricultural reform. They only represent incipient, albeit far-ranging, changes designed to disrupt a series of causally connected relationships that thwart a Christian ethic of gratitude from becoming embodied in Corn Belt agriculture.

Land Reform: Reduction of Farm Size

The first, and by far the most important, necessary structural adjustment is land reform decreasing the size of farms in the Corn Belt.

Instead of reiterating the litany of ills associated with large farms, perhaps the best way to illustrate the multifaceted benefits of smaller farm size is to imagine the Corn Belt as comprised of farms no larger than three hundred acres. In other words, let us assume that the most land that can be owned and operated by one family is three hundred acres, and no absentee or corporate ownership[3] exists. How would the effects of such an agricultural system most likely differ from ours?

First, rural communities would almost assuredly be healthier and more vibrant. Rural populations would be larger, more money would be circulating longer in farming-dependent communities, which in turn would mean better support for local businesses, and the large number of services dependent on the public tax base would be improved. More people would take an active role in local politics, thereby preventing a small group from disproportionately influencing a community's political decisions. Expansionistic tendencies and cannibalistic behavior of gobbling up neighbors' farms would be nonexistent, two prime factors undermining communal solidarity and neighborliness.

Second, agriculture would be less capital intensive, due primarily to the lack of need for large, powerful, expensive machinery and implements, which would mean a more favorable debt-to-asset ratio that would militate against economic fragility. Moreover, the smaller scale would increase the probability that economic setbacks could be dealt with effectively through personal frugality or savings, thereby obviating the need for credit.

Third, more opportunities would exist to adopt beneficial alternatives. The smaller scale would be conducive to biological methods of pest control, since a farmer could now physically inspect enough of his or her farmland to determine whether pests were becoming problematic. Farmers could also substitute human labor to control weeds (in cases where no-till methods have not been adopted) instead of using herbicides. It would also be likelier that enough animal manure could be acquired to be a sufficient substitute for synthetic nitrogen, which would also increase the topsoil's organic matter content. Not only would these alternatives be cost-effective for many farmers, but they would minimize dependencies, resistance in insect and weed populations, and chemical treadmills and would reduce the cancers and other maladies associated with agricultural chemical use.

Fourth, absentee ownership, corporate ownership, and the tenant farming associated with both would decrease, probably substantially. This would be very advantageous in promoting sustainability. Topsoil erosion on land farmed by tenants, for instance, is 40 percent higher than on land farmed by the owner himself or herself.[4] The reason for this disparity is the lack of long-term self-interest in promoting topsoil retention. Because tenants do not own the land they farm and cannot bequeath it to their descendants, there is less motivation to practice soil conservation measures that benefit future generations of farmers.

Fifth, if small farms today are indicative of the way farms would have been structured if American agriculture had developed under the stipulated size constraint, they would be far more diverse in terms of the variety of plants and animals produced. This would open new avenues for beneficial relationships such as intercropping, which helps control insect populations; pasturing animals on steeply sloped land highly susceptible to erosion; the use of animal manure to augment soil fertility; and more extensive crop rotations to grow feed for animals, which also helps suppress insect problems, reduces the need for synthetic chemicals, and prevents erosion. In addition, diversity has substantial economic advantages insofar as it increases the probability that low commodity prices for one product can be offset by the sale of other, more profitable farm products.

Of course, the standard objection to reducing farm size in the Corn Belt is that productivity would suffer. I have already shown why productivity in itself is not a moral criterion, so we should immediately take this claim with a grain of salt and insist on applying the correct moral standard: Does our agricultural system produce a sufficient amount of safe, nutritious food? According to this standard, it might be very advantageous to reduce corn and soybean production in the Corn Belt, since producing different crops might result in more people having access to healthier foods. But apart from these considerations, the standard objection that productivity would suffer is misplaced. To a great extent, the American public has been duped into equating productivity with total output. On the contrary, the more germane issue is the efficiency of certain production methods, measured by the amount of inputs required to produce a specified amount of grain. Any farmer could temporarily increase productivity by spending hundreds of dollars more per acre on herbicides, fertilizers, and pesticides, but such inputs would represent extreme overkill since the return would be minuscule relative to the resources expended to increase yields. On the other hand, an increase in productivity coupled with a reduction of inputs would be momentous. This truly represents productive farming. If productivity is understood in this manner, smaller farms would be a boon to the Corn Belt. Studies indicate that farms around three hundred acres in size are far and away the most productive today, and that as farms cross this size threshold and become larger, their productivity steadily diminishes.[5] The superior productivity of smaller sized farms has been corroborated extensively by studies of agricultural systems worldwide. A recent study of two hundred agricultural projects in fifty-two different countries documents "an average 93 per cent increase in per hectare food production" among small farms during the last decade alone.[6] Time after time, the reigning assumption that large farms are more productive turns out to be nothing more than a myth.

In my opinion, there is no other single structural element of American agriculture that exercises such a disproportionate degree of influence over the entire system than farm size. Nor is there any doubt in my mind that large farms represent the element most inimical to the tenets of a Christian ethic of gratitude. If the current trend of increasing average farm size continues, it will spell long-term disaster for agriculture in the Corn Belt. Therefore, the first order of business for agriculture reform is to begin breaking up large farms and establishing policies to ensure that this trend is never repeated.

The political viability of reorganizing land ownership on a wide-spread basis, I realize, is exceedingly tenuous. There are numerous vested interests in maintaining a network of large farms in the Corn Belt, especially among major corporations which have bene-fited greatly from the technologies and chemical inputs required to operate on such a large scale. Nor is my proposal likely to gain a re-ceptive audience from farmers themselves. The American tradition of land ownership and property rights, which regards land as an instru-mental commodity to promote personal self-interest, creates a wide zone of legal liberty for property owners in terms of the amount of land owned and the manner in which it is used.[7] While farmers today have begrudgingly accepted some restrictions on land-use practices, the vast majority are deeply opposed to any external entity imposing restrictions on the amount of land owned by a farmer.

This is precisely where the American and Judeo-Christian tradi-tions of land ownership diverge. In the latter tradition, land ownership is subservient to social, economic, and political objectives, and when the dynamics impelling the development of an agricultural system cul-minate in arrangements that interfere with or possibly preclude the realization of these objectives, then land gets redistributed. Nor is the practice of land redistribution, as we have seen, a historical aberra-tion in this tradition, employed only in the rarest circumstances to rectify a patently egregious situation. On the contrary, the Jubilee institutionalized periodic land redistribution to counteract accumu-lation of land and poverty, marginalization, and vulnerability. While our cultural biases cause a considerable degree of fear, trepidation, and outrage whenever someone advocates land redistribution, these biases thwart our ability to construct an agricultural system consistent with a Christian ethic of gratitude and contravene God's intentions for this slice of creation. Land redistribution is needed in American agriculture more today than ever before, and Christians should not regard this reordering as a lamentable state of affairs but as moment pregnant with fruitful, imaginative possibilities to create something pleasing in God's eyes.

Federal Agricultural Policies

The second necessary structural adjustment that would have a sub-stantial ratchet effect on various dimensions of Corn Belt agriculture involves federal policies, especially economic incentives. While re-forming the federal government's agricultural policies certainly cannot realize all the criteria of a Christian ethic of gratitude, few would deny that the federal government is the most formative influence on Amer-ican agriculture in recent times.[8] Let me briefly present the major lineaments of federal intervention in American agriculture and its effects, then suggest some needed modifications.

Prior to the twentieth century, the federal government's inter-vention in American agriculture focused on encouraging the settle-ment of the frontier[9] and creating the infrastructure and knowledge needed to supply growing urban areas with food. The federal gov-ernment's activity in American agriculture during this period was relatively limited: the highlights were a series of bills passed in the 1800s, which made land available to settlers for a nominal fee, and the creation of the United States Department of Agriculture and of land-grant colleges to disseminate information to farmers.[10] The Great Depression represented a watershed event in national agricultural pol-icy. Faced with widespread poverty in rural areas and the specter of increasing concentration in agricultural production due to foreclosures of family farms, the federal government assumed a robust intervention-ist role in American agriculture and sought to stabilize and increase farm incomes through a series of measures, including acreage allot-ments, tariffs, tax benefits, quotas, crop insurance, low-interest loans, and direct subsidies,[11] with the latter representing the most influential device for the federal government.

From the 1930s until 1996, subsidies were awarded for a handful of crops: corn, wheat, sorghum, barley, oats, rice, and cotton were sub-sidized for the entirety of this period, and soybeans and some oilseed crops were added later. Subsidies were awarded to individual property owners on the basis of acres recently planted in program crops and the average yields per acre.[12] Beginning in 1996, the so-called Freedom to Farm Act passed by Congress eliminated the link between subsidies and these program crops; farmers now were able to grow any crops they chose while remaining eligible for subsidy payments, which supposedly gave them greater freedom to respond to the market's demand for certain foodstuffs.[13]

Several features of federal commodity policies deserve attention. Unwittingly or not, direct subsidies have encouraged the growth of farm size. By basing subsidy payments on overall production (base acres = average number of acres x average yield per acre), a property owner is rewarded financially for increasing farm size, since this increases production and generates more income from subsidy payments. Not surprisingly, large farms capture a disproportionate amount of the subsidy monies offered by the federal government every year,[14] sometimes to a shocking degree. According to the Center for Rural Affairs, for instance, under the provisions of the 2002 farm bill a twenty-five-thousand-acre California cotton farm would be eligible for $8.4 million in subsidy payments.[15] This favoring of large farms through subsidy payments, in turn, has indirectly given rise to many of the trends discussed in chapter 2: capital intensiveness; economic fragility; expensive, complex technologies; specialization; use of synthetic chemicals; and the genetic homogeneity of our major cash crops.

Notice in the preceding paragraph that the recipient of subsidy payments is called a "property owner" rather than a "farmer." This is because subsidy payments are given to property owners, not necessarily to the people who farm the land. Sometimes these coincide, but increasingly they do not, and this practice has engendered absentee ownership, usually by an urban elite, who typically purchase farmland for the financial benefits it provides later when the land is sold. Subsidy payments reduce the economic risk of land ownership, which encourages nonfarmers to buy farmland, but other factors are operative too: a buyer's investment is protected against inflation and in many instances purchasing farmland provides significant tax benefits. Whatever the reason, this phenomenon of land speculation artificially inflates land prices, sometimes to the point where farmers cannot purchase farmland because no money can be made by actually farming the land. When this occurs, land typically becomes available only to corporations and wealthy individuals in urban areas who possess the economic wherewithal to purchase farmland and then wait years until a handsome profit can be made by selling it after land prices have risen steadily. In the meantime, the land is rented to and farmed by tenants.[16] As we have seen already, the most serious drawback to absentee ownership and tenancy is that profits usually go to individuals or organizations located in distant cities, with fewer monies left for farming communities and their local businesses and public services. The tenancy associated with absentee ownership also fosters apathy in community involvement and political decision making.

Yet another negative consequence of federal subsidies is constant overproduction of (former) program crops such as corn and soybeans. Given the choice to receive federal subsidies by growing corn and soybeans or to grow nonprogram crops that were ineligible for federal monies, Midwestern farmers have almost universally opted for the former (the Amish being the one notable exception; they do not accept direct subsidy monies from the federal government). While it might boost our national pride to know that American agriculture is renowned worldwide for its productivity, the fact is that the glut of corn and soybeans produced by American farmers every year has been a perennial problem for the federal government, and many programs have been implemented to reduce production of these crops, including the popular Conservation Reserve Program (CRP), which pays farmers for leaving farmland fallow and not producing grain on this land for a specified time period. This policy of encouraging the production of corn and soybeans through subsidies while simultaneously discouraging their production through other subsidies (set-aside programs) is borderline schizophrenic, to say the least. But the main problem with chronic overproduction is that it creates low commodity prices for farmers, which causes a number of undesirable behaviors to compensate for low revenues: bringing highly erodable, marginal land into cultivation to increase production; adopting new, capital intensive technologies, which is usually accompanied by more debt and places pressure on other farmers to adopt similar technologies as overproduction causes commodity prices to fall even further; expansion of farm size as farmers seek to produce more grain to sell on the open market; and greater use of synthetic chemicals to boost production.

Awarding federal subsidies on the basis of production levels has also contributed to other problems. It has encouraged the genetic truncation of corn and soybeans, since farmers favor genetic strains that are the best producers, which in turn makes American agriculture more vulnerable to widespread crop loss and limits future plant breeding options insofar as the pool of genes available to insert into lines of crops is greatly diminished (assuming transspecies genetic engineering is not employed). It has encouraged regional specialization because the Corn Belt happens to be the geographical area most conducive to producing the greatest amount of corn and soybeans. To a certain degree, regional specialization makes sense, but it also creates an enormous amount of waste and pollution as producers and consumers are separated geographically, mutually beneficial relationships between animals and crops are severed, and food needs to be transported over long distances.

Perhaps the best aspect of federal agricultural programs is the recent emphasis on soil conservation through the CRP, cost-sharing programs for farmers to enact soil conservation measures (terraces, windbreaks, etc.), the encouragement of no-till methods through the Environmental Quality Incentives Program, and Conservation Compliance, which mandates certain practices and environmentally friendly structures in order for a farmer to be eligible for commodity payments. The bulk of conservation program monies since 1988, approximately 70 percent, have been directed toward taking land out of production, with the CRP being the principal beneficiary. Interestingly, commentators have noted that while topsoil erosion on CRP land was reduced by over 400 million tons per year from 1982 to the late 1990s, this impressive benefit was offset by increased soil erosion rates on non-CRP farmland. As a result of better corn and soybean prices resulting from the decreased production engendered by the CRP, many farmers began converting hay and pasture ground back into corn and soybean production, which suffered higher soil erosion rates than before.[17] Commentators have also noted that the federal government's conservation programs are exceedingly limited in their potential, since they simply take for granted certain structural aspects of contemporary American agriculture — large farm size, chemical intensiveness, mechanization, specialization, capital intensiveness — and working within these constraints try to reduce the most unsavory effects without ever attempting to alter the structural factors responsible for the effects in the first place. This tinkering on the periphery of American agriculture will never amount to much without substantively altering the system itself. As one scholar writes, "There is only so much tweaking that can be done to make an inherently flawed policy more sustainable."[18]

Other than these few isolated instances, the federal government's intervention throughout the twentieth century has generally resulted in a pattern of agricultural development contrary to most elements of a Christian ethic of gratitude. This does not imply, however, that federal intervention in American agriculture in the form of subsidies and other financial incentives should cease, as some have suggested.[19] Withdrawing financial support and leaving American agriculture exposed to the vagaries of the market would almost certainly exacerbate the trends discussed and criticized in chapter 2 and greatly reduce the amount of leverage that could be applied to produce much-needed structural changes.[20] Absent some colossal shift in our national consciousness and value system, I see no way of fostering the tenets of a Christian ethic of gratitude in American agriculture if federal financial incentives are jettisoned. At least for the time being, government, whether federal, state, or local, will be a pivotal instrument for change in the agricultural sector.

Government financial incentives should be redirected on the basis of criteria that are consistent with a Christian ethic of gratitude. Based on these criteria, an index would be formulated to determine the level of financial support awarded to each farmer based on the degree of compliance (similar to the way various USDA indices are used today). Such a policy would not compel any farmer to modify his or her current practices; instead, this policy would rely on incentives to induce positive structural change, and farmers would be free to decide whether, and to what degree, they wish to comply. While I cannot delve into the subtleties and minutiae of government subsidies in any great detail, I want to present a brief sketch of the criteria that make up the index. Given the fact that the reasons for many of the criteria have been discussed in earlier chapters, I will try to avoid territory already well trod in order to avoid unnecessary repetition.

The criteria are based on the following characteristics:

1. ownership and active participation

2. farm size

3. nutritional content of food grown

4. diversity

5. soil conservation

6. organic farming practices

7. animal habitat

8. solar power

9. crop rotations

10. production for local community.

Criterion 1 requires that eligibility for government subsidies is dependent upon a person owning and working the farmland. Absentee or corporate ownership of farmland is an automatic disqualification for government subsidies, and hired labor reduces the amount of subsidies.

Criterion 2 requires that farms be medium sized or smaller for the owner/operator to be eligible for subsidies, and that no subsidies be given for crops produced on land over and above a predetermined limit. In the context of Corn Belt agriculture, a "medium sized" farm would be approximately three hundred acres. On farms larger than three hundred acres, subsidies would be awarded for the lowest producing parcels of land, which would discourage farmers from bringing marginal land into production.

Criterion 3 recognizes that foods differ in their nutritional content and that farmers should be rewarded for growing healthier foods. In my mind, there is a qualitative difference between a farmer growing field corn and soybeans, which are fed to cows to make beef, and a farmer who grows broccoli, spinach, carrots, lettuce, and beets (or even a farmer growing just one of these). Quite bluntly, the former is involved in creating a product that is not as valuable in promoting human health. Especially in the United States, which is currently experiencing a national obesity epidemic, the government should not artificially deflate the price of unhealthy foods and make them more accessible to consumers. Of course, this criterion is difficult to apply in practice, since many crops are used in manifold ways (corn, for instance, can be fed to beef cows or dairy cows, or chickens, or hogs, or used to produce ethanol, cooking oil, sweeteners, or lubricants, or used for emergency food relief overseas). The occasional complexity of determining a crop's relationship to the goal of promoting human health, however, should not undermine the general proposition that the government should discriminate among foods. Let the government's "cheap food" policy continue, but let it be limited to foods that make for well-functioning bodies and minds.

Diversity is a laudable national goal on a number of levels.[21] Genetic diversity helps ensure the long-term viability of American agriculture by maximizing the number of beneficial genes capable of being inserted into lines of popular crops (absent transspecies genetic engineering). This large gene pool helps mitigate stresses due to pests, pathogens, climatic conditions, and other factors, and presents the best way to insulate our agricultural system from foreseeable and unforeseeable vicissitudes. Regional diversity makes available a wider range of fresher foods at the local level and helps reduce the pollution and costs associated with transportation. Diversity on individual farms creates various beneficial relationships between animals and plants and between various plant species, which has the potential to increase soil fertility, reduce fertilizer applications, help control unwanted bug populations biologically, and reduce a farmer's economic vulnerability to low commodity prices. Virtually all the ills associated with specialization discussed in chapter 2 are mitigated by criterion 4.

Criterion 5 rewards farmers not only for conserving topsoil, but also for improving the topsoil's structure and fertility. For the better part of the twentieth century, the federal government pursued the former robustly, with moderate success. But absent the latter, sheer bulk matters little: I have encountered very flat fields in Iowa that had suffered little topsoil loss through wind or water erosion, but were so compacted by the weight of heavy machinery that it was difficult to dig a shallow hole in the soil with a sharp spade. Needless to say, while these fields contained ample topsoil in which to grow crops, their productivity was sharply diminished by their poor tilth. The key to criterion 5 is requiring demonstrable results. Currently, the government only requires certain features or practices (terraces, windbreaks, etc.) to be eligible for commodity programs.[22] However, if windbreaks are positioned poorly or if water simply runs to the end of a terrace and escapes with topsoil in tow, the purpose of these soil conservation measures is thwarted.

Criterion 6 gives preference to farmers that forego the use of synthetic chemicals. In one specific respect, encouraging organic farming is worrisome. Organic farming is usually accompanied by increased cultivation to remove undesirable weeds, which keeps the topsoil in a disturbed state and typically leads to higher levels of erosion. I hedge somewhat in the preceding sentence because there is evidence that soil perturbation does not inevitably lead to more soil erosion. The Amish, for instance, who plow their fields every year and cultivate as needed throughout the growing season (both practices are becoming much rarer today with the advent of no-till farming), experience less soil erosion than farmers employing no-till methods, which are commonly touted as the best soil conservation measures today.[23] The reason is that the Amish incorporate much more organic matter into the soil, especially through extensive animal manure applications, which greatly increases the soil's ability to absorb and retain water. Thus, the typical link between cultivation and erosion is not necessary, depending on the quality of the topsoil.

Criterion 7 rewards farmers for creating more habitat for animals to exist and flourish, either by supporting greater diversification of wild animal species on the farm or by supporting greater numbers of wild animals. This incentive to make agriculture friendlier to nonhuman animals might take the form of temporarily or permanently retiring land from cultivation.[24] But it is a mistake to think that retiring land represents the only, or best, method of creating habitat for wild animals. While the creation of wildlife habitat and farming the land are often portrayed as mutually exclusive, there are a number of ways to improve both: crop diversification improves soil quality and inhibits insect outbreaks, and provides a greater range of ground cover for animals; planting trees in fencerows helps prevent soil erosion and provides food and shelter for a number of birds and cavity-dwelling animals; grass strips along waterways prevent erosion and add habitat; preserving wetlands is a boon for many species of animals, especially migratory birds, and they help filter out harmful farm chemical runoff.

Criterion 8 favors farmers who rely more on solar power than fossil fuels for energy on the farm. As I argued earlier, a predominantly solar-powered agricultural system will be less susceptible to the vicissitudes associated with fossil-fuel use, which in turn makes American agriculture more structurally secure.

Criterion 9 offers a financial incentive to farmers who practice crop rotations, as these help prevent soil erosion, break the cycle of insect infestations, reduce the need for synthetic chemical applications, and take advantage of mutually beneficial relationships among different plant species.

The last criterion promotes producing for a local market. While verification might be difficult in some cases, producing food for the local community is highly beneficial for a number of reasons. It allows money to circulate longer in rural towns and cities, which counteracts the economic decline documented by rural sociologists for the past fifty years. It promotes crop diversification and its associated benefits, because people want to eat a variety of foods. It reduces transportation-related pollution. Perhaps most important, it creates the possibility of growing more nutritious food. Plant breeders typically select crop varieties for their transportability over long distances (and also their ability to withstand mechanical harvesting); nutritional content is usually a secondary or tertiary concern, if it is considered at all. Quite predictably, given these plant-breeding priorities, most of the produce on grocery store shelves is nutritionally deficient relative to the same produce fifty years ago. Producing for the local community and eliminating long, time-consuming transportation routes between producer and consumer allow farmers to grow crops that are tastier and richer in vitamins and nutrients.

These two substantive shifts in American agriculture — smaller farm size and redirected government financial supports — represent the sine qua non for creating an agricultural system consistent with a Christian ethic of gratitude. Change these two aspects, and a series of new dynamics are introduced into our agricultural system that strongly counteract the trends criticized in chapter 2, allowing for a morally desirable food production system to emerge, take root, and eventually become institutionalized. If implemented and maintained in the long term, these structural renovations would almost completely revamp the contours of American agriculture, making it more sustainable, more secure from internal and external threats, more hospitable to nonhuman animals, less dependent on harmful synthetic chemicals, more favorable to the revitalization of rural America, and more diverse and locally based. Not a bad beginning for an agricultural system that is begging for reform.

Let us now move beyond necessary structural adjustments and consider several concrete agricultural systems that more fully embody a Christian ethic of gratitude. While I have been highly critical of the dominant agricultural system in the Corn Belt, the fact remains that there exists a great deal of hope on the horizon in the form of working food-production systems that meet most of the moral criteria presented in earlier chapters, and at the very least represent a vast moral improvement over current Corn Belt agriculture. In many cases, these "alternative" agricultural systems have been marginalized and underappreciated because they do not quite fit the mold of contemporary American agriculture in all its aspects: specialized, chemical intensive, large-scale, mechanized, technologically sophisticated, capital intensive, and market oriented. These alternative food production systems, however, have many lessons to offer and represent the future of American agriculture.

Embodiments of a Christian Ethic of Gratitude: Alternative Agricultural Systems

Gardening: Intensive Agriculture

While it might sound laughable to recommend gardening as an alternative to contemporary American agriculture, the fact is that gardens are far and away the most productive agricultural systems today in terms of providing the most food per square foot of land. Although most Americans are likely to regard gardening as nothing more than a quaint hobby, gardening serves a very different function in poor countries.[25] Especially during the last two decades, urban gardens have become increasingly popular in Third and Fourth World countries, and the reason for their popularity is not only their incomparable ability to provide the poor with a safe, inexpensive supply of fresh, nutritious food, but also the fact that gardening does not require high startup or maintenance costs or expensive technologies. Anyone with access to a small plot of land, a few simple tools, and a small amount of money for seeds can start a garden. Gardening for the world's poor, quite simply, is one of the easiest ways to ensure food security for themselves and their families.

Given that the possibilities for gardening are so varied, ranging from small raised beds outside the kitchen door containing a couple of tomato plants and herbs, to large half-acre to one-acre plots that produce enough vegetables to feed a family of four for the better part of a year, generalizing about gardening and the various comparative benefits gardens provide has its limitations. Moreover, since most gardens are site-specific and tailored to an individual person's or family's needs and resources, a garden's real value often emerges only in the finer details of its actual social, ecological, economic, and political functions. Thus, to put a face, so to speak, on the broad category of "gardening," let me discuss an agricultural system with which I have extensive firsthand experience, my family's vegetable garden, and the ways it either coheres or conflicts with a Christian ethic of gratitude.

Our backyard vegetable garden is twenty-three feet by nineteen feet, or approximately one one-hundredth of an acre, and every year we usually grow six to ten tomato plants, a dozen potato plants, three rows of onions, three rows of carrots, one row of peas, two rows of spinach, two rows of lettuce, three eggplants, twenty-five broccoli plants, four cabbage plants, two acorn squash plants, two butternut squash plants, two summer squash plants, twenty cloves of garlic, two cucumber plants, two zucchini plants, three rows of beets, two rows of radishes, one row of green beans, one row of edible soybeans, and a few herbs. Due to our hospitable climate for gardening in southeastern Pennsylvania (planting usually begins in March and production ends in November), we are able to produce two crops of some plants per growing season. When production begins slowing down in late summer, we plant another round of cold-weather crops (broccoli, spinach, and lettuce), which usually mature before the first hard frost.

Our garden's soil fertility is enhanced in several ways. We compost all kitchen waste produced throughout the year and apply it uniformly over the garden annually, which increases the nutrient content of our soil. All plant matter such as leaves and stems not known to pose a threat to plants the following year is left on the garden to decay. We save our lawn clippings and use the grass as mulch between rows. Before tilling at the beginning of the growing season, we distribute a half dozen large bags of aged, brittle leaves and sometimes a small bale of straw over the garden, and then work everything thoroughly into the ground. During the fall, a nitrogen-fixing cover crop is planted, which is also tilled into the ground in the spring. We rotate our crops every year and try to maximize beneficial relationships between plants (e.g., following the nitrogen fixers with plants having high nitrogen requirements). To date, no commercial fertilizer has been applied on our garden, nor have any of our vegetables seemed to suffer for lack of fertilizer.

The straw, leaves, compost, and cover crop help prevent soil erosion. All these increase our garden topsoil's organic matter content and its ability to absorb and retain water. Since our garden is surrounded by grass for hundreds of feet on each side, any soil dislodged during rainfalls probably does not go far, and almost certainly does not make its way to the nearest waterway. I have checked for visible signs of erosion after rainstorms, but have never found any. Perhaps the best soil retention device, however, is the layer of mulch applied on our garden between rows of plants. This mulch shelters our topsoil from high winds, and during rainstorms it shields the soil from direct collisions with raindrops and acts as a formidable barrier against soil particles being washed away by water.

The need for pest control has been nonexistent. Crop rotations help reduce bug problems, and the health of our topsoil helps create strong, vibrant plants that are usually able to withstand pest-induced stresses. But probably the main reason for our lack of need for pest control, I admit, is our extremely high tolerance for pests. My wife and I agreed long ago never to let our garden become a battleground against crop loss. We have always accepted the fact that bugs, rabbits, an occasional groundhog, and the family dog supplementing his diet with garden vegetables would decrease our yields. In the larger scheme of things, however, these losses are offset in other ways: our dog does an admirable job of keeping rabbits and groundhogs out of our backyard; he eats less commercial dog food when consuming garden vegetables every day; and our garden attracts a healthy number of beneficial predators that keep insect populations in check.

Animal life abounds in our garden. In addition to the usual insects that invariably prey on garden vegetables, we have a dozen or more species of birds visiting our garden regularly, and ladybugs, preying mantises, toads, snakes, butterflies, caterpillars, inchworms, many species of spiders, and mice are frequent visitors. Last year, a rabbit burrowed into the ground and built a nest under a canopy of broccoli leaves, where she housed about a half dozen babies. Rarely can one visit our garden without encountering some creature foraging for its next meal.

Without question, those benefiting most from our garden are our children. Our oldest child, Peter (age two and a half; our daughter, Hannah, is nine months old and not walking yet), is something of an outdoor maladroit, and the garden is a constant source of wonder and delight for him. He spends innumerable hours scouring the undersides of leaves looking for insects, digging in the dirt, hunting for earthworms and grubs, looking for vegetables hidden under dense mats of foliage, picking cherry tomatoes for him or the dog to eat, chasing butterflies, studying insect behavior, and helping us with the mundane tasks of planting, weeding, mulching, and picking. For Pete, our garden is not simply a food production system; it is a combination playground, schoolhouse, entomology exhibit, botanical center, zoo, hands-on science museum, and grocery store all rolled into one.

The nutritional benefits for our children are considerable. Most of our meals during the growing season center around whatever is ripe and ready to eat, and our vegetables are usually consumed within a couple of hours after being picked. This short time lag between picking and eating maximizes the nutritional content of the vegetables consumed. The texture and flavor of fresh vegetables offer considerable advantages over the mushy, bland canned vegetables and the tough, fibrous grocery store produce that has usually been picked days (if not weeks) earlier. I am convinced that the palatability of our garden vegetables have had an enormous effect on Pete's food preferences. Given the choice, Pete will almost always choose a salad, green beans, carrot sticks, or a head of broccoli over the typical junk foods most American kids consume (hot dogs, hamburgers, pizza, etc.), and Pete's between-meals snacks during the growing season are whatever strikes his fancy in the garden. Needless to say, as a parent it is highly satisfying to be able to offer fresh, nutritious, chemical-free, tasty food to your child and to create a child so psychologically receptive to, even desirous of, healthy foods.

In addition to its dietary benefits, our garden provides many social opportunities. Almost every evening during the growing season involves a trip to the garden, either as a family or with me or my wife accompanying Pete to the garden to pick vegetables, water the tomatoes, do some weeding, check on the status of our plants, or simply to "dink around," as I call it. This unstructured time together is greatly appreciated by everyone involved, and it offers opportunities to talk, play, and enjoy one another without the distractions of modern American life. The social utility of our garden, however, extends beyond our family. We share the bounty of our garden with others, and about once a week we gather an assortment of vegetables and distribute them to a neighbor. Our neighbors always enjoy seeing the kids again, and the face-to-face contact and friendly conversations that typically ensue are good ways to solidify existing relationships and to foster a climate of goodwill with those in our neighborhood.

In terms of the end result of providing food for people to eat, the contrast between our garden and the same sized plot of land in the Corn Belt could not be sharper. Iowa farmers, for instance, averaged 157 bushels of corn per acre in 2003, the second highest production level ever recorded in Iowa. This means that on one one-hundredth of an acre (our garden's size) an Iowa farmer yields 1.57 bushels of corn per year, which weigh approximately eighty-eight pounds. The majority of this corn is fed to cows to create beef for human consumption, and given a grain-to-meat conversion ratio of 16:1,[26] the end result is five and one-half pounds of beef. Although I have never kept precise measurements of our garden's output throughout the year, the following represent my best estimates (all estimates are according to volume, since it is easier for most people to visualize pints, quarts, gallons, and five-gallon buckets rather than weights): fifteen gallons of tomatoes; ten gallons of potatoes; five gallons of onions; three gallons of carrots; one quart of peas; five gallons of spinach (precooked and uncompressed); ten gallons of lettuce; three gallons of eggplants; five gallons of broccoli heads; five gallons of acorn squashes; five gallons of butternut squashes; three gallons of summer squashes; one quart of garlic cloves; one gallon of cucumbers; five gallons of zucchinis; four gallons of beets; two gallons of radishes; two gallons of green beans; one quart of edible soybeans; one pint of basil; and one pint of cilantro. In terms of sheer bulk, our garden is the clear winner. To give a visual presentation, this is comparable to a standard-sized plastic bread bag filled with beef placed next to two medium-sized garbage cans filled with garden produce. But focusing only on quantity is likely to belie a more important fact: the array of vitamins and nutrients our garden vegetables provide for our family is much more conducive to our physical health than the end result of a similar-sized strip of Iowa cornfield, namely, five and one-half pounds of beef.

Extending the comparative analysis further to include more criteria of a Christian ethic of gratitude reveals other advantages of our garden. More of our garden's inputs are supplied locally, and some of these are produced directly on our property. The principal energy sources (solar power and human labor) are renewable. Neither our neighbors nor people downstream from us have their physical health undermined by synthetic chemical runoff. The diversity of animal life found in our garden on a regular basis is far greater than that found in a typical Midwestern cornfield of the same size. Given the same practices, our garden is sustainable (at least according to common indicators of sustainability) and would provide food indefinitely for future generations. Vicissitudes of an economic or political nature would have little disruptive effect on our garden. No known internal conditions or dynamics are present that might gradually undermine our garden's health and fertility. The total distance each food item from our garden travels between producer and consumer is approximately one hundred feet, which greatly reduces the pollution associated with transportation.

Waste elimination is another advantage of our garden. Hundreds of pounds of kitchen scraps are composted every year and distributed over our garden, which transforms household garbage into valuable soil additives. Grass clippings, leaves, and pine needles are also applied directly to the garden or composted. In addition to increasing our garden soil's fertility and organic matter content, recycling these waste products saves space in landfills. Yet our garden's capacity to reduce waste occurs in other ways as well. By providing food and reducing our demand for foodstuffs at the local grocery store, our garden helps eliminate a great deal of waste that often goes unnoticed: plastic or paper grocery bags, pine pallets used for bulk delivery, cardboard boxes, individual containers, and gas to move food from producer to processor to distributor to grocery store to personal residence. To offer an accurate appraisal of the waste eliminated by our garden, however, it would probably be necessary to include the vast array of negative indirect effects that do not occur because our garden reduces our demand for food products purchased at the grocery store.

By almost all the moral criteria specified earlier, our garden represents a far superior agricultural system. The major limitation of our garden, of course, is its inability to provide enough food for our family. While it probably provides the equivalent of one full meal each day for every person in our family during the peak season (June, July, and August), it only supplements the foodstuffs we need to purchase elsewhere. This is the undeniable fact true of all small-scale gardening: despite its appeal on many moral fronts, it can never fulfill the moral criterion of providing a sufficient amount of food.

Although gardening will never represent anything more than a partial solution to constructing an agricultural system consistent with a

Christian ethic of gratitude, our survey of the possibilities presented by gardening sharply counteracts the common American conception of gardening simply as an enjoyable hobby. Gardening is certainly enjoyable in many ways, but its theological meaning far transcends the categories of individual preferences and fulfillment commonly supplied by the dominant ideology of expressive individualism. At its best, gardening is a way to realize a host of valuable moral objectives and to make a small part of our food production complex a little kinder to the land, to ourselves, to our neighbors, to our wild friends, and to future generations.

Community-Supported Agriculture

Community-supported agriculture (CSA) began approximately thirty years ago in Japan as an attempt to personalize relationships between producer and consumer and to encourage local food self-sufficiency. A decade after its inception, the idea migrated to the eastern United States, and within several years spread from the eastern seaboard to virtually all major metropolitan areas in the contiguous forty-eight states.[27]

While the phenomenon of CSA is just as varied as gardening in its structure and detail, let me offer a few generalizations about CSA farms. For a CSA farmer, the first order of business is soliciting subscribers during the late winter for the upcoming growing season. Subscribers purchase a "share" (or multiple shares), which means a certain amount of produce each week, relative to what is in season. Early in the year, a share might mean only one plastic grocery store bag of cold-weather crops such as lettuce, spinach, and broccoli; during the middle of summer, a share might mean a half-dozen bags filled with a dozen or more types of vegetables and fruits every week. By contracting during the winter, a farmer's produce is sold before the season begins, and the benefit of this arrangement is that a farmer has available a sufficient amount of cash to cover all the costs associated with running his or her farm that year, which mitigates the need for credit, indebtedness, and interest payments.

While CSA farmers always incur normal risks associated with any business, most of the risk is assumed by the subscriber. Since a share is relative to the produce available each week, a subscriber's share can be affected by a number of variables influencing production: rainfall, cloudiness, pests, low or high temperatures, etc. Sometimes growing conditions are near-perfect, resulting in an unusually large share; other seasons are marked by low productivity due to the aforementioned conditions, which means that a subscriber gets less for his or her money.

Produce is usually available to a subscriber once per week, and is either delivered to a few centrally located drop-off points where they are picked up by subscribers, or the subscribers travel to the CSA farm and gather their produce there.

Diversity is at a premium on CSA farms. Since a CSA farm provides food to individuals or families who will be consuming the food directly, it is necessary to provide the greatest range of produce that can be grown in a respective area. CSAs, in consequence, grow a wide variety of vegetables, many cultivate patches of berry bushes and tend an assortment of fruit trees, and many provide eggs and various forms of meat to increase their offerings.

In many other ways, CSA farms tend to go against the grain of mainstream American agriculture: they are small, usually never larger than twenty-five acres; they rely heavily on simple, inexpensive technologies such as hoes, spades, trowels, garden claws, etc.; they tend to be organic; they rely extensively on local inputs that can be acquired on the farm; they are human labor intensive; and their market is local, usually within ten or fifteen miles of the farm.

Although it is somewhat misleading to think of CSA as gardening on a larger scale, the parallels between the two are significant, especially in light of a Christian ethic of gratitude. Like gardening, CSA provides fresh, (usually) chemical-free food to consumers; it is less dependent on unreliable inputs, such as fossil fuels; it is insulated better from external circumstances (lower prices due to overproduction, etc.); the negative side effects associated with transportation are much less; it transforms waste into valuable soil additives; its crop diversity provides a more hospitable environment for animals; and at its best it is sustainable.

The substantial difference between gardening and CSA, however, is the latter's ability to feed more people. Gardening's potential as a viable alternative to agriculture in the Corn Belt is limited by the time constraints of contemporary American life and the lack of access to land. CSA is not similarly limited: the time needed to pick up produce from a CSA farm or delivery location is usually comparable to the time needed for a short trip to the grocery store, and one does not need to own land personally to reap the benefits of CSA. As such, CSA can play a larger structural role in making American agriculture more consistent with a Christian ethic of gratitude.

There are other important aspects of CSA to mention. CSA has been touted by many as community-friendly agriculture. Some CSAs require that subscribers perform a specified number of hours of work on the farm as part of their contractual obligation, which brings together community members and offers opportunities to meet new local people. Many also provide after-hours social events, such as potluck dinners, socials, and dances, and workshops and seminars open to the public are common. CSAs are also child-friendly and encourage parents to bring children to the farm to pick produce, to run around and burn off some energy, and to meet other kids. Many also have a "children's garden," where kids are encouraged to tend their own small plot of ground. In the sense of providing multiple venues for people to get to know others in their local community better, there is little doubt that CSAs create possibilities for more enriching communal relationships.[28]

Yet this represents only one facet of community building. As we discussed in chapter 2, the deterioration of rural communities in the latter half of the twentieth century was caused principally by the economic strangulation induced by large farms. The larger farms became, the more businesses, public services, and personal incomes suffered in farming-dependent towns. The chief advantage of CSA is that it eliminates scores of intermediaries between producers and consumers that are effectively capturing a greater percentage of a product's sales price, which translates into more money for farmers and their communities.[29] Especially if the ethos of a particular community is sufficiently imbued with a commitment to buy locally, this can result in money circulating several times in a rural town before it finally exits and heads elsewhere. This is precisely the dynamic that supports the economic revitalization of rural America and its manifold positive side effects.

Another advantage of CSA is the degree of control and knowledge it offers to subscribers. For approximately three decades, Wendell Berry has been driving home the point that the distance between consumer and producer created by our contemporary food production system effectively precludes us from gathering much morally relevant data about the food we consume. On both counts, Berry is correct. Consider shopping at the typical chain grocery store in America. A consumer's control over the foods offered for sale is virtually nonexistent. Gaining access to someone with the authority to alter the selection of foods on the grocery store shelves typically involves multiple conversations that gradually ascend the managerial chain of command, beginning with low-level, part-time workers who are usually most accessible as they stock shelves, then midlevel, full-time employees, and then an assistant manager who possesses the authority to make the desired change, if he or she is so inclined. Yet even if one has the persistence to pursue this activity to its end, the fact remains that the large number of people patronizing the typical American chain grocery store, sometimes thousands or tens of thousands every week, greatly reduces the political clout of the individual consumer. In the large scheme of things, one customer's business is almost meaningless in this context, which means that a chain grocery store has little or no incentive to take seriously the customer's request.

The knowledge that can be acquired about foods in chain grocery stores is exceedingly thin. While product labels sometimes convey basic information that might or might not be helpful, the consumer is largely left in the dark about conditions surrounding the production of the foodstuff. Imagine pulling a can of peas off a grocery store shelf, locating the store manager, and asking him or her a series of questions: Were pesticides applied to these peas? If so, which particular pesticides? Were any synthetic chemicals used on the farm? What type of soil conservation measures does the farm employ? Is the farm comprised of monocultures, or does it practice crop rotations and produce multiple crops every year? What is the quality of the topsoil on the farm? Is the farm highly mechanized? Does the farm employ migrant laborers? If so, what are their hourly wages and working conditions? Does the farm try to create habitat for animals? Does the farm try to purchase inputs locally? Amusement, bewilderment, and annoyance are the likeliest responses to these questions, and I doubt that even the most competent store manager would be able to answer even a small fraction of them.

The situation is entirely different on a CSA farm. Answers to these questions are readily forthcoming either by strolling around the farm and observing conditions firsthand or by asking the owner/operator or farm manager, who is usually intentionally accessible on food distribution days to interact with subscribers, to gather information, and to answer any queries that might arise. Unlike grocery store employees, CSA personnel are involved in every facet of production, which enables them to accumulate an extraordinary degree of practical knowledge about their crops, methods of production, and farm conditions that can be very useful to someone interested in supporting a particular type of agriculture.

Individual CSA subscribers also enjoy more political leverage, and their preferences and comments carry greater weight. The much smaller customer base of CSAs means that a CSA farmer has more to lose by ignoring or alienating a subscriber, which usually translates into greater responsiveness to an individual's requests. Especially given the fact that CSAs usually generate new business by word of mouth, it is incumbent on CSA owners not to treat subscribers poorly and thereby to create the situation in which a few disgruntled patrons sow sour grapes in the local community and tarnish the CSA's reputation.

Please do not mistake these comments as praise for expanding the personal choice of consumers, which is usually linked to a philosophical or theological worldview that promotes individual freedom and places a premium on the satisfaction of individual desires. My intention is neither to solidify the expressive individualism that is already well entrenched in the United States, nor to laud the ability of CSAs to cater to individual whims and fancies,[30] but to highlight the fact that CSA represents a form of agricultural production that is malleable and to some extent controllable by ordinary individual citizens. This is an important point. The small-scale nature of CSAs and the personal interaction that usually characterizes the owner-subscriber relationship lend themselves to a quasi-democratic form of participation and governance, in which the individual's voice is heard and often makes a difference. While extensive, coordinated political action is usually needed to gain access to the corridors of power charged with formulating governmental or business policy affecting the agricultural sector, which effectively vitiates the ability of small groups or individuals to enact meaningful change, CSA offers direct access, relevant and fairly comprehensive knowledge, responsiveness to the smallest bases of power, and the ability to implement certain policies, practices, or methods of production immediately without having to wallow through layers of institutional bureaucracy.

In my mind, CSA can and should play a pivotal role in reshaping American agriculture according to the tenets of a Christian ethic of gratitude. While retaining the many moral benefits of gardening, CSA also offers the possibility of overcoming the fact that most Americans lack the resources to grow their own food and must rely on others for their daily sustenance. CSA, then, offers an alternative to mainstream Corn Belt agriculture that is far more promising on a broader scale. Unfortunately, many CSAs currently cater to the economic elite and often reflect their eccentric tastes for novelties that symbolize their sense of privilege and status. It is no accident that CSAs tend to be located within a short driving distance of affluent suburban areas that are typically associated with well-educated white-collar workers, soccer moms, spacious houses, and high-performance automobiles.

There is no reason, however, that CSAs need to be located near major metropolitan areas or to cater to the well-to-do in order to survive and flourish. In fact, the greatest area of promise for CSA lies in the small towns of rural America that have been ravaged economically over the last fifty years. Why? First, many citizens of small rural communities have been involved in farming their entire lives and possess an extraordinary degree of knowledge about the nuts-and-bolts of managing and operating a farm. To a great extent, the knowledge base necessary to begin CSAs on a widespread basis is already present in abundance in rural America.[31]

Second, many of these citizens are former farmers who could not make an adequate living at traditional corn and soybean production, but would relish the opportunity to get back into farming if the right opportunity presented itself. I suspect that many of these former Midwestern farmers simply have not been exposed to anything resembling CSA and have not seriously entertained the idea that farming can be something other than capital-intensive, technologically sophisticated, large-scale, and market-oriented monocultures of corn and soybeans.

Third, out of all the casualties of the economic decline in rural America, the disappearance of the local grocery store strikes a particularly sour chord in the citizens of small rural towns. While many are annoyed at the fact that purchasing high-ticket items now usually involves a lengthy trip to a distant large city, having to travel once or twice per week to other towns or cities to secure basic necessities such as groceries evokes an unparalleled degree of anger and frustration. Nor are these negative emotions associated simply with the inconvenience of frequent travel. Grocery stores in small rural communities function as cultural and social centers, where people exchange news, renew friendships, conduct informal business, and chat with the store employees and patrons. Understandably, the disappearance of the local grocery store has impoverished community life and made it more difficult to find satisfactory venues for regular social intercourse. The allure of CSA is its potential to fill both gaps. During the growing season, a CSA can eliminate the need for many of the trips to other towns to buy groceries, and it can serve as a central meeting place on distribution days or provide social opportunities through on-farm work, potlucks, or educational seminars.

Fourth, starting up a CSA is a possibility for a greater number of people, especially the lower and middle classes who will never be in the financial situation to begin farming in the traditional mode of Corn Belt agriculture. While anyone uninvolved in the daily operation of a CSA is likely to underestimate the amount of resources needed to make it function smoothly, it seems safe to say that a CSA requires neither a large amount of land nor expensive machinery, buildings, implements, or inputs. A few acres, a collection of hand tools, a reliable tiller or two, a few large compost bins, a storage building, money for seeds, a greenhouse to start seeds indoors, sufficient knowledge and managerial skills, an adequate amount of manual labor, and certain odds and ends (boxes, buckets, tables, etc.) seem to be the bare necessities for getting a CSA up and running. The comparatively low start-up costs associated with this type of agriculture create opportunities for a broad range of people and strongly corroborate our egalitarian tendencies to look favorably upon institutions that do not make economic privilege a necessary prerequisite for admission.

Finally, the small-scale nature of a CSA coupled with the fact that people in rural communities almost always live in close proximity to farmland means that CSAs should be able to be situated in prime locations, which are usually as close to the subscribers as possible. For a typical corn and soybean farmer who deals in large tracts of land, finding a hundred acres of farmland for sale within a one-mile radius of the city limits is virtually impossible; the odds of acquiring farmland similarly situated increases exponentially when only a few acres are needed.

While I have lauded the potential of CSA to contribute to the revitalization of rural America, the fact is that the benefits of CSA can accrue in virtually any setting across the United States. Given the vast potential of CSA to move a substantial portion of our food production system closer to the tenets of a Christian ethic of gratitude, it is incumbent upon us not only to support CSAs financially as far as possible and to be active participants in CSAs to ensure that they do not succumb to the temptations that have besieged American farmers and led to the trends criticized in the preceding chapter, but also to strive to institutionalize measures that create a relatively permanent demand for CSAs and their foods at the local level. CSA currently functions as a voluntary association between private individuals (subscribers and CSA owners), and while this arrangement offers many advantages for both, it leaves intact existing economic institutions and patterns of behavior that often force CSA into the role of serving a niche market.[32]

While many institutional remedies at various levels would be beneficial, let me suggest a few that are the most feasible at the local level. Public and parochial schools should be encouraged to form partnerships with CSAs, either by subscribing to an already existing CSA or, if no CSA exists in the immediate vicinity, by soliciting local farmers to start a CSA that would be awarded a contract to supply the school with food for its hot lunch program. In addition to this arrangement's obvious benefits (fresh food for the children, a source of income for the farmer, and an economic boost for the local community), it also could provide valuable educational opportunities for the students as they become more aware of the story behind the food they consume and perhaps even actively participate on the farm itself and learn about the many fascinating aspects of growing food.

In a similar way, grocery stores need to be pressured to offer CSA food on their shelves. This is an uphill battle, but one that is very worthwhile. The main element militating against a close working relationship between a grocery store and a CSA is the former's need for delivery of certain crops consistently every week throughout the year. A grocery store does not want to be limited by the seasonal nature of agriculture, so that it has available on its shelves broccoli only during May and June, and then again in October and November, or acorn squash available only during August and September. No, a grocery store wants select foodstuffs available on its shelves every day of the year, and the easiest way to accomplish this is to contract with a distributor capable of reaching across the globe to ensure a steady supply of desired foods. From the grocery store's perspective, trying to forge a partnership with a CSA only creates unnecessary work, logistical problems, and potential issues with a reliable distributor.

This being said, forging partnerships with grocery stores would be a boon to CSA. Perhaps I am capitulating too easily to the contemporary consumer mentality that treasures convenience, but one major disadvantage of joining a CSA is the additional time and travel it requires. In addition to a trip to a CSA, a subscriber also needs to visit a grocery store to obtain needed items not offered by the CSA. If CSA produce were available at the local grocery store, I strongly suspect that people would be more willing to support CSA.

Cafés, restaurants, Meals on Wheels programs, food banks, caterers, and all the other different types of businesses and institutions that prepare or distribute food also represent a promising area for CSA. There is a growing trend among local restaurants (by which I mean restaurants not part of a national chain) to tailor their menus around produce in season in their respective area, and many have effectively fostered a cultural and moral shift among local citizens that makes them more supportive of CSA and aware of the many benefits CSA offers.

Of course, many other structural adjustments beneficial to CSA could be mentioned, but my purpose is not to develop a blueprint for making CSA more mainstream. The point I wish to emphasize is that CSA offers an alternative to Corn Belt agriculture that better embodies a Christian ethic of gratitude, and it behooves us to implement institutional measures that create a consistent demand for CSA and the many food products it provides. Without this institutional basis, CSA still might flourish through the support of individual subscribers; but the more CSA is weaved into the structures upon which we depend regularly, the more the positive benefits of CSA will begin to accrue at many levels and the more CSA will enjoy the prospect of a long-term future in the United States. The time for CSA has come, and Christians of all stripes should support CSA in whatever way possible to make our agricultural system more consonant with God's desires.

Cuba: Low-Input Agriculture

Cuba is probably the most remarkable success story in contemporary agriculture. Not only is the almost complete structural renovation of Cuba's agricultural system virtually unprecedented in its depth and breadth, but the food production system currently in place in Cuba turns on its head deeply embedded assumptions and prevailing wisdom in the mainstream agricultural sector of the United States, which have given impetus to the trends discussed in chapter 2. Cuban agriculture offers a healthy dose of optimism about the feasibility of accomplishing structural change while simultaneously demonstrating the viability of alternative forms of production that are consistent with a Christian ethic of gratitude.

Recent Cuban agricultural history is frequently divided into three periods: prerevolution (ca. 1900–1959), postrevolution (1959–1990), and contemporary (1990–present). Like most colonized countries whose economies are geared toward producing exports (mostly foodstuffs or raw materials) for wealthier, more industrialized First World countries,[33] during the prerevolution period Cuban agriculture sought to maximize its comparative advantage by producing a small handful of cash crops, especially sugar cane and tobacco. Coupled with the ideology of agricultural modernization that emerged in the first half of the twentieth century, which eventually culminated in the "Green Revolution" that transformed Third and Fourth World agricultural systems worldwide, as well as the influence of American corporations[34] and their preferred notion of agricultural development, which at this time controlled a large proportion of farmland and sugar cane production in Cuba, Cuban agriculture followed a path of development during this period that strongly paralleled that of the Corn Belt in the United States: capital intensive, large farm size, mechanized, fossil fuel intensive, technologically sophisticated, and productive of monocultures.[35]

The Revolution of 1959 and subsequent economic embargo by the United States left Cuba with far fewer markets for an agricultural system that depended extensively on exports. This potential economic crisis was averted, however, by forming a trade alliance with the Socialist Bloc, especially the former Soviet Union. This was mutually advantageous for all parties involved. Cuba had already established itself as a major producer of a few valuable food items and had a well-oiled, export-oriented agricultural system. By forging a strong economic relationship with Cuba, the Soviet Union had access to a few desirable agricultural products that were hard to acquire from other socialist countries. In return, the Soviet Union functioned as a virtual life-support system for Cuba, supplying foodstuffs, agricultural inputs, petroleum, heavy machinery, and a number of other manufactured goods.[36] Especially given the extremely favorable terms of trade for sugar offered by the Soviet Union, which during certain periods was over five times the average price on the international market, Cuba converted much of its arable land to sugar cane production, including land that had formerly been used to grow food for domestic consumption.[37]

While this relationship brought significant benefits to Cubans as measured by several indices of human well-being, its dark side was the degree of dependency it created. Large-scale, capital-intensive, monocrop agriculture is notorious for being dependent on external inputs, and this was certainly true for Cuban agriculture. Yet the dependency was not limited to the production of the major export crop, sugar, but extended to the entire domestic food supply. Approximately three times more land was devoted to sugar production than to production of food crops for domestic consumption, and an astonishing 57 percent of the total calories consumed on a daily basis by Cubans were imported, making Cuba one of the most food-dependent countries in the world.[38]

Cuba's day of reckoning arrived with the collapse of the Soviet Union. By 1989, Cuba's trade relationship with the Soviet Union began unraveling, and within a short period of time all the crucial inputs upon which Cuban agriculture necessarily depended became unavailable. Almost overnight, Cuba was plunged into a state of desperation: protein and fat consumption was reduced by 80 percent; the amount of fertilizers and pesticides available was reduced by 80 percent;[39] petroleum by 66 percent; wheats and grains by 50 percent; and new agricultural machinery, implements, and spare parts were almost nonexistent.[40] The average daily caloric intake of Cubans fell by 30 percent,[41] and hunger became a common element of daily life in Cuba.

The Cuban government's response to this crisis was a national effort to convert their agricultural system into one that could function effectively under such conditions of scarcity. This meant diversified, low-input agriculture that relied on locally available resources. As substitutes for synthetic chemicals, Cuban farmers began controlling pests through natural biopesticides, microbial antagonists, and intercropping to attract beneficial predators; crop rotations, organic fertilizers, animal and green manures, and compost augmented soil fertility; and weed control was attained by better crop rotations and cover crops. The absence of tractors, petroleum, and spare parts was overcome by a "sweeping return to animal traction."[42] Another component of the Cuban government's program was the restoration of land that was formerly abused after decades of intensive monocropping, which damaged the soil considerably and reduced its productivity. To boost production levels on this land, Cuban farmers focused on "conservation tillage, contour plowing, cover cropping, incorporation of biomass and biologically active forest soils, and other methods to restore soil structure and fertility."[43]

The response to this new input substitution form of agriculture was mixed. The large state-run farms, which composed approximately 80 percent of Cuba's arable farmland, experienced a precipitous decline in production levels, while the small-scale peasant farms that made up the remaining 20 percent of arable farmland increased production.[44] While the inability of the large state-run farms to adapt well to the conditions of restraint can be attributed partially to managerial shortcomings, economy of scale was the fundamental flaw. Large farms, as we have seen already, are fragile in a number of respects and find it very difficult, if not impossible, to transition to low-input forms of production. Whether it be insufficient amounts of local inputs, an inability to substitute different technologies, dwindling soil fertility, the inability to adopt natural insect control, or some other reason, the fact is that large farms are rigid and incapable of functioning outside the context of a high degree of external inputs.

Based on the early success of the small-scale peasant farms and the failure of the large state-run farms, in 1993 the Cuban government took extraordinary actions: first, it secured land use rights for urban gardeners to bring any unused land into cultivation, which produced a vast network of urban gardens and farmers' markets in metropolitan areas;[45] second, the large state-run farms were abolished and the land was privatized and turned over to the workers in the form of worker-owned cooperatives. These cooperatives still had to fulfill annual quotas for certain crops, and property rights were retained by the state (although farmland was leased for free in perpetuity), but the effectiveness of these two measures was astonishing: acute food shortages disappeared by 1995,[46] production levels of most major foodstuffs continued to increase, and Cuba today is one of the world's most self-sufficient countries in food production.

Cuba's resounding success with organic, low-input, small-scale, diversified farming is living testimony to the feasibility of a different agricultural paradigm that is almost diametrically opposed to that underlying mainstream Corn Belt agriculture today. One scholar put it as follows:

[C]ontemporary Cuba turned conventional wisdom completely on its head. We are told that small countries cannot feed themselves, that they need imports to cover the deficiency of their local agriculture. Yet Cuba has taken enormous strides toward self-reliance since it lost its key trade relations. We hear that a country can't feed its people without synthetic farm chemicals, yet Cuba is virtually doing so. We are told that we need the efficiency of large-scale corporate or state farms in order to produce enough food, yet we find small farmers and gardeners in the vanguard of Cuba's recovery from a food crisis.[47]

The value of Cuba's example, however, lies not only in its power to debunk many of the myths often used to legitimate contemporary American agriculture and its preferred form of production, but also in the elements that fostered the successful structural renovation of Cuban agriculture and provide an incipient model that can be instructive for the development of agriculture in the Corn Belt. In fact, the most striking aspect of Cuban agriculture's structural features is the degree of similarity with indigenous agricultural systems, which were discussed in chapter 1: small farm size, diversity of plants and animals, use of local inputs, multiple recycling processes, optimization of biological interactions to maximize symbiotic relationships, soil conservation, and production for the local community. This likeness to indigenous agricultural systems is not accidental. The peasant farmers who proved so successful in boosting production levels during the food crisis and prompted the Cuban government to follow their lead as the structure of Cuban agriculture was reconstituted were simply incorporating the methods and practices handed down from past generations of farmers that had withstood the test of time and proven to be successful.[48] The principal savior of Cuban agriculture, in other words, was not more sophisticated technology, more capital, or more powerful machinery, but the accumulated wisdom of farmers who practiced a very different form of agriculture under conditions of scarcity, which eventually was highly beneficial when similar conditions obtained.

The importance of traditional agricultural knowledge was recognized by the Cuban government decades before the food crisis began, fostered in great part by the ecology movement which was highly skeptical of the Green Revolution and its model of agricultural development and which placed considerable pressure on the Cuban government to redirect agricultural research to the study of traditional agricultural systems. This younger generation of scientists found a receptive ear in the Cuban government, and building on the insights gathered from traditional agricultural systems, their research and development programs produced many innovative methods, technologies, and products. Granted, the fruits of this research were not in great demand before the food crisis and were mostly confined to small-scale operations. Yet in the absence of external inputs experienced with the collapse of trade relations with Socialist Bloc countries, the research of these scientists was invaluable — and their knowledge and pretested products, already available and waiting to be employed and used — greatly eased the pains associated with this transition.[49]

In my opinion, the knowledge base offered by Cuba's peasant farmers and by scientists operating outside the mode of mainstream agriculture was the linchpin for Cuba's agricultural success story, and without this repertoire of knowledge Cuba's agricultural experiment would probably have turned out much differently — and tragically. It is important, however, to be very precise about the knowledge base that functioned so effectively for Cuban agriculture. In the context of American agriculture, the term "knowledge" typically conjures up images of a cadre of PhDs who specialize in one particular area, carry out their research in laboratories for major corporations, possess a technical vocabulary, help create highly sophisticated products, and are imbued with scientific reductionism that understands reality by breaking it down into its smallest component parts. The prestige and respect associated with this notion of knowledge typically engenders a great deal of deference and passivity in the layperson, who simply takes the products created by the experts and uses them according to the user's instructions. This understanding of knowledge, however, functions as a one-way street, with the experts creating the specific products and technologies that are offered to the agricultural sector and thereby controlling the way in which agriculture develops.

This is not the paradigm of "knowledge" that saved Cuban agriculture. Experts were not regarded as having a monopoly on relevant knowledge. Indeed, the Cuban government recognized that relevant knowledge would emanate from a number of diverse sources that could contribute insights into low-input, diversified, organic, low-technology farming and that the success of their new agricultural system would depend on the ability to collect, disseminate, and improve upon the knowledge available from all these sources. To foster this process, the Ministry of Agriculture inaugurated a program in the study of Cuban indigenous agriculture, since it had evolved and flourished in the context of resource scarcity and its traditions and practices had been highly advantageous during the transition period.[50]

The Cuban government also began a massive retraining program for experts committed to a Green Revolution model of agriculture and its defining characteristics: heavy dependence on capital, synthetic chemicals, hybrid crops, heavy machinery, and sophisticated technology. These experts, the Cuban government reasoned, would be a formidable liability to agricultural reform unless their basic model for agriculture was displaced and their energy focused on different objectives and research agendas.[51] In addition to this effort focused on agricultural experts, the Cuban government sought to establish a strong foothold for low-input agriculture in the academy by creating new university programs in agroecology at the undergraduate and graduate levels and by greatly expanding agricultural education and training programs at rural vocational high schools to expose future farmers to the principles of low-input agriculture.[52]

Yet another method valuable for collecting and disseminating relevant agricultural information was bringing farmers together physically to share insights. Recognizing that farmers practicing low-input agriculture and experimenting with different strategies, methods of production, and technologies were likely to possess practical knowledge beneficial to other farmers, the Cuban government began sponsoring mobile seminars and workshops designed to facilitate informational exchanges and to create links between local farmers.[53]

This paradigm of agricultural knowledge, suffice it to say, is very different from that in the United States. It is more multidirectional in the flow of knowledge, more broadly based in the number and type of people brought into the discussion, and more receptive to practitioners (farmers) having substantial input and sharing ideas with one another. In short, by recognizing that the loci of relevant agricultural knowledge are diffuse and by institutionalizing measures designed to tap into these different knowledge bases, Cuba has maximized the odds that beneficial insights will be uncovered, recognized, disseminated, implemented, and eventually improved upon as farmers and others search for better ways to practice low-input agriculture.

Another lesson gleaned from the Cuban food crisis and the restructuring of Cuban agriculture is the necessity of structural redesign to accomplish certain objectives in the agricultural sector. As I argued earlier, economy of scale is probably the most formative structural aspect of an agricultural system, insofar as it strongly prefers certain methods, practices, policies, relationships, technologies, and types of knowledge over others and thereby functions as a ratchet ordering various components of the system in a particular manner. Cuba's firsthand experience with a negative economy of scale quickly confirmed the significant drawbacks of large farms that functioned as immovable white elephants unable to adapt to conditions of scarcity and thereby exacerbating a national food crisis. It is no accident that one of the Cuban government's first measures was the elimination of these large farms.

Yet the range of possibilities created by a network of smaller farms is perhaps the more important lesson. With farms much smaller, Cuban farmers could now use biological methods to control pests; enjoy the multiple benefits of diversification; create beneficial relationships between crops and animals; substitute animals for traction power; substitute human labor for synthetic chemicals; gain access to appropriate and relatively inexpensive technologies; become more familiar with the uniqueness of particular patches of land and tailor land-use practices accordingly; enhance soil fertility through the use of manure, compost, and other locally accessible resources; and increase production levels. None of these would have been possible in the context of a network of large farms and the type of arrangements they typically engender. The shift in farm size, of course, is not the only structural adjustment contributing to Cuba's success, and the viability of many of these practices consistent with low-input agriculture will depend on continuing support from the Cuban government, educators, and farmers.

Due to the relative infancy of Cuba's low-input agricultural system, it is difficult to address the larger question of its sustainability. To a great extent, sustainability can be ascribed to an agricultural system only after undergoing the test of time; in most instances, however, indicators of sustainability are inferred from common characteristics of sustainable agricultural systems or they are simply well-educated hypotheses about necessary factors that contribute to an agricultural system's ability to persist in the long term. While the surety of attributing sustainability to Cuba's new agricultural system does not rise to the level of the first standard, there is every reason to suspect that it meets the second. Not only is the archetype for Cuba's low-input agricultural system — indigenous agriculture — one of the securest and most dependable forms of agricultural production throughout recorded human history, but all the characteristics that contribute to sustainability that were discussed in chapter 1 are well represented in current Cuban agriculture and are explicit objectives of Cuban national agricultural policy.

Cuba's experiment in low-input agriculture deserves the closest attention as it develops over the next few decades and their farmers and scientists perfect techniques, methods of production, and technologies suited to this form of agriculture. Cubans have already developed some of the most effective locally available, biological insect controls in the world, and the signs are promising that many innovative breakthroughs are on the horizon that will make low-input agriculture even more attractive. Yet in the larger picture, attention is owed to Cuban agriculture because it represents a form of food production almost diametrically opposed to that of the Corn Belt, and one that could provide valuable information if our country ever seriously entertains a structural renovation of our agricultural system. If, as I suspect, we will someday have no choice but to revamp Corn Belt agriculture, Cuban agriculture could play a large role in making our food production system more consistent with a Christian ethic of gratitude.

The Old Order Amish: Tradition-Based Agriculture

The bulwark supporting contemporary Amish agriculture is a centuries-old agricultural tradition, forged under inhospitable conditions when the Amish were expelled from their land in sixteenth-century Europe and forced to farm highly marginal ground,[54] and perfected over time as Amish farmers experimented, learned, adapted, and through this process discovered a recipe, so to speak, for sustainable agriculture that has been transmitted from generation to generation. While many question marks often surround the sustainability of agricultural systems due to their relative infancy, Amish agriculture is comparatively unambiguous; it has persisted for centuries in a number of different environmental and regional contexts.

The sustainability of Amish agriculture, however, is not simply a byproduct of the innovation, skills, and adaptability commonly fostered by the necessity of farming under less than ideal conditions, but is tied to a religious ethos that regards certain core values as virtually inviolable, which in turn function as limiting principles that dictate the shape and content of Amish agriculture and thereby contribute to its sustainability. This might seem odd to contemporary Americans, who are likely to regard strong religious-moral proscriptions as unpalatable restrictions of freedom and progress that cannot avoid being counterproductive or highly detrimental in the long run, but these self-imposed restrictions based on foundational religious beliefs seem to be a pivotal reason that Amish agriculture is sustainable. Of course, the Amish adhere to their religious beliefs because they regard them as true, not because they have the functional effect of producing a sustainable agricultural system. Yet the Amish illustrate a common pattern among sustainable agricultural systems: all operate under conditions of restraint, whether self-imposed or not, that (compared to the conditions of contemporary American agriculture) place sharp limits on available inputs, economy of scale, technologies employed, and farm structure.

Let me explain two of these religious beliefs, separation from the world and the importance of community, and the cluster of practical implications they entail that affect the sustainability of Amish agriculture. Central to the Amish religious self-identity is St. Paul's exhortation in Romans 12:2, "Do not be conformed to this world, but be transformed by the renewing of your minds, so that you may discern what is the will of God — what is good and acceptable and perfect."[55] The Amish believe that God's true church is completely different from the corrupt world and that the church's members, as strangers to and pilgrims in this terrestrial life, must intentionally distance themselves from secular life and its trappings. Yet the last word of the Romans passage is equally relevant: the reason for separation from the world is to achieve perfection in God's eyes, to become the type of persons that God intended the chosen people to be. This notion of perfection interjects a great deal of rigor and austerity into Amish life by insisting on nothing less than complete obedience to God's will, whether easy or difficult.

Given these religious beliefs, the Amish are extremely cautious about the particular things appropriated from outside their community and are also very reluctant about situations that might entail compromising their beliefs. In an agricultural context, this translates into a robust conservatism that prefers the known over the new and novel, an agricultural system developed within the Amish community rather than by experts and agribusinesses, and an abiding skepticism about any technology, relationship, or product that breeds dependency and subtly erodes a commitment to perfection. So, for instance, the Amish are not enamored by new agricultural technologies; on the contrary, they are deeply skeptical of them[56] since their full effects are largely unknown and their high purchase price often entails debt, which leads to vulnerability and possible compromise as farmers struggle to make enough money to repay loans. This conservatism also places a premium on self-reliance, since the best way to avoid becoming entangled in situations that limit freedom, breed dependency, and thereby create the temptation to violate the commitment to perfection is to limit intercourse with others and to use one's own skills and resources as much as possible to avoid relying on others. This is why the Amish consistently substitute human labor on the farm whenever feasible (contrary to the trend in American agriculture to substitute capital for human labor), since by performing tasks oneself it is possible to avoid purchasing machinery, petroleum, and other items that often create economic pressures which could lead to compromises.

The second foundational religious belief, the importance of community, stems from a theological anthropology that understands human beings as fallen, disordered creatures who are inclined toward self-exaltation and pride, which becomes manifest in a variety of ways: "self-seeking, personal power, wealth, and status."[57] Absent any countervailing force, this inclination would eventually dominate a person and lead to a downward spiral of moral depravity. The local Amish community offers a powerful check on this negative tendency by providing guidance, assistance, and reproof when needed and by enforcing the regulations of the *Ordnung* (a body of rules governing all aspects of Amish life). Furthermore, the community is vested with a broad-based authority that supersedes each individual's judgment and requires that each Amish person submit to his or her community's directive.

For the Amish, the stakes are exceedingly high in maintaining the appropriate kind of community, for it represents the most capable front-line defense against inherent, pernicious human urges which, if not resisted, are likely to culminate in eternal perdition. Community, then, is a spiritual lifeline of the utmost importance, providing the appropriate guidance to direct its members to life with God. This strong communitarianism functions as a limiting principle in Amish agriculture in several important ways. First, it limits technological innovation, since the adoption of any new technology requires an extended communal discussion about the respective technology's effects on family life, farming methods, religious observances, and other facets of Amish life. Only after the community has engaged in this deliberative process and decided to accept the new technology is an individual allowed to adopt it.

Second, it has helped curtail the expansion of farm size among the Amish. A community cannot fulfill its purpose when considerable distance separates members and the nearest neighbor is a mile or more down the road; close physical proximity is the cornerstone for the type of interaction and involvement in one another's lives needed for a community to know about its members sufficiently and to exercise influence over their behavior. Because of this distinct notion of community, the predatory behavior of owners of large farms gobbling up nearby smaller farms, which has been prevalent in the Corn Belt for the past half-century and has engendered an extraordinary amount of resentment, anger, and ill will in rural America, is nonexistent in Amish communities. The Amish do not look upon a neighbor's farmland as an opportunity to increase one's profit margin; economic gain pales in comparison to the value of having a neighbor who can help promote the religious goals of the community and contribute integrally to the salvation of its members.

While these practical effects of Amish foundational religious beliefs are not the exclusive reasons for the sustainability of Amish agriculture, they play an integral part. Strong communal controls over technology have helped the Amish avoid the infamous technological treadmill that creates debt, generates a need for additional income, and pressures farmers to purchase cutting-edge machinery and implements. Their relative lack of indebtedness has created a zone of freedom for Amish farmers to be more discriminating about the technologies appropriated by the Amish community and to be able to incorporate technologies that best fit into their preferred agricultural system.

Limitations on technology have also produced positive side effects that contribute to the vitality of Amish communities. The Amish are perhaps most famous for rejecting automobile ownership and the use of tractors for field work (although tractors are sometimes used to power equipment such as augers and conveyor belts),[58] preferring instead to use horses for transportation and traction power in the fields. While most Americans are likely to view an Amish horse-drawn carriage tooling down a rural highway as an amusing artifact of bygone days, this mobility limitation has a very beneficial function. A typical American farmer can drive for hours a day to purchase agricultural machinery and implements, high-ticket items, and household goods in distant cities, a pattern of behavior that has become more common as farms have grown larger in the United States. Of course, the effect of this behavior is less money circulating in the local community, which as we have seen affects businesses, government services, education, and many other important facets of rural life. Due to their decreased mobility, Amish farmers do not enjoy comparable opportunities to make purchases in distant locales and must instead conduct more of their business locally. As one Amish farmer writes, the horse is a major reason for the health and vitality of Amish communities: "If we Amish in northeastern Ohio look at our community and all its small villages... that are thriving in spite of a Wal-Mart ten miles away, we can see it is because of the horse. Seldom do we travel farther than five or six miles to do our business. Some may go to Wal-Mart, but not on a weekly basis. The standardbred horse helps us, even if we think globally, to act locally."[59]

In a roundabout way, the Amish's communitarianism, which has effectively limited farm size (very few Amish farms exceed 150 acres, which is small by today's standard for farm size in the Corn Belt), has engendered a great deal of diversity in Amish agriculture. It is virtually impossible on a small farm to make a living wage by growing only corn and soybeans. Add an array of animals and different crops into the mix, however, and the economic potential of a small farm increases dramatically. Input substitution becomes a regular feature (manure applications reduce the need for fertilizers, and crop rotations help break pest cycles and reduce the need for pesticides, both of which are money-saving practices), the diversity provides insulation against low commodity prices for certain products, feed crops can be grown on the farm rather than purchased on the market, and human labor can be used more efficiently on a diversified farm. Yet the benefits of diversity are equally advantageous in promoting sustainability. Applying animal manure "increases fertility, improves soil structure, [and] improves both water holding-capacity and drainage."[60] Diversity allows for better crop rotations, which allows a farmer to maximize beneficial relationships between plant species. Diversity provides more opportunities to match particular parcels of land with certain crops or practices (e.g., growing trees or pasturing animals on steeply sloped, highly erodable soil), thereby minimizing deleterious side effects.

Gauged by other sustainability indicators, the Amish fare exceptionally well. The Amish are widely acknowledged as some of the best tenders of topsoil in the world. When banished from their homes in sixteenth-century Europe and forced to farm land with marginal soil, the Amish became adept at developing techniques to create and enhance topsoil, and this body of knowledge has been employed by Amish farmers ever since. Even compared to some of the best soil management methods favored by proponents of industrialized agriculture (e.g., no-till), the Amish are still able to create topsoil better in virtually all categories indicating soil health and fertility.[61] As one scholar writes, soil on Amish farms "exhibited higher rates of water infiltration, higher levels of alkaline-phosphatase activity, less compaction, and more organic matter than the non-Amish farm."[62]

Amish agriculture also relies more extensively on solar energy. While almost every aspect of production on a conventional farm is dependent directly or indirectly on fossil fuels (the production of heavy machinery, the use of tractors and combines, drying grain, the production of synthetic chemicals, etc.), the Amish try to minimize their reliance on fossil fuels through input substitution whenever possible. The most apparent contrast between these two forms of agricultural production is the Amish's use of horses for field work instead of tractors, combines, and other heavy machines. Horses, of course, get their energy from grasses and grains, which in turn get their energy from the sun. Yet the energy required for traction power is not the only difference. The manure produced by horses decreases the need for petroleum-based fertilizers; pest control is fostered by crop rotations and on-farm diversity, which decrease the need for synthetic pesticides; cultivating decreases the need for herbicides; widespread planting of legumes decreases the need for synthetic nitrogen; and human labor is substituted for machine power for a variety of field tasks. In study after study, the comparative energy efficiency of Amish farms over conventional farms has been documented,[63] and the degree of energy independence attained by Amish farms is enviable. While the growing scarcity of fossil fuels bodes ill for the future of conventional Corn Belt agriculture, Amish agriculture is relatively unaffected by the vicissitudes associated with fossil-fuel dependency. In short, Amish agriculture's energy independence makes this form of food production far more secure and stable.

On another indicator of sustainability, too, Amish agriculture offers a marked comparative advantage. The Amish rely far more extensively on local inputs to maintain necessary relationships and dynamics. Given their preference for self-sufficiency, which minimizes the degree to which the Amish become dependent on outsiders and thereby might be tempted to compromise their moral beliefs, Amish agriculture is intentionally designed around available local inputs. The key to this design is diversity: to produce the many inputs needed for a well-functioning farm, a diverse array of elements is needed. On a conventional Corn Belt farm, the degree of homogeneity militates against creating needed inputs, most of which need to be transported to the farm from elsewhere. On an Amish farm, a far greater number of inputs can be produced by exploiting the many beneficial relationships enjoyed in a more diverse setting.

I doubt that anyone would argue that conventional Corn Belt agriculture is more sustainable than Amish agriculture. According to every sustainability indicator, Amish agriculture is the clear winner. Yet sustainability represents only one element of a Christian ethic of gratitude, and when other moral benchmarks are considered, the benefits of Amish agriculture become even more apparent. Although there are regional differences among the Amish regarding the use of synthetic chemicals, the Amish as a group apply less synthetic chemicals to their fields that could cause serious physical health problems for residents of rural areas.[64] Due to their widespread practice of input substitution, Amish agriculture requires less synthetic chemicals to grow crops. From an economic standpoint, this makes good sense: Why pay for synthetic chemicals when other less expensive, on-farm alternatives are available? Yet economic motivations are not the only relevant factor. Religious injunctions, and more specifically the mandate to love one's neighbor, also seem to play a role in minimizing chemical use. As one Amish farmer asks, "I was recently told that during late spring and early summer every raindrop in the eastern corn belt contains minute parts of *Lasso*, a popular corn herbicide and suspected carcinogen. Can you love your neighbor and do this?"[65] While no more than a small fraction of the Amish practice near-organic agriculture, these considerations converge to produce a disinclination to use synthetic chemicals.

Amish agriculture presents considerable benefits to a broader range of animal species compared to conventional Corn Belt agriculture. Although a "garden mentality" that regards anything not brought into agricultural production as a waste is prevalent in both sectors, the diversity of Amish farms minimizes the negative effects of this mentality for animal life. For a conventional Corn Belt farmer, succumbing to the urge to till as much land as possible typically results in ponds and wetlands being drained, fencerows begin removed, woodlots being cleared, and abandoned farm buildings being razed to make way for more bushels of corn and soybeans, all of which reduce available habitat for many species of animals. Take the same garden mentality and let it function unrestrained in the context of diversified Amish agriculture, and the result is very different. Woodlots are regarded no longer as impediments to corn and soybean production, but as valuable sources of food (nuts, wild berries, mushrooms, wild game) and wood that can be used to make furniture or buggies, burned for fuel in the winter, or sold for profit. Woodlots can also be managed for maple sugar production and provide out-of-the-way locations for beehives. Fencerows are good places to grow berry bushes, fruit-bearing trees, and other perennial plants that thrive without frequent human intervention. Ponds are watering holes for horses, cows, pigs, and sheep, homes for domesticated geese and ducks, and a source of fish for consumption. This degree of diversity clearly supports a much greater array of wild animals than a conventional corn and soybean farm. The diversity of cultivated land on an Amish farm and its benefits to wildlife also should not be overlooked. The standard three- to five-year rotation of hay-hay-corn-oats-winter–wheat provides better ground cover for many small animals and birds, which in turn supports greater numbers of predators such as minks, foxes, badgers, raccoons, coyotes, and birds of prey.

The Amish exemplify the idea that agriculture need not be inimical to wild animals and strongly undermine the common assumption that the only way to create habitat for our wild friends to live and to flourish is to remove land from agricultural production and to cease and desist human activity in these areas. While any type of human activity in nature necessarily favors certain species over others, the perceived irreconcilable conflict between agricultural production and animal species presupposes a certain form of agriculture — monocultures of corn and soybeans found everywhere in the Corn Belt — that greatly simplifies ecosystems and proves disadvantageous to all but a handful of animals. If Corn Belt agriculture were dominated by diverse farms similar to the Amish's, the heartland would not be such a desertlike abode for its wild denizens, but a place where a greater array of animals could make a home.

One objection to promoting Amish agriculture as an alternative model for Corn Belt agriculture is the common perception that this type of farming cannot generate sufficient income: Amish farms are simply too small to produce enough profit to provide a family with a decent material lifestyle. If true, this objection would limit the degree to which Amish agriculture is a viable alternative to conventional Corn Belt agriculture, at least on a widespread basis. Claims like this, of course, are laden with assumptions about social prestige and standing, which regard certain material goods as necessary for a life well lived, and determining whether this form of agriculture can provide a "decent" lifestyle depends on whether one has in mind a lavishly furnished three-thousand-square-foot house, four automobiles, regular vacations, and an annual two-month respite from harsh Midwestern winters in some southern state or whether a more modest lifestyle is considered decent.

I also suspect that another important assumption underlies this type of objection. Most middle-class Americans would look at an Amish farm and immediately conclude that this type of farming generates less income that a conventional farm. Why? Because there are no common indicators of an economically lucrative agricultural operation: no expensive, heavy machinery, no new automobiles parked in the garage, no recreational vehicles or boats sitting behind buildings, no large machine sheds, no modern appliances in the kitchen, and no ornate furnishings in the house. This lack of items associated with wealth in a Midwestern agricultural setting, however, has nothing to do with less income generated by the farm. The Amish would not purchase these items even if they could afford them because they either serve no valuable purpose in the context of Amish agriculture or they contradict their religious beliefs. For the Amish, striving to acquire material goods that most middle-class Americans would consider borderline necessities "is nothing more than the worship of the golden calf."[66]

These assumptions aside, the profitability of Amish agriculture is indisputable. In fact, empirical data show that Amish agriculture is consistently more profitable than conventional Corn Belt agriculture in terms of gross and net farm-related income per hectare.[67] To a great extent, this finding is unsurprising given the many cost-saving and income-generating practices of the Amish: substituting human labor for capital, producing many inputs on the farm, creating economic value from waste, diversifying farm production and thereby maintaining multiple revenue sources, and foregoing the use of expensive technologies. The profitability of Amish agriculture is astonishing, however, insofar as the Amish refuse to accept direct cash subsidies from the government,[68] which represent a considerable economic boost for many conventional corn and soybean farmers and are often the exclusive reason these farmers are not continually teetering on the verge of bankruptcy. Yet despite this formidable handicap, Amish farmers are still able to be more profitable than their conventional Midwestern counterparts.

While I have tried to dispel the common myth that Amish agriculture is unprofitable, in the final analysis it is wise not to place a great deal of stock in economic considerations. Profit is affected by so many variables (commodity prices, government subsidies, weather, insect infestations, international production levels, expansion or contraction of markets, the price of oil and steel, to mention but a few) and often so disconnected from good farming practices that it is difficult to determine what profitability really means. But more important, profitability is a moot issue in American agriculture. We really have no choice: We need farmers and the food they produce, and farming will be made profitable in order to get the food we desire. The only relevant questions are, who will profit, and, from which type of agricultural system?

In my opinion, a more pertinent drawback of Amish agriculture is the number of animals raised on the typical Amish farm. The Amish not only use horses for traction power in the field, but keep on their farms a sizeable array of other animals (relative to conventional Corn Belt farms). These animals serve key functions on an Amish farm: the sale of meat is financially lucrative — and the principal reason for the comparative profitability of Amish farms — and the manure they produce and apply to their fields plays a vital role in maintaining topsoil quality and quantity. National animal production at the level of the Amish, however, is unrealistic and undesirable. Not only would this produce a glut of animal products for which there would be insufficient demand, but the increased level of crop production necessary to feed these animals would be staggering. As one commentator writes, "more than triple the harvested crop production of the U.S. would be required to feed [this] increased level of animal production."[69]

While this suggests that Amish agriculture, as currently practiced, cannot be adopted nationally, it does not foreclose the possibility that Amish agriculture can be a model for agricultural development on a smaller basis, nor does it eliminate a modified form of Amish agriculture as a potential solution with broader applicability. For instance, other methods of soil augmentation might adequately compensate for reduced manure applications without sacrificing the system's sustainability or negatively altering internal farm dynamics.

In the final analysis, we should be grateful to have in our midst the Amish practicing a centuries-old form of agriculture. Their spirit of resistance to the American cultural milieu that has engendered many unpalatable trends in American agriculture has kept alive an agricultural tradition that offers a clear and distinct alternative to business as usual in the agricultural sector. The sustainability of Amish agriculture offers lessons and insights into the structural dynamics and relationships necessary to create a food production system that can benefit generations far into the future. Their agricultural system demonstrates that food production need not be overtly hostile to the formation of supportive, vibrant communities that can provide a nurturing atmosphere for people to live, work, and raise families. The degree of security against a host of vicissitudes, due to extensive input substitution and reliance on local resources, makes Amish agriculture capable of withstanding foreseeable and unforeseeable disruptions that would have a calamitous effect on conventional Corn Belt agriculture. And as humans extend our influence farther around the globe, appropriating and altering ecosystems and competing with wild animals for resources and space, the Amish have found a way to make their small slice of creation more conducive to the diversity that seems so pleasing to God.[70] An impressive list of accomplishments consistent with a

Christian ethic of gratitude and a clearly preferable alternative to conventional Corn Belt agriculture — not a bad place to glean insights into the future development of American agriculture.

Wes Jackson: Natural Systems Agriculture

One of the most promising approaches to making American agriculture more conducive to realizing the moral objectives of a Christian ethic of gratitude comes from Wes Jackson and his colleagues at the Land Institute, an independent agricultural research and testing center in Salina, Kansas. Jackson believes that contemporary American agriculture, indeed all agricultural systems fitting the industrial paradigm, are so destructive[71] that they are properly likened to a disease. Jackson writes in his landmark *New Roots for Agriculture:*

> This book calls essentially all till agriculture, almost from the beginning, into question, not because sustainable till agriculture can't be practiced, but because it isn't and hasn't been, except in small pockets scattered over the globe. So destructive has the agricultural revolution been that, geologically speaking, it surely stands as the most significant and explosive event to appear on the face of the earth, changing the earth even faster than did the origin of life. Volcanoes erupt in small areas, and mountain ranges require so long in their uplift that adjustments to changing conditions by the life forms are smooth and easy. But agriculture has come on the global scene so rapidly that the life-support system has not had time to adjust to the changing circumstances. In this sense, then, till agriculture is a global disease, which in a few places has been well-managed, but overall has steadily eroded the land. In some areas, such as the U.S., it is advancing at an alarming rate. Unless this disease is checked, the human race will wilt like any other crop.[72]

Although Jackson is critical of many of American agriculture's effects, including chemical contamination due to synthetic pesticide, fertilizer, and herbicide use; decreasing genetic diversity of our major cash crops; and our extensive reliance on nonrenewable fossil fuels, Jackson is most concerned about topsoil erosion, which makes our agricultural system internally self-destructive. Fertile topsoil in sufficient quantity is agriculture's lifeblood, and with every inch of topsoil lost or degraded, the productivity of American agriculture declines.[73] The problem, Jackson writes, is the extraordinary lengths of time needed to create topsoil, coupled with topsoil erosion rates produced by our agricultural system. Under natural conditions, it takes between three hundred and a thousand years to create one inch of topsoil; if organic matter is allowed to accumulate on farm fields, approximately thirty years is needed for one inch of topsoil to form.[74] Given the topsoil erosion rates this past century, the amount of time needed to return topsoil levels to their original position before the introduction of intensive farming methods in America is staggering. In one year alone, the United States loses over 4 billion tons of topsoil; or to given a more visual presentation, if the topsoil eroding every year were placed in freight cars loaded to their rated capacity, the chain of cars would encircle our planet twenty-four times, and this is only during one year.[75]

It is tempting, Jackson explains, to regard topsoil erosion as a problem that can be remedied by better farming methods, conservation techniques, or farm implements. This is the typical response of the mainstream agricultural sector, which understands topsoil erosion — as well as virtually all other negative effects created by contemporary industrialized agricultural systems — as a "problem in agriculture,"[76] as Jackson calls it, that can be remedied by American ingenuity overcoming isolated flaws. What this response ignores or fails to recognize is that American agriculture as we know it is itself the problem, and no amount of tinkering at the fringes of our agricultural system will transform it into a truly sustainable enterprise. In other words, Jackson recommends rethinking the presuppositions upon which American agriculture is based, and subsequently undergoing a thorough structural renovation of our food production system.

Jackson's proposed alternative, what he calls "natural systems agriculture," is premised on the idea that native biological communities that have emerged and evolved through the process of natural selection are best adapted to exist and thrive in their particular locales. Absent human interventions that cause decline or destruction, the internal dynamics of these native ecosystems are beneficial to all plants within the ecosystem, which in turn allow it to persist indefinitely (or at least for very long periods of time). Stated a little differently, these native ecosystems are sustainable, and Jackson thinks that if American agriculture is going to become sustainable, it must attempt to mimic the conditions of the native ecosystems that it has replaced.

In his study of the native tallgrass prairie in Kansas, Jackson observed four characteristics essential to its sustainability (these characteristics can also be generalized to cover other ecosystems as well).[77] First, it "maintains or builds its natural capital." Although many factors fall under the category of "natural capital," the most important is fertile topsoil. Over time, the native tallgrass prairie actually accumulates topsoil. The main reason is that the native tallgrass prairie is composed primarily of perennial grasses, which hold topsoil in place much more securely than the annual crops dominant in contemporary American agriculture. As a general rule, annuals devote more energy to seed production, and less to growing deep, widespread root systems. Perennials are just the opposite, and the extensive root systems they produce are much better at holding topsoil in place during rain and windstorms. Furthermore, annuals require a farmer to keep topsoil in a more disturbed state (although no-till methods have decreased the soil disturbance necessary), and this soil perturbation increases the likelihood of soil erosion. In contrast, once perennials are established, no subsequent topsoil disturbance is needed.

The second characteristic making the native prairie sustainable is its ability to fix and hold nutrients. The key to this characteristic is complementary diversity, in which a combination of a wide range of perennial plants, or polyculture, provides a series of beneficial relationships that allow the ecosystem to function well. Although nutrient cycles are highly complex and involve numerous variables, the general idea behind complementary diversity is that every plant both needs and produces certain nutrients during its life, and given the right combination of plants in close physical proximity, a plant's nutrient needs will be supplied regularly by other plants, and the nutrients a plant produces will in turn be advantageous to other plants. As Jackson explains, "In a polyculture of plants, one species that fixes nitrogen complements others that are unable to fix nitrogen. Another species may do a better job of pulling up trace elements necessary for the nitrogen fixer and other species as well."[78] In this way, nutrient flows are multiple, relatively constant, and in a natural recycling program in which waste from one plant becomes nutrition for another.

This is not the case in contemporary American agriculture, which is dominated by monocultures. In these agricultural systems, nutrient flows are one-way, from the industrial source of chemical fertilizers to the field; they are sporadic; and little recycling of nutrients occurs. The reason is quite simple: lack of crop diversity prevents any mutually advantageous relationship between plants.[79]

The third characteristic of the native tallgrass prairie is its ability to adapt to periodic stresses such as drought, excessive rainfall, or hail. Diversity of plant species minimizes the degree to which these periodic stresses can cause large-scale destruction in the native prairie. Small-sized hail, for example, might injure or kill a few species of plants with narrow, fragile stalks, while leaving the remainder of the native prairie unharmed. In an agricultural system dominated by monocultures, the same small-sized hail, in contrast, might kill almost entire fields of soybeans or knock most of the soybean pods to the ground, ruining the harvest.

Drought and excessive rainfall pose less of a danger to the native tallgrass prairie because its topsoil absorbs and retains water better. Due to its high organic-matter content, the native tallgrass prairie's topsoil is light and porous, similar to the high-grade potting soil that can be purchased in garden stores across the United States. Its porosity allows water to seep further down into the topsoil, which means it is able to retain water in greater quantities and for longer periods of time. Its superior water absorption ability means that it takes far more rain to saturate the topsoil, at which point water starts running across the soil's surface and causes erosion.

The final characteristic Jackson mentions is the native prairie's ability to manage its weed, pest, and pathogen populations. Once again, complementary diversity is the essential ingredient for fulfilling this function. Take insect control, for example. The ideal scenario is to have a field of plants that attract as many beneficial predators as possible, and to make the undesirable insects expend as much energy as possible in their feeding route by spacing plants apart, which weakens them and makes them more susceptible to disease and predators. On a comparative basis, both conditions are realized to a much greater degree in the native prairie's polyculture than in the monocultures of contemporary American agriculture. The diversity of plants in the native prairie attracts a greater number of natural predators, which helps keep unwanted insect populations in check. The wider dispersion of plant species in a polyculture also makes insects move or fly greater distances to get their next meal.

Based on these four characteristics that Jackson claims are the backbone of sustainable ecosystems, he proposes that grain production in the United States should eventually transition to a network of fields dominated by perennial crops grown in mixtures. To this end, Jackson and the researchers at the Land Institute have embarked on a hundred-year plant breeding project intended to increase the productivity of perennials and to identify combinations of plants that attain the desired degree of complementary diversity. The first objective is necessary since perennials typically produce much less grain than annuals, and it would be desirable for a number of reasons to have perennials produce more grain. The second objective is probably more difficult — and more crucial to Jackson's crop breeding program — since the scores of variables involved in attaining complementary diversity in a polyculture interject a considerable degree of mental complexity into the process. This is precisely why Jackson's program is so lengthy: understanding the dynamics and relationships involved in growing combinations of plants together is difficult and will probably take many decades to grasp fully, even though Jackson and his colleagues have documented some impressive results in their breeding program and have developed different polycultures that show considerable promise.[80]

If Jackson's plant breeding program and research agenda eventually culminate in polycultures of perennials that fulfill his objectives, the benefits would be breathtaking, and his natural systems agriculture could turn out to be one of the greatest achievements in human history. Since a polyculture of perennials, once established, requires no further perturbation of the topsoil, and since it would provide a thick protective canopy covering the ground, wind and water erosion would be virtually nonexistent, and topsoil could actually start to accumulate on a widespread basis. Declining topsoil fertility due to erosion would become a thing of the past, and streams, rivers, and lakes would no longer be choked by sediment coming from agricultural fields.

A polyculture of perennials would rely on solar energy far more than a typical corn or soybean field in the Corn Belt. Use of petroleum-based chemicals could be foregone entirely, or reduced considerably, in a polyculture of perennials. There would be less need for synthetic pesticides because species diversity within fields would provide better biological pest controls by attracting a wider variety of beneficial predators.[81] In turn, fewer people would suffer and die from diseases caused by pesticide exposure or ingestion. There would be less need for synthetic fertilizers because a plant's nutritional requirements would be met by its neighbors through natural processes. This would also reduce contamination of groundwater supplies and algae blooms associated with fertilizer runoff. Demand for synthetic herbicides would also decrease, especially after the polyculture becomes established and chokes out any competing weeds. Not only does this reduced demand for fossil fuels in the form of petroleum-based chemicals represent considerable financial savings for farmers, but it also makes a polyculture of perennials more insulated from the many vicissitudes associated with fossil-fuel dependency.

A polyculture of perennials also relies more extensively on local inputs. In fact, it eliminates the need for many inputs. While a typical corn or soybean field in the Corn Belt requires a bevy of synthetic chemicals, the manufacturing of which requires a coordinated network of relationships and a resource base extending across the globe, the complementary diversity of a polyculture of perennials provides many necessary ingredients on the farm itself to ensure its continued smooth functioning.

Another considerable advantage of polycultures is the animal habitat they create. At their best, corn and soybean fields provide food and/or shelter only for a handful of opportunistic animal species for approximately five months per year (summer to fall). During the remainder of the year, these fields are barren and support little animal life. With few exceptions, conventional Midwestern corn and soybean production involves a massive simplification of former ecosystems that is highly deleterious to most animal species. Consider, in contrast, Jackson's proposed polycultures of perennials: not only would their plant diversity be more hospitable to a wider variety of animals, but they would provide yearlong ground cover and valuable habitat for a greater range and number of wild animals. Of course, it is impossible to know exactly how polycultures of perennials would affect animal populations since Jackson's work is still under way and thus the constitutions of the various polycultures are unknown. But there is almost no way they could be worse for animals than conventional corn and soybean production; and if they even moderately resemble the native tallgrass prairie that once flourished across the Corn Belt, it would be a boon to the animal kingdom and might even allow the reintroduction of endangered animal species that have found Corn Belt agriculture such a hostile environment in which to live.

In my mind, Jackson's proposed natural systems agriculture represents a highly promising future for American agriculture. If his project is successful and polycultures of perennials eventually replace the monocultures of corn and soybeans across the Corn Belt, this agricultural system would be sustainable, it would be better insulated against a variety of negative variables, it would rely more on solar power, it would rely more extensively on local inputs, it would spare scores of people from disease and destruction, and it would be a friendlier place for many more animals. Yet the tangible benefits of polycultures of perennials are not the only valuable aspects of Jackson's proposal. Even if the quest for viable polycultures of perennials proves to be elusive after a hundred years of plant breeding, experiments, and field tests, Jackson and his colleagues at the Land Institute have started something of a revolution by making native ecosystems a model for agricultural development and by taking practical steps to make this model a living reality. Not only does Jackson's work provide a foundation upon which other scientists can build, but his natural systems agriculture forces a paradigm shift in agricultural thought that will bear fruit for centuries to come. This turn to nature as a repository of wisdom for agricultural development already has garnered the allegiance of a number of influential scientists, and as conventional American agriculture continues toward its inevitable demise and the need for an alternative agricultural system becomes more pressing, there is little doubt that something akin to Jackson's natural systems agriculture will emerge as a prime contender to secure the long-term health and vitality of American agriculture.

There are, of course, critical questions surrounding Jackson's proposal. One, which I already mentioned briefly, is whether perennials can be altered or created in order to produce acceptable levels of grain.[82] Jackson and his colleagues are working against a formidable deficit: throughout human history, perennials have been largely ignored by plant breeders since they yield less than their annual counterparts. Thus, there is scant accumulated knowledge about perennials and little effort expended historically to improve the productive capacity of perennials in agricultural settings. While this does not pose any intractable problem in principle, it means that Jackson's plant breeding program is largely starting from scratch and that the process of creating new strains of perennials might be long in the making.

Another major issue concerns Jackson's holism and whether the scientific ingenuity can be mustered to move from testing to commercial production. Although the term "holism" has become firmly embedded in a number of academic disciplines today, from psychology to medicine to theology, and the impression is often given (erroneously so, in my estimation) that a "holistic perspective" is easily understandable and attainable, this is hardly the case in agriculture. While it might be easy to understand the mechanisms operative in one plant species, when you add another in close proximity, then another, then another into the equation, which could be likely in a field of mixed perennial grain crops, the sheer number of variables and relationships, both positive and negative, becomes considerable. In this sense, Jackson's agenda for American agriculture is far more complex than the simplistic, reductive mentality that now dominates our approach to agricultural problems.[83] Within the latter paradigm, the network of wider relationships is largely ignored (and along with it potentially valuable solutions), and a rather straightforward remedy is usually applied: if bugs are the problem, douse them with chemicals to kill them; if a lack of nutrients is the problem, apply a synthetic fertilizer to fulfill the plant's needs. Jackson, of course, eschews such reductionism; yet by insisting on understanding ecosystems holistically and modeling agriculture on native ecosystems, his natural systems agriculture could prove to be a more complicated food production system than conventional agriculture.

Jackson's critics maintain that polycultures of perennials pose distinct obstacles to harvest, especially highly diverse polycultures containing a number of different plant species. While a polyculture of two different plants might not present unusual challenges to harvest, more diverse polycultures containing plants varying in height, seed location, and maturation schedules would most likely be a more complicated affair. Furthermore, since the chief advantage of perennials over annuals is that they require less soil perturbation, it is vital not to destroy perennials during the harvesting process, which would require replanting and soil disturbance leading to erosion. Combines traditionally used to harvest corn, soybeans, and other grains are probably inadequate for this job: their weight would injure or kill a large proportion of the perennials, and they are equipped to harvest only one type of grain at a time.[84] Yet these concerns about harvesting might be overblown. According to Jerry Glover, a soil scientist at the Land Institute, annual farm equipment traffic has not proven to be problematic thus far, and a machine has been developed to harvest multiple seeds. Recently, for instance, mixtures consisting of corn, sunflower, sorghum, and soybean were harvested together and the seeds were separated postharvest. While the seed separation process concerned the Land Institute researchers the most, it turned out to be easier than they thought it would be.[85]

The potential complexity of Jackson's project, however, should not stifle enthusiasm for the Land Institute's work and research. In fact, Jackson's natural systems agriculture is precisely the idea that should garner our unflinching long-term national support. For too long, American agriculture has operated under the premise that nature is something to be subdued, manipulated, overcome, and brought under control, and that human wisdom and resourcefulness provide the necessary tools for this task. Yet this dominant worldview in the agricultural sector not only has led to a food production system that is sowing the seeds of its own destruction, but also violates some of the most deeply held Christian moral principles. Now, with Jackson's natural systems agriculture, we are finally in a position to reshape our agricultural system according to a model honed by evolutionary processes for millennia and withstanding the test of time, and to uncover insights into the dynamics of native ecosystems that have been neglected due to human arrogance and naïve faith in our mental prowess. This bodes exceedingly well for the future of American agriculture: not only would this model make our food production system more secure, sustainable, and consistent with other tenets of a Christian ethic of gratitude; it also represents an alternative to corn and soybean production that could be adopted on a broad scale in the Corn Belt.

The stakes are exceedingly high in Jackson's project. If ultimately unsuccessful, Jackson's research might still prove to be beneficial to scientists willing to continue work on natural systems agriculture, and maybe after decades or perhaps even centuries this line of inquiry will reap considerable tangible results. But if Jackson and his colleagues hit the mother lode and begin creating viable polycultures of perennials that can be used commercially on a broad scale, and if others contribute to overcoming the aforementioned obstacles in the path of making natural systems agriculture a practical reality, then American agriculture could enter a new phase of production for the foreseeable future. There is no project worthier of our time, attention, and support, and it behooves us to promote Jackson's agenda to the fullest extent possible.

Conclusion

Americans are blessed by abundant land and fertile soil that is the envy of the world. We are blessed by hospitable climates, adequate rainfall, and all the ingredients that make the heartland so conducive to farming — the pulverizing force of glaciers that swept across North America, the buffalo that once roamed the prairies and deposited their nutrient-rich manure across the ground, the earthworms that churn tons of soil upward and emit valuable excreta, and the formerly dominant native tallgrass prairie and its yearly cycle of life and death that fertilized and created topsoil in quantities found nowhere else on this planet. We are blessed by farmers and the virtues they incarnate. We are blessed by farm communities and the children they produce, who continue the noble vocation of farming. We are blessed by the food produced in the Corn Belt and the sustenance it provides every single day of our lives. We are blessed by God, the source and sustainer of everything that exists and the creative force responsible for the good land we enjoy.

Americans are graced by all these blessings flowing from God, and it would be a shame — no, a desecration — to squander the enormous gifts we have been given by standing by idly as forces converge to erode our soil, pollute our land, destroy our farm communities, poison rural citizens, create one of the most structurally vulnerable agricultural systems in human history, and unravel God's benevolent work that has been in process for millions of years. Yet despite the lamentable state of contemporary American agriculture, hope is on the horizon. There is nothing inevitable about the decline of American agriculture, and there are preferable alternatives either long in existence but now marginalized, ignored, or largely forgotten or still in the experimental stage, each of which better coheres with a Christian ethic of gratitude and makes our little segment of creation a little more pleasing to God.

This is a moment of opportunity for America, an opportunity to further God's work in this world by rebuilding a national treasure. The work might be arduous and lengthy, but its eventual completion signals good news for many as the blessings we have inherited fulfill their intended purpose. There are few gifts as precious as a healthy, vibrant agricultural system, and it would be truly marvelous to bequeath a gift of this magnitude to future generations.

Notes

Chapter One: Theology, Ethics, and Agriculture

1. Richard Manning, *Grassland: The History, Biology, Politics, and Promise of the American Prairie* (New York: Viking Penguin, 1995), 45–46.

2. O. J. Reichman, *Konza Prairie: A Tallgrass Natural History* (Lawrence: University Press of Kansas, 1987), 148.

3. Ibid., 60–61.

4. Ibid., 107–10.

5. Peter Farb, *Face of North America: The Natural History of a Continent* (New York: Harper & Row, 1963), 209.

6. Reichman, *Konza Prairie*, 156.

7. This phrase is taken from Wendell Berry, *The Gift of Good Land: Further Essays Cultural and Agricultural* (New York: North Point Press, 1981).

8. James Gustafson, *Ethics from a Theocentric Perspective*, vol. 1, *Theology and Ethics* (Chicago: University of Chicago Press, 1981), 131.

9. Brian Childs, "Gratitude," in *Dictionary of Pastoral Care and Counseling*, ed. Rodney Hunter (Nashville: Abingdon, 1990), 470–71.

10. Enda McDonagh, *Gift and Call* (St. Meinrad, Ind.: Abbey Press, 1975), 86.

11. Richard Gula, *Reason Informed by Faith* (Mahwah, N.J.: Paulist Press, 1989), 52.

12. Joseph Fletcher, *Situation Ethics* (Philadelphia: Westminster Press, 1966), 156.

13. Eph. 5:20; 1 Thess. 5:18; and 1 Tim. 4:4.

14. My thanks to Edward Vacek, S.J., who helped clarify this point in a personal conversation.

15. Gustafson, *Ethics from a Theocentric Perspective*, 1:209–10.

16. The general definition is adapted from Paul F. Camenisch, "Gift and Gratitude in Ethics," *Journal of Religious Ethics* 9 (Spring 1981): 2.

17. Of course, it could be argued that even apparently futile benevolent actions can indirectly benefit someone by inspiring others to perform similar actions. While this might be true, since accidental benefits are unintentional (more on this below), they do not warrant a grateful response.

18. Fred R. Berger, "Gratitude," *Ethics* 85 (July 1975): 299.

207

19. Terrance McConnell, *Gratitude* (Philadelphia: Temple University Press, 1993), 41–45.

20. A. D. M. Walker, "Gratefulness and Gratitude," *Proceedings of the Aristotelian Society* 81 (1981): 43.

21. Berger, "Gratitude," 299; A. John Simmons, *Moral Principles and Political Obligations* (Princeton, N.J.: Princeton University Press, 1979), 171–72; Camenisch, "Gift and Gratitude in Ethics," 2; and Edward C. Vacek, "Gifts, God, Generosity, and Gratitude," in *Spirituality and Moral Theology: Essays from a Pastoral Perspective*, ed. James Keating (New York: Paulist, 2000), 85.

22. Patrick Fitzgerald, "Gratitude and Justice," *Ethics* 109 (October 1998): 121.

23. Vacek, "Gifts, God, Generosity, and Gratitude," 89–90.

24. Cf. Thomas Aquinas, *Summa Theologiae*, II-II.106.3 ad. 2, who argues that even lacking a benevolent motive, the recipient still must express gratitude to the benefactor.

25. McConnell, *Gratitude*, 19–26, makes similar arguments.

26. Of course, in some cases entering a contract might be motivated by a desire to help another. In these situations, gratitude would be the appropriate response.

27. Berger, "Gratitude," 300.

28. Victor Hugo, *Les Misérables*, trans. Lee Fahnestock and Norman MacAfee (New York: Penguin, 1987), 113.

29. Camenisch, "Gift and Gratitude in Ethics," 16.

30. McConnell, *Gratitude*, 38.

31. Camenisch, "Gift and Gratitude in Ethics," 10–11.

32. McConnell, *Gratitude*, 56.

33. Camenisch, "Gift and Gratitude in Ethics," 8–10.

34. Ibid., 15.

35. Roslyn Weiss, "The Moral and Social Dimensions of Gratitude," *Southern Journal of Philosophy* 23 (1985): 491–501, for example, denies that accepting a gift obligates the recipient in any way.

36. Camenisch, "Gift and Gratitude in Ethics," 5.

37. Berger, "Gratitude," 305; Fitzgerald, "Gratitude and Justice," 146; Walker, "Gratefulness and Gratitude," 52; Vacek, "Gifts, God, Generosity, and Gratitude," 104–5; Claudia Card, "Gratitude and Obligation," *American Philosophical Quarterly* 25 (1988): 121–25; Gilbert Meilaender, *The Theory and Practice of Virtue* (Notre Dame, Ind.: University of Notre Dame Press, 1984), 156–69; Mike W. Martin, "Good Fortune Obligates," *Southern Journal of Philosophy* 37 (1999): 63–65; and James M. Gustafson, *Can Ethics Be Christian?* (Chicago: University of Chicago Press, 1975), 101. Christopher Heath Wellman, "Gratitude as a Virtue," *Pacific Philosophical Quarterly* 80

(1999): 284–300, claims that condemnatory moral judgments directed toward a recipient who fails to requite to a benefactor are based not on any duty to the benefactor, but on the recipient's lack of character, which causes an undervaluation of the benefactor.

38. For a thorough deconstruction of a balance-sheet mentality in ethics, see Mark Johnson, *Moral Imagination: Implications of Cognitive Science for Ethics* (Chicago: University of Chicago Press, 1993), 40–50.

39. McConnell, *Gratitude*, 58.

40. Camenisch, "Gift and Gratitude in Ethics," 10.

41. Meilaender, "The Virtue of Gratitude," in *The Theory and Practice of Virtue*, 161–62; and Camenisch, "Gift and Gratitude in Ethics," 9.

42. Of course, contrary to the benefactor's express or implied intention, a recipient might be highly creative and novel in his or her use of a gift, which might be highly pleasing to — although completely unforeseen by — the benefactor. Situations like this constitute appropriate use of the gift, even though the benefactor's intent was contravened. Paul Camensich prefers to call this an "enlarge[ment] upon the donor's intentions" since the benefactor would have approved the particular use of the gift if he or she had considered it fully (Camenisch, "Gift and Gratitude in Ethics," 10).

43. Ibid.

44. For interesting parallels with Native American theology, see John Hart, *The Spirit of the Earth* (New York: Paulist Press, 1984), 41–46.

45. M. Douglas Meeks, "God and Land," *Agriculture and Human Values* 2 (1985): 18.

46. Lev. 25:23; Deut. 10:14–15; and Ps. 24:1.

47. Norman C. Habel, *The Land Is Mine* (Minneapolis: Fortress Press, 1995), 98; Christopher J. H. Wright, *God's People in God's Land* (Grand Rapids: William B. Eerdmans, 1990), 115–16; and Hart, *The Spirit of the Earth*, 69–71.

48. Gen. 1:29; Exod. 3:7–8; Lev. 26:3–5; and Num. 33:53.

49. Pope John Paul II, "God Has Destined the Earth for All Men," in *The Pope Speaks* 24 (1979): 339; National Conference of Catholic Bishops, "For I Was Hungry and You Gave Me Food," November 2003, 5, accessed at *www.usccb.org/bishops/agricultural.htm*; United Methodist Church, "U.S. Agriculture and Rural Communities in Crisis," 1996, 1, accessed at *www.umc-gbcs.org/issues/resolutions.php?resolutionid=31*; and Evangelical Lutheran Church in America, "A Social Statement on Caring for Creation: Vision, Hope, and Justice," 1993, 2–3, accessed at *www.elca.org/dcs/environment/html*.

50. C. Dean Freudenberger, *The Gift of Land: A Judeo-Christian Perspective on Value and Lifestyle Change in a Threatened World* (Los Angeles: Franciscan Communications, 1981), 6–8; Meeks, "God and Land," 20; Hart,

The Spirit of the Earth, 4; and L. Shannon Jung, "Agricultural Technology As If God Were Involved," *Reformed Review* 41 (Spring 1988): 206.

51. National Catholic Rural Life Conference, "A Catholic Rural Ethic for Agriculture, Environment, Food, and Earth," n.d., accessed at *www.ncrlc.com/ruralethic.htm*.

52. For a number of examples, see Daniel Hillel, *Out of the Earth: Civilization and the Life of the Soil* (Berkeley: University of California Press, 1991).

53. Pope John Paul II, "God Has Destined the Earth for All Men," 339 (my italics). See also his "Address of John Paul II to the Participants in the World Conference on Agrarian Reform and Rural Development," 1979, 1, accessed online at *www.Vatican.va/holy_father/john_paul_ii/speeches/1979/july/documents/hf?jp-ii_sp.htm*, where the pope writes, "[A]ll the goods of the earth are meant to benefit all the members of the *human family*" (my italics).

54. H. Paul Santmire's *Nature Reborn: The Ecological and Cosmic Promise of Christian Theology* (Minneapolis: Fortress Press, 2000) offers a helpful overview on the contours and substance of this debate.

55. Ps. 104:21.

56. Job 40:15–32.

57. Gen. 9:10.

58. Luke 12:6.

59. Isa. 11:6–9.

60. Col. 1:19–20.

61. Santmire, *Nature Reborn*, 37.

62. Gustafson, *Ethics from a Theocentric Perspective*, 1:96.

63. R. Neil Sampson, *Farmland or Wasteland: A Time to Choose* (Emmaus, Pa.: Rodale Press, 1981), 9.

64. Wes Jackson, *New Roots for Agriculture* (San Francisco: Friends of the Earth; Salina, Kans.: Land Institute, 1980), 2.

65. Meeks, "God and Land," 25; and the North Dakota Catholic Conference, "Giving Thanks through Action: A Statement by the Roman Catholic Bishops of North Dakota on the Crisis in Rural Life," 1998, 2, accessed at *www.ndcatholic.org/ruralstmt.htm*.

66. For a comparison of Protestant and Catholic moral theologians on the issue of divine freedom, see Mark E. Graham, *Josef Fuchs on Natural Law* (Washington, D.C.: Georgetown University Press, 2002), 14–16.

67. My working notion of freedom is the ability to act otherwise. Some theologians, in contrast, maintain that freedom only exists if an option does not present itself as the best course of action morally. Thus to choose freely, it is necessary that all possible courses of action be equally good, since if one option is better morally then an agent must pursue it.

68. Karl Barth, *Church Dogmatics*, vol. 2, bk. 1, *The Doctrine of God*, trans. T. H. L. Parker et al., ed. G. W. Bromiley and T. F. Torrance (Edinburgh: T. & T. Clark, 1957), 301.

69. Graham, *Josef Fuchs on Natural Law*, 16.

70. Keith Ward, *Religion and Creation* (Oxford: Clarendon Press, 1996), 159–91.

71. Jürgen Moltmann, *God in Creation* (Minneapolis: Fortress Press, 1993), 76.

72. Karl Rahner, *Foundations of Christian Faith: An Introduction to the Idea of Christianity*, trans. William V. Dych (New York: Crossroad, 1989), 201.

73. Ibid., 190.

74. William C. Spohn, *Go and Do Likewise: Jesus and Ethics* (New York: Continuum, 1999), 89–91.

75. Matt. 14:14; Luke 7:13; Matt. 20:34; and Mark 8:2.

76. For an informative survey of major Christian denominational statements on agriculture, see Stanislaus J. Dundon, "Sources of First Principles for an Agricultural Ethic," in *Ethics and Agriculture: An Anthology on Current Issues in World Context*, ed. Charles V. Blatz (Moscow: University of Idaho Press, 1991), 63–74. My thanks to Professor Dundon, who provided helpful information through personal correspondence.

77. Exod. 23:10–11 and Lev. 25:2–7.

78. While not specified explicitly in the biblical texts, the Sabbatical Year probably was not observed by all farmers simultaneously, but individually during different years. It would have been far more beneficial for the poor to have access to a few farms every year, rather than access to every farm every seventh year. As Christopher Wright points out, "The poor of the people and the wild beasts would derive little sustenance from a single fallow every seven years, but the continuous presence of some land lying fallow in every locality would obviously provide some relief" (*God's People in God's Land*, 145).

79. Hart, *The Spirit of the Earth*, 72; Habel, *The Land Is Mine*, 102; Wright, *God's People in God's Land*, 144; and Aloys Hüttermann, *The Ecological Message of the Torah* (Atlanta: Scholars Press, 1999), 89.

80. Exod. 23:11. It should be noted that the "wild beasts" are also to benefit from this access, which is another instance of God's care and concern for nonhuman creation.

81. Richard Cartwright Austin, *Hope for the Land: Nature in the Bible* (Atlanta: John Knox Press, 1988), 100–101.

82. Lev. 19:9–10 and Deut. 24:19–22.

83. Deut. 24:19–22.

84. It is disputed how widely the Jubilee Year was observed in practice and to what degree, even though it is mandated in Leviticus and Deuteronomy.

85. Hart, *The Spirit of the Earth*, 76–77.

86. "Woe to those who join house to house, who add field to field, until there is no more room, and you are made to dwell alone in the midst of the land. The Lord of hosts has sworn in my hearing: 'Surely many houses shall be desolate, large and beautiful houses, without inhabitant. For ten acres of vineyard shall yield but one bath, and a homer of seed shall yield but an ephah'" (Isa. 5:8–10, RSV).

87. For statements about the social nature of the human person in official documents, see David J. O'Brien and Thomas A. Shannon, eds., *Catholic Social Thought: The Documentary Heritage* (Maryknoll, N.Y.: Orbis Books, 1992).

88. For practical illustrations of the crippling effects of poverty, see Jonathan Kozol, *Amazing Grace: The Lives of Children and the Conscience of a Nation* (New York: Crown, 1995); and David Hilfiker, *Not All of Us Are Saints: A Doctor's Journey with the Poor* (New York: Ballantine Books, 1994).

89. Julia Meaton and David Morrice, "The Ethics and Politics of Private Automobile Use," *Environmental Ethics* 18 (1996): 42–44.

90. Pope John Paul II, *Veritatis Splendor*, Vatican translation (Boston: St. Paul Books & Media, 1993), nos. 71–78.

91. Eberhard Schockenhoff, *Natural Law and Human Dignity: Universal Ethics in an Historical World*, trans. Brian McNeil (Washington, D.C.: Catholic University of America Press, 2003), 216.

92. National Council of Catholic Bishops, *The Challenge of Peace: God's Promise and Our Response* (Washington, D.C.: United States Catholic Conference, 1983), no. 105.

93. *Catechism of the Catholic Church* (Mahwah, N.J.: Paulist Press, 1994), no. 2296.

94. John 8:1–11.

95. Matt. 12:1–14.

96. Matt. 9:36; 14:13–21; 20:29–34; Mark 8:1–10; and Luke 7:11–17.

97. Matt. 5:38–39, 43–45.

98. Luke 16:19–31.

99. Derek Parfit, *Reasons and Persons* (Oxford: Clarendon Press, 1984), 511.

100. For a thorough analysis of this tendency to abstract, see Charles R. Pinches, *Theology and Action: After Theory in Christian Ethics* (Grand Rapids: William B. Eerdmans, 2002).

101. Mark E. Graham, "Rethinking Morality's Relationship to Salvation: Josef Fuchs, S.J., on Moral Goodness," *Theological Studies* 64 (2003): 750–72.

102. Andrew Marshall, "Sustaining Sustainable Agriculture: The Rise and Fall of the Fund for Rural America," *Agriculture and Human Values* 17 (2000): 268.

103. For a survey of positions on agricultural sustainability, see Charles Francis, "Research and Extension Agenda for Sustainable Agriculture," *American Journal of Alternative Agriculture* 3 (1988): 123–26; National Research Council, Board on Agriculture, *Alternative Agriculture* (Washington, D.C.: National Academy Press, 1989); Gordon and Jane Douglass, "Creation, Reformed Faith, and Sustainable Food Systems," in *Reformed Faith and Economics*, ed. Robert L. Stivers (Lanham, Md.: University Press of America, 1989), 117–44; and William Lockeretz, "Open Questions in Sustainable Agriculture," *American Journal of Alternative Agriculture* 3 (1988): 174–81.

104. Jules N. Pretty, "Supportive Policies and Practice for Scaling Up Sustainable Agriculture," in *Facilitating Sustainable Agriculture*, ed. N. G. Roling and M. A. E. Wagemakers (Cambridge: Cambridge University Press, 1998), 25.

105. Jules Pretty, *The Living Land: Agriculture, Food and Community Regeneration in Rural Europe* (London: Earthscan Publications, 1998), 20.

106. Paul B. Thompson, *The Spirit of the Soil: Agriculture and Environmental Ethics* (New York: Routledge, 1995), 165.

107. Ibid., 155.

108. John A. Hostetler, *Amish Society*, 4th ed. (Baltimore: Johns Hopkins University Press, 1993), 119.

109. Hillel, *Out of the Earth*, 20.

110. Ibid., 153–54.

111. Francis Moore Lappé, *Diet for a Small Planet* (New York: Ballantine Books, 1982), 70.

112. Jeremy Rifkin, *Beyond Beef: The Rise and Fall of the Cattle Culture* (New York: Penguin Books, 1992), 154.

113. For a masterful treatment on the hidden presuppositions behind technology, contemporary political institutions, and the phenomenon of capitalism, see Murray Jardine, *The Making and Unmaking of Technological Society: How Christianity Can Save Modernity from Itself* (Grand Rapids: Brazos Press, 2004).

114. Unless noted otherwise, the following structural characteristics of indigenous agricultural systems are taken from Miguel A. Altieri, "Why Study Traditional Agriculture?" in *Agroecology*, ed. C. Ronald Carroll, John H. Vandermeer, and Peter Rosset (New York: McGraw-Hill, 1990), 551–64.

115. Dennis Michael Warren, "Indigenous Agricultural Knowledge, Technology, and Social Change," in *Sustainable Agriculture in the American Midwest*, ed. William R. Edwards and Gregory McIsaac (Chicago: University of Illinois Press, 1994), 37.

116. Berry, *The Gift of Good Land*, 9.

117. Stephen R. Gliessman, *Agroecosystem Sustainability: Developing Practical Strategies* (New York: CRC Press, 2000), 6.

118. Berry, *The Gift of Good Land*, 29–30.

119. These are not the only factors related to diminished nutritional content. Processing and breeding plants for cosmetic perfection and the ability to be harvested mechanically also exacerbate this problem.

120. A synopsis of this Canadian study can be accessed at *www.findarticles.com/cf_dls/m0FKA/10_64/91563473/p1/article.jhtml.*

121. Bt corn has been genetically modified to express botulism at the cellular level. Thus, every cell of a Bt corn plant contains botulism, a highly effective pesticide. Proponents argue that this will reduce the amount of pesticides needed to control pernicious insects and decrease the various side effects of pesticide use.

Chapter Two: Trends in American Argiculture

1. Adrienne Koch and William Peden, eds., *The Life and Selected Writings of Thomas Jefferson* (New York: Random House, 1944), 280.

2. Richard Cartwright Austin, "Rights for Life: Rebuilding Human Relationships with Land," in *Theology of the Land*, ed. Bernard F. Evans and Gregory D. Cusack (Collegeville, Minn.: Liturgical Press, 1987), 113.

3. J. G. A. Pocock, *The Machiavellian Moment: Florentine Political Thought and the Atlantic Republican Tradition* (Princeton, N.J.: Princeton University Press, 1975), 533; and Paul B. Thompson, "Thomas Jefferson and Agrarian Philosophy," in *The Agrarian Roots of Pragmatism*, ed. Paul B. Thompson and Thomas C. Hilde (Nashville: Vanderbilt University Press, 2000), 130.

4. Koch and Peden, *The Life and Selected Writings of Thomas Jefferson*, 324.

5. John M. Brewster, "The Relevance of the Jeffersonian Dream Today," in *Land Use Policy and Problems in the United States*, ed. Howard W. Ottoson (Lincoln: University of Nebraska Press, 1963), 97.

6. John Hart, *The Spirit of the Earth* (New York: Paulist Press, 1984), 88.

7. Victor Davis Hanson, *The Other Greeks: The Family Farm and the Agrarian Roots of Western Civilization* (New York: Free Press, 1995), 6.

8. Wendell Berry, "Whose Head Is the Farmer Using? Whose Head Is Using the Farmer?" in *Meeting the Expectations of the Land*, ed. Wes Jackson, Wendell Berry, and Bruce Colman (San Francisco: North Point Press, 1984), 24.

9. For a detailed examination of the development of American agriculture, see Willard W. Cochrane, *The Development of American Agriculture: An Historical Analysis* (Minneapolis: University of Minnesota Press, 1993), 13–170.

10. C. Dean Freudenberger, *The Gift of Land: A Judeo-Christian Perspective on Value and Lifestyle Change in a Threatened World* (Los Angeles: Franciscan Communications, 1981); C. Dean Freudenberger, *Food for Tomorrow?* (Minneapolis: Augsburg Publishing House, 1984); C. Dean Freudenberger, *Global Dust Bowl: Can We Stop the Destruction of the Land Before It's Too Late?* (Minneapolis: Augsburg Publishing House, 1990); Richard Cartwright Austin, *Beauty of the Lord: Awakening the Senses* (Atlanta: John Knox Press, 1988); Wendell Berry, *The Unsettling of America: Culture and Agriculture,* 3rd ed. (San Francisco: Sierra Club, 1996); Marty Strange, *Family Farming: A New Economic Vision* (Lincoln: University of Nebraska Press, 1988); Jay Staten, *The Embattled Farmer* (Golden, Colo.: Fulcrum, 1987); Gene Logsdon, *At Nature's Pace: Farming and the American Dream* (New York: Pantheon Books, 1994); Wes Jackson, *Becoming Native to This Place* (Washington, D.C.: Counterpoint, 1996); Wes Jackson, *Altars of Unhewn Stone: Science and the Earth* (New York: North Point Press, 1987); Wes Jackson, *New Roots for Agriculture* (San Francisco: Friends of the Earth; Salina, Kans.: Land Institute, 1980); Ed Ayres, *God's Last Offer: Negotiating for a Sustainable Future* (New York: Four Walls Eight Windows, 1999); and Helena Norberg-Hodge, Peter Goering, and John Page, *From the Ground Up: Rethinking Industrial Agriculture,* rev. ed. (New York: Zed Books, 2001).

11. Dan. 5:27.

12. George M. Boody, "Agriculture as a Public Good," in *The Farm as Natural Habitat: Reconnecting Food Systems with Ecosystems,* ed. Dana L. Jackson and Laura L. Jackson (Washington, D.C.: Island Press, 2002), 262.

13. Staten, *The Embattled Farmer,* 7–9.

14. Cochrane, *The Development of American Agriculture,* 53.

15. Ibid., 28–29; and National Agricultural Statistics Service, *Census of Agriculture, 2002,* accessed at *www.nass.usda.gov/census/census02/preliminary/cenpre02.txt.*

16. Strange, *Family Farming,* 41.

17. The claim that the declining number of farmers has created a large block of people available for work elsewhere, which is almost always regarded positively, represents a highly dubious assessment of farming's value and worth. If farming were considered a socially beneficial occupation that was highly satisfying to the farmers themselves, one would probably bemoan the fact that so many farmers have been displaced and are no longer able to enjoy the farming life.

18. Goldschmidt's study, sponsored by the federal government's Bureau of Agricultural Economics, was highly controversial at the time. As Marty Strange writes, it was "politically suppressed, [Goldschmidt] was drummed out of the agency, and subsequently, the agency itself was dismantled" (Strange, *Family Farming,* 57).

19. Walter Goldschmidt, *As You Sow* (New York: Harcourt, Brace and Company, 1947), 189, 203.

20. Ibid., 186–220.

21. Ingolf Vogeler, *The Myth of the Family Farm: Agribusiness Dominance of U.S. Agriculture* (Boulder, Colo.: Westview Press, 1981), 251.

22. Ibid., 256–64.

23. Strange, *Family Farming*, 87.

24. David G. Francis, *Family Agriculture: Tradition and Transformation* (London: Earthscan Publications, 1994), 116–17.

25. Dean MacCannell, "Agribusiness and the Small Community," quoted in Strange, *Family Farming*, 87.

26. Kathryn Marie Dudley, "The Entrepreneurial Self: Identity and Morality in a Midwestern Farming Community," in *Fighting for the Farm: Rural America Transformed*, ed. Jane Adam (Philadelphia: University of Pennsylvania Press, 2003), 191.

27. A debt-to-asset ratio of 30 percent, for example, means that for every one hundred dollars in assets, a farmer has thirty dollars in debts.

28. Joseph N. Belden, *Dirt Rich, Dirt Poor: America's Food and Farm Crisis* (New York: Routledge and Kegan Paul, 1986), 32–33.

29. Strange, *Family Farming*, 107.

30. Staten, *The Embattled Farmer*, 150.

31. Strange, *Family Farming*, 107.

32. Staten, *The Embattled Farmer*, 90.

33. Ibid., 95–96; B. Delworth Gardner, *Plowing Ground in Washington: The Political Economy of U.S. Agriculture* (San Francisco: Pacific Research Institute for Public Policy, 1995), 115–39; and Kenneth L. Robinson, *Farm and Food Policies and Their Consequences* (Englewood Cliffs, N.J.: Prentice Hall, 1989), 71–74.

34. Peggy F. Bartlett and Peter J. Brown, "Agricultural Development and the Quality of Life: An Anthropological View," *Agriculture and Human Values* 2 (1985): 31.

35. Strange, *Family Farming*, 111.

36. There were other means to enhance soil fertility (distributing leaves, wood ashes, gypsum, marls, and bone meal over a field), but these had less impact overall than crop rotation and spreading manure. For an analysis of the various mechanisms employed to increase soil fertility, see Hans Jenny, "The Making and Unmaking of a Fertile Soil," in *Meeting the Expectations of the Land*, eds. Wes Jackson, Wendell Berry, and Bruce Colman (San Francisco: North Point Press, 1984), 42–55.

37. The use of animal manure to add organic matter is feasible only in a diversified agricultural system, in which farmers grow plants and raise animals on the same farm. Today specialization occurs along geographical

lines, so that most animals are raised in the southwestern United States, corn is grown in the Midwest, wheat in the Great Plains, cotton in the Deep South, etc. In this context, animal manure has become a monumental problem, since transporting it to grain-producing regions, sometimes hundreds of miles away, becomes financially burdensome.

38. The one exception is the Amish, who still practice crop rotations.

39. Jackson, *New Roots for Agriculture*, 24.

40. Amory Lovins, L. Hunter Lovins, and Marty Bender, "Energy and Agriculture," in *Meeting the Expectations of the Land*, ed. Wes Jackson, Wendell Berry, and Bruce Colman (San Francisco: North Point Press, 1984), 73.

41. Hybrid seeds also contributed to increases in productivity.

42. Judith D. Soule and Jon K. Piper, *Farming in Nature's Image: An Ecological Approach to Agriculture* (Washington, D.C.: Island Press, 1992), 32.

43. Judy Soule, Danielle Carré, and Wes Jackson, "Ecological Impact of Modern Agriculture," in *Agroecology*, ed. C. Ronald Carroll, John H. Vandermeer, and Peter Rosset (New York: McGraw Hill, 1990), 178–80; and Norberg-Hodge et al., *From the Ground Up*, 13.

44. National Research Council, Board on Agriculture, *Alternative Agriculture* (Washington, D.C.: National Academy Press, 1989), 100.

45. Norberg-Hodge et al., *From the Ground Up*, 15.

46. Soule and Piper, *Farming in Nature's Image*, 33.

47. Common usage of the term "pesticide" refers to insect control by synthetic chemicals. Technicians would opt for more specific terms, such as insecticides for insect control, rodenticides for rodent control, etc. I use the common term "pesticide" throughout when discussing insect control.

48. Soule and Piper, *Farming in Nature's Image*, 128–29. See also Jeffrey W. Bentley and Robert J. O'Neill, "On the Ethics of Biological Control of Insect Pests," *Agriculture and Human Values* 14 (1997): 284, for practical examples of natural pest control.

49. Bentley and O'Neill, "On the Ethics of Biological Control of Insect Pests," 286. Soule and Piper cite a slightly lower number (*Farming in Nature's Image*, 46).

50. Soule and Piper, *Farming in Nature's Image*, 46; National Research Council, Board on Agriculture, *Alternative Agriculture*, 124.

51. Robert van den Bosch, *The Pesticide Conspiracy* (Garden City, N.Y.: Doubleday, 1978), 17–35.

52. The average effective life of a pesticide today is only five or six years, since within this span of time insect populations have usually become resistant.

53. Bentley and O'Neill, "On the Ethics of Biological Control of Insect Pests," 286.

54. Soule and Piper, *Farming in Nature's Image*, 48–49.

55. Kristin Shrader-Frechette, "Pesticide Policy and Ethics," in *Ethics and Agriculture: An Anthropology on Current Issues in World Context*, ed. Charles V. Blatz (Moscow: University of Idaho Press, 1991), 426.

56. Soule, Carré, and Jackson, "Ecological Impact of Modern Agriculture," 181.

57. Soule and Piper, *Farming in Nature's Image*, 36–38.

58. Canadian Institute for Environmental Law and Policy, "A Green Food and Agriculture Agenda for Ontario," 1999, 1, accessed at *www.cielap.org/infocent/research/agri.htm*.

59. Especially with low-level pesticide exposure, which commonly causes headaches, nausea, drowsiness, confusion, and depression, it is difficult to determine the cause precisely since these symptoms can also be caused by a wide variety of other ailments.

60. Soule and Piper, *Farming in Nature's Image*, 40.

61. Shrader-Frechette, "Pesticide Policy and Ethics," 428.

62. Van den Bosch, *The Pesticide Conspiracy*, 27–28.

63. Shrader-Frechette offers an excellent example of the often unforeseeable negative side effects of pesticide use: "Several year[s] ago, the [World Health Organization] used DDT to kill off malaria-carrying mosquitos in Borneo. The chemicals killed the mosquitos but not the roaches, which accumulated the pesticide in their bodies. When the long-tailed lizards, called geckos, ate the roaches, the DDT in their prey caused disorders in their nervous systems. The geckos became sluggish and fell victim to the village cats, who ate them and died from the DDT in the lizards. Rats, carrying the threat of a plague epidemic, moved in from the Borneo forests, and cats had to be flown into the villages to catch the rats. The cats controlled the rat population, but the roofs of the people's huts began caving in because the lizards, now gone, had formerly eaten the caterpillars that ate the roof thatching" ("Pesticide Policy and Ethics," 426).

64. Van den Bosch, *The Pesticide Conspiracy*, 34.

65. John Fraser Hart, *The Land That Feeds Us* (New York: W. W. Norton, 1991), 23.

66. Ibid., 19–40.

67. My thanks to Steve Koop, an Iowa farmer, for a lengthy conversation on this matter.

68. Lovins, Lovins, and Bender, "Energy and Agriculture," 68.

69. Evan Eisenberg, *The Ecology of Eden* (New York: Vintage Books, 1998), 412–21; Bill McKibben, *The End of Nature* (New York: Random House, 1989), 26–31; and Christopher Flavin, "The Heat Is On: The Greenhouse Effect," in *Environmental Ethics*, ed. Louis Pojman (Boston: Jones and Bartlett, 1994), 371–78.

70. William C. French, "Ecological Security and Policies of Restraint," in *Christianity and Ecology*, ed. Dieter T. Hessel and Rosemary Radford Ruether (Cambridge, Mass.: Harvard University Press, 2000), 482.

71. Cultivating soil is becoming much less popular with the advent of "no-till" farming techniques in which the seeds are drilled directly into the ground, planted closely together, and weeds are controlled by herbicides. The no-till method has eliminated the need for cultivation and plowing, two factors frequently contributing to topsoil erosion.

72. Logsdon, *At Nature's Pace*, 87–88.

73. Strange, *Family Farming*, 113.

74. Clive Ponting, *A Green History of the World: The Environment and the Collapse of Great Civilizations* (New York: Penguin Books, 1991), 267.

75. John A. Hostetler, *Amish Society*, 4th ed. (Baltimore: Johns Hopkins University Press, 1993), 122–25.

76. Wendell Berry, *The Gift of Good Land* (New York: North Point Press, 1981), 130.

77. Soule and Piper, *Farming in Nature's Image*, 23.

78. Belden, *Dirt Rich, Dirt Poor*, 79–80.

79. Ibid., 81.

80. David Pimentel and Wen Dazhong, "Technological Changes in Energy Use in U.S. Agricultural Production," in *Agroecology*, ed. C. Ronald Carroll, John H. Vandermeer, and Peter Rosset (New York: McGraw Hill Publishing, 1990), 158.

81. Soule and Piper, *Farming in Nature's Image*, 24.

82. Lovins, Lovins, and Bender, "Energy and Agriculture," 68–69.

83. Pimentel and Dazhong, "Technological Changes in Energy Use," 159.

84. An interesting and thorough comparative analysis of substituting draft horses for traction power in American agriculture is provided by Marty Bender, "Industrial Versus Biological Traction on the Farm," in *Meeting the Expectations of the Land*, eds. Wes Jackson, Wendell Berry, and Marty Bender (San Francisco: North Point Press, 1984), 87–105.

85. While the United States accounts for 4–5 percent of the world's population, Americans are responsible for 30 percent of the world's energy consumption. See Ponting, *A Green History of the World*, 292.

86. Miguel A. Altieri, "Why Study Traditional Agriculture?" in *Agroecology*, ed. C. Ronald Carroll, John H. Vandermeer, and Peter Rosset (New York: McGraw Hill, 1990), 560.

87. Ibid., 558.

88. Philip McMichael, "The Power of Food," *Agriculture and Human Values* (March 2000): 26, quoting Jeremy Rifkin, *The Biotech Century: Harnessing the Gene and Remaking the World* (New York: Tarcher/Putnam, 1998), 110–11.

89. Belden, *Dirt Rich, Dirt Poor*, 85.

90. Donald N. Duvick, "Genetic Diversity and Plant Breeding," in *Ethics and Agriculture: An Anthology on Current Issues in World Context*, ed. Charles V. Blatz (Moscow: University of Idaho Press, 1991), 495–96.

91. Soule and Piper, *Farming in Nature's Image*, 18–19.

92. Jane Rissler and Margaret Mellon, *The Ecological Risks of Engineered Crops* (Cambridge, Mass.: MIT Press, 1996), 10.

93. Ibid., 15.

94. Bryan J. Hubbell and Rick Welsh, "Transgenic Crops: Engineering a More Sustainable Agriculture?" *Agriculture and Human Values* 15 (1998): 44.

95. Keith Douglass Warner, *Questioning the Promise: Critical Reflections on Agricultural Biotechnology from the Perspective of Catholic Teaching* (Des Moines, Iowa: National Catholic Rural Life Conference, 2000), 6.

96. Rissler and Mellon, *The Ecological Risks of Engineered Crops*, x–xi. For a thorough assessment of many of the critics' concerns about genetic engineering, see Gary L. Comstock, *Vexing Nature? On the Ethical Case against Agricultural Biotechnology* (Boston: Kluwer Academic, 2000), 175–288.

97. For an assessment of biotechnology's possible beneficial applications see Donald Duvick, "Biotechnology Is Compatible with Sustainable Agriculture," *Journal of Agricultural and Environmental Ethics* 8 (1995): 112–25; and Donald Duvick, "Our Vision for the Agricultural Sciences Needs to Include Biotechnology," *Journal of Agricultural and Environmental Ethics* 4 (1991): 200–206.

98. Christian J. Peters, "Genetic Engineering in Agriculture: Who Stands to Benefit?" *Journal of Agricultural and Environmental Ethics* 13 (2000): 317.

99. Ibid., 323.

100. Warner, *Questioning the Promise*, 15–16.

101. Hubbell and Welsh, "Transgenic Crops," 49.

102. Warner, *Questioning the Promise*, 17.

103. For endorsements of a precautionary approach to biotechnology, see National Catholic Rural Life Conference, "Agricultural Biotechnology: A Catholic Rural Life Perspective," June 2002, 1–4, accessed at *www.ncrlc.com/NCRLC_GE_webstatement.html*; and Warner, *Questioning the Promise*, 27–32.

104. Rissler and Mellon, *The Ecological Risks of Engineered Crops*, 24–25.

105. These questions are raised in ibid., 27–70.

106. Peters, "Genetic Engineering in Agriculture," 315–20; Miguel Altieri and Peter Rosset, "Ten Reasons Why Biotechnology Will Not Ensure Food Security, Protect the Environment and Reduce Poverty in the Developing World," October 1999, accessed at *www.foodfirst.org/progs/global/ge/altieri-11-99.html*; and Warner, "Critical Reflections on Agricultural Biotechnology," 13–15.

107. Jacques Ellul, *The Technological Bluff*, trans. Geoffrey W. Bromiley (Grand Rapids: William B. Eerdmans, 1990), 132.

108. Cochrane, *The Development of American Agriculture*, 126.

109. These characteristics are synthesized from Langdon Winner, *Autonomous Technology: Technics-out-of-Control as a Theme in Political Thought* (Cambridge: Massachusetts Institute of Technology Press, 1977), and Ellul, *The Technological Bluff*.

110. This figure was gathered by surveying the classified advertisements of a half dozen American Web sites related to draft horses and averaging the sales prices of approximately thirty horses.

111. Ellul, *The Technological Bluff*, 35–39.

112. Jerry Mander, *In the Absence of the Sacred* (San Francisco: Sierra Club, 1991), 48.

113. It should be noted that the draining of wetlands was not only motivated by a need to remove impediments, but also to increase productivity and profit by bringing more land into cultivation.

114. The creation of small trenches between rows of crops is becoming rarer today in American agriculture due to the increasing popularity of no-till farming. While certainly better at retaining topsoil, commentators have noted that no-till farming sharply increases the amount of herbicides applied to fields.

115. Ellul, *The Technological Bluff*, 71.

116. See Bender, "Industrial Versus Biological Traction on the Farm," 87–105.

117. Albert Borgmann, *Power Failure: Christianity in the Culture of Technology* (Grand Rapids: Brazos Press, 2003), 122.

118. Dudley, "The Entrepreneurial Self," 184.

119. David Kline, "Great Possessions," in *The New Agrarianism: Land, Culture, and the Community of Life*, ed. Eric T. Freyfogle (Washington, D.C.: Island Press, 2001), 186.

120. Ian Barbour, *Ethics in an Age of Technology* (San Francisco: Harper, 1993), 96.

121. See, for example, Joseph Mendelson, "Roundup: The World's Biggest-Selling Herbicide," *Ecologist* 28 (1998): 270–75.

122. Eisenberg, *The Ecology of Eden*, 31.

123. David Toolan, *At Home in the Cosmos* (Maryknoll, N.Y.: Orbis Books, 2001), 96.

Chapter Three: An Alternative Vision for American Agriculture

1. Ellen Meiksins Wood, "The Agrarian Origins of Capitalism," in *Hungry for Profit*, ed. Fred Magdoff, John Bellamy Foster, and Frederick H. Buttel (New York: Monthly Review Press, 2000), 23–41.

2. Helena Norberg-Hodge, Peter Goering, and John Page, "From Global to Local: Sowing the Seeds of Community," in *The Ethics of Food: A Reader for the 21st Century*, ed. Gregory E. Pence (Lanham, Md.: Rowman and Littlefield, 2002), 196.

3. By "corporate ownership" I mean the possession of legal title to farmland by an entity composed of individuals seeking only to further their economic self-interest, which also offers stock to the public. Largely because of tax benefits, the legal instrument of incorporation is often used by what are traditionally considered "family farmers," although their concerns are not solely economic, nor is stock in the corporation offered to non–family members. I want to exclude the latter from the meaning of "corporation."

4. Ian Barbour, *Ethics in an Age of Technology* (San Francisco: Harper, 1993), 96.

5. Marty Strange, *Family Farming: A New Economic Vision* (Lincoln: University of Nebraska Press, 1988), 91–103.

6. Jules Pretty, *Agri-Culture: Reconnecting People, Land and Nature* (London: Earthscan Publications, 2002), 82–85.

7. Eugene C. Hargrove, "Anglo-American Land Use Attitudes," in *Environmental Ethics: Divergence and Convergence*, 3rd ed., ed. Susan J. Armstrong and Richard G. Botzler (New York: McGraw-Hill, 2004), 164–76.

8. Cf. Kathleen A. Merrigan, "Government Pathways to True Food Security," in *Visions of American Agriculture*, ed. William Lockeretz (Ames: Iowa State University Press, 1997), 155–72.

9. Karl Stauber, "Envisioning a Thriving Rural America through Agriculture," in *Visions of American Agriculture*, ed. William Lockeretz (Ames: Iowa State University Press, 1997), 109.

10. Jay Staten, *The Embattled Farmer* (Golden, Colo.: Fulcrum, 1987), 5–16.

11. There are several types of direct federal subsidies, but for the sake of simplicity I lump these into one broad category.

12. George M. Boody, "Agriculture as a Public Good," in *The Farm as Natural Habitat: Reconnecting Food Systems with Ecosystems*, ed. Dana L. Jackson and Laura L. Jackson (Washington, D.C.: Island Press, 2002), 263.

13. Neill Schaller, "Sustainability and Public Policy," in *Sustainability in Agricultural and Rural Development*, ed. Gerard E. D'Souza (Brookfield, Vt.: Ashgate, 1998), 159–60.

14. Ingolf Vogeler, "The Structure of U.S. Agriculture: Agribusiness or Family Farms?" in *Ethics and Agriculture: An Anthology on Current Issues in World Context*, ed. Charles V. Blatz (Moscow: University of Idaho Press, 1991), 153–55.

15. Center for Rural Affairs, "Farm Bill Summary," accessed at *www.cfra .org/resources/2002_FarmBill.htm*.

16. Bread for the World Institute, *Agriculture in the Global Economy: Hunger 2003* (Washington, D.C.: Bread for the World Institute, 2003), 40.

17. Boody, "Agriculture as a Public Good," 264–67.

18. Ibid., 267.

19. See Bread for the World Institute, *Agriculture in the Global Economy*.

20. Merrigan, "Government Pathways to True Food Security," 155–58.

21. Ibid., 162–65.

22. Boody, "Agriculture as a Public Good," 272.

23. David Kline, *Great Possessions: An Amish Farmer's Journal* (San Francisco: North Point Press, 1990), xvii.

24. For a study of agricultural programs and their effect on wildlife populations, see William R. Edwards, "Agriculture and Wildlife in the Midwest," in *Sustainable Agriculture in the American Midwest*, ed. William R. Edwards and Gregory McIsaac (Chicago: University of Illinois Press, 1994), 95–123.

25. For information on urban gardening, see Annu Ratta and Jac Smit, "Urban Agriculture: It's About Much More Than Food," *WHY Magazine* 13 (Summer 1993): 26–29; Catherine Murphy, *Cultivating Havana: Urban Agriculture and Food Security in the Years of Crisis* (Oakland: Food First, 1999), 1–4; and Lauren Baker and Jin Huh, "Rich Harvest," *Alternatives Journal* 29 (Winter 2003): 21–25. For a thorough analysis of Third and Fourth World agriculture, see Bread for the World Institute, *Agriculture in the Global Economy: Hunger 2003*.

26. Francis Moore Lappé, *Diet for a Small Planet* (New York: Ballantine Books, 1982), 70.

27. Jim Heffern, "Putting Local Food on the Table: Sustainable Rural Economy Depends on Keeping Regional Connections," *National Catholic Reporter* 38 (June 7, 2002): 2 (downloadable version).

28. Critics argue that the community-friendly aspect of CSA is largely window dressing. See for example, Laura B. DeLind, "Place, Work, and Civic Agriculture: Common Fields for Cultivation," *Agriculture and Human Values* 19 (2002): 217–24; and Laura B. DeLind, "Considerably More Than Vegetables, a Lot Less Than Community: The Dilemma of Community Supported Agriculture," in *Fighting for the Farm: Rural America Transformed*, ed. Jane Adams (Philadelphia: University of Pennsylvania Press, 2003), 192–206.

29. Helena Norberg-Hodge, Peter Goering, and John Page, *From the Ground Up: Rethinking Industrial Agriculture*, rev. ed. (New York: Zed Books, 2001), xxx.

30. See DeLind, "Considerably More Than Vegetables," and DeLind, "Place, Work, and Civic Agriculture" for critiques of this mentality.

31. I have one reservation about this statement. In some instances, the knowledge generated from direct involvement in agriculture would be inapplicable to operating a CSA because it is based on the presuppositions

and mental habits of industrialized agriculture. Needless to say, bringing this mind-set to a CSA and attempting to model a CSA on the agricultural system currently present in the Corn Belt would vitiate many of the benefits of CSA.

32. DeLind, "Considerably More Than Vegetables," 202.

33. For an extended discussion of the dynamics and techniques involved in colonizing agricultural production, see Clive Ponting, *A Green History of the World: The Environment and the Collapse of Great Civilizations* (New York: Penguin, 1991), 194–223.

34. Armando Nova, "Cuban Agriculture before 1990," in *Sustainable Agriculture and Resistance: Transforming Food Production in Cuba*, ed. Fernando Funes, Luis García, Martin Bourque, Nilda Pérez, and Peter Rosset (Oakland: Food First, 2002), 27.

35. Brian H. Pollitt, "The Transition to Socialist Agriculture in Cuba: Some Salient Features," *Bulletin of the Institute of Development Studies* 13 (1982): 12.

36. Peter M. Rosset, "Cuba: Ethics, Biological Control, and Crisis," *Agriculture and Human Values* 14 (1997): 292.

37. Ivette Perfecto, "Sustainable Agriculture Embedded in a Global Sustainable Future: Agriculture in the United States and Cuba," in *Environmental Justice: Issues, Policies, and Solutions*, ed. Bunyan Bryant (Washington, D.C.: Island Press, 1995), 179.

38. Peter M. Rosset, "Cuba: A Successful Case Study of Sustainable Agriculture," in *Hungry for Profit*, ed. Fred Magdoff, John Bellamy Foster, and Frederick H. Buttel (New York: Monthly Review, 2000), 205.

39. Hugh Warwick, "Cuba's Organic Revolution," *Ecologist* 29 (1999): 457.

40. Fernando Funes, "The Organic Farming Movement in Cuba," in *Sustainable Agriculture and Resistance: Transforming Food Production in Cuba*, ed. Fernando Funes, Luis García, Martin Bourque, Nilda Pérez, and Peter Rosset (Oakland: Food First, 2002), 6.

41. Rosset, "Cuba: Ethics, Biological Control, and Crisis," 293.

42. Peter M. Rosset, "Alternative Agriculture Works: The Case of Cuba," *Monthly Review* 50 (July–August 1998): 2.

43. Rosset, "Cuba: Ethics, Biological Control, and Crisis," 294.

44. Rosset, "Cuba: A Successful Case Study of Sustainable Agriculture," 207–8.

45. Miguel A. Altieri, Nelso Companioni, Kristina Canizares, et al., "The Greening of the 'Barrios': Urban Agriculture for Food Security in Cuba," *Agriculture and Human Values* 16 (1999): 134.

46. Rosset, "Cuba: Ethics, Biological Control, and Crisis," 297.

47. Rosset, "Alternative Agriculture Works: The Case of Cuba," 4.

48. Rosset, "Cuba: Ethics, Biological Control, and Crisis," 296.

49. Ibid., 293.

50. Ibid., 300.

51. Luis García, "Agroecological Education and Training," in *Sustainable Agriculture and Resistance: Transforming Food Production in Cuba*, ed. Fernando Funes, Luis García, Martin Bourque, Nilda Pérez, and Peter Rosset (Oakland: Food First, 2002), 90.

52. Ibid., 98–103.

53. Rosset, "Cuba: Ethics, Biological Control, and Crisis," 300.

54. John A. Hostetler, *Amish Society*, 4th ed. (Baltimore: Johns Hopkins University Press, 1993), 115.

55. Ibid., 75.

56. Lee Zook, "The Amish Farm and Alternative Agriculture: A Comparison," *Journal of Sustainable Agriculture* 4 (1994): 26.

57. Hostetler, *Amish Society*, 84.

58. David Walbert, *Garden Spot: Lancaster County, the Old Order Amish, and the Selling of Rural America* (New York: Oxford University Press, 2002), 111–12.

59. David Kline, *Scratching the Woodchuck: Nature on an Amish Farm* (Athens: University of Georgia Press, 1997), 195–96. As Kline writes elsewhere, the horse also contributes to Amish family life: "Not only does working with horses limit farm size, but horses are ideally suited to family life. With horses you unhitch at noon to water and feed the teams and then the family eats what we still call dinner. While the teams rest there is usually time for a short nap. And because God didn't create the horse with headlights, we don't work nights" ("Great Possessions," in *The New Agrarianism: Land, Culture, and the Community of Life*, ed. Eric T. Freyfogle [Washington, D.C.: Island Press, 2001], 192).

60. Wendell Berry, *The Gift of Good Land: Further Essays Cultural and Agricultural* (New York: North Point Press, 1981), 251.

61. Kline, *Great Possessions*, xvii–xviii; and Berry, *The Gift of Good Land*, 249–53.

62. Katharine V. Blake, Enrico A. Cardamone, Steven D. Hall, et al., "Modern Amish Farming as Ecological Agriculture," *Society and Natural Resources* 10 (1997): 145.

63. Deborah H. Stinner, M. G. Paoletti, and B. R. Stinner, "In Search of Traditional Farm Wisdom for a More Sustainable Agriculture: A Study of Amish Farming and Society," *Agriculture, Ecosystems, and Environment* 27 (1989): 85.

64. Ibid., 83.

65. Kline, *Great Possessions*, xviii.

66. Hostetler, *Amish Society*, 131, quoting an unidentified Amish patriarch.

67. Marty Bender, "An Economic Comparison of Traditional and Conventional Agricultural Systems at a County Level," *American Journal of Alternative Agriculture* 16 (January 2001): 7–9.

68. David G. Sommers and Ted L. Napier, "Comparison of Amish and Non-Amish Farmers: A Diffusion/Farm-Structure Perspective," *Rural Sociology* 58 (1993): 135.

69. Bender, "An Economic Comparison of Traditional and Conventional Agricultural Systems," 10.

70. See Gen. 1.

71. Jackson writes, "Agriculture may be our most noble invention, but in my view, it is the most devastating phenomenon to have occurred on our planet. The plow may have destroyed more options for future generations than the sword" (Wes Jackson, "Ecosystem Agriculture: The Marriage of Ecology and Agriculture," in *Global Perspectives on Agroecology and Sustainable Agricultural Systems*, ed. Patricia Allen and Debra Van Dusen [Santa Cruz: Agroecology Program, University of California, 1988], 15).

72. Wes Jackson, *New Roots for Agriculture* (San Francisco: Friends of the Earth; Salina, Kans.: Land Institute, 1980), 2.

73. R. Neil Sampson, *Farmland or Wasteland: A Time to Choose* (Emmaus Pa.: Rodale Press, 1981), 126–27.

74. Jackson, *New Roots for Agriculture*, 17.

75. The introduction of no-till farming methods, which involve much less topsoil disturbance than plowing and cultivating, have reduced topsoil erosion considerably since the publication of Jackson's 1980 *New Roots for Agriculture*. The problem with no-till farming, however, is the need for many more chemicals such as pesticides and herbicides compared to traditional tillage farming.

76. Wes Jackson, "Why Natural Systems Agriculture?" *www.landinstitute .org/vnews/display.v/ART/2000/08/01/37e288b43?in_archive=1.*

77. The four characteristics of sustainable ecosystems are taken from Jackson, "Why Natural Systems Agriculture?"

78. Wes Jackson, "A Search for the Unifying Concept for Sustainable Agriculture," in *Meeting the Expectations of the Land*, ed. Wes Jackson, Wendell Berry, and Bruce Colman (San Francisco: North Point Press, 1984), 221.

79. Judith D. Soule and Jon K. Piper, *Farming in Nature's Image: An Ecological Approach to Agriculture* (Washington, D.C.: Island Press, 1992), 115–16.

80. For a list of papers outlining the Land Institute's successes, see *www.landinstitute.org/vnews/display.v/SEC/Publications%3E%EScience+publ.*

81. Wes Jackson, *Altars of Unhewn Stone: Science and the Earth* (New York: North Point Press, 1987), 113–14.

82. "Acceptable" is the important adjective when considering production levels. I have already explained why the term "production" is highly relative and why it conveys very little morally relevant information by itself. Thus, increased or decreased production always must be situated in the appropriate moral context, namely, providing a sufficient amount of safe, nutritious food.

83. For a decisive refutation of this reductionism, see Frederick Ferré, *Hellfire and Lightning Rods: Liberating Science, Technology, and Religion* (Maryknoll, N.Y.: Orbis Books, 1993), 11–23.

84. Paul B. Thompson, *The Spirit of the Soil: Agriculture and Environmental Ethics* (New York: Routledge, 1995), 124–25.

85. Jerry Glover, personal communication, January 10, 2005. Glover graciously read the natural systems agriculture section of my manuscript and offered helpful clarifications. I am grateful for his time and energy.

Bibliography

Altieri, Miguel A. "Why Study Traditional Agriculture?" In *Agroecology*, ed. C. Ronald Carroll, John H. Vandermeer, and Peter Rosset, 551–64. New York: McGraw-Hill, 1990.

Altieri, Miguel A., Nelso Companioni, Kristina Canizares, et al. "The Greening of the 'Barrios': Urban Agriculture for Food Security in Cuba." *Agriculture and Human Values* 16 (1999): 131–40.

Altieri, Miguel A., and Peter Rosset. "Ten Reasons Why Biotechnology Will Not Ensure Food Security, Protect the Environment and Reduce Poverty in the Developing World." October 1999. Accessed at *www.foodfirst.org/progs/global/ge/altieri-11-99.html*.

Aquinas, Thomas. *Summa Theologica*. 5 volumes. Trans. Fathers of the English Dominican Province. 1911; reprint, Westminster, Md.: Christian Classics, 1981.

Austin, Richard Cartwright. *Beauty of the Lord: Awakening the Senses*. Atlanta: John Knox Press, 1988.

———. *Hope for the Land: Nature in the Bible*. Atlanta: John Knox Press, 1988.

———. "Rights for Life: Rebuilding Human Relationships with Land." In *Theology of the Land*, ed. Bernard F. Evans and Gregory D. Cusack, 103–26. Collegeville, Minn.: Liturgical Press, 1987.

Ayres, Ed. *God's Last Offer: Negotiating for a Sustainable Future*. New York: Four Walls Eight Windows, 1999.

Baker, Lauren, and Jin Huh. "Rich Harvest." *Alternatives Journal* 29 (Winter 2003): 21–25.

Barbour, Ian. *Ethics in an Age of Technology*. San Francisco: Harper, 1993.

Barth, Karl. *Church Dogmatics*. Volume 2. Book 1. *The Doctrine of God*. Trans. T. H. L. Parker et al. Ed. G. W. Bromiley and T. F. Torrance. Edinburgh: T. & T. Clark, 1957.

Bartlett, Peggy F., and Peter J. Brown. "Agricultural Development and the Quality of Life: An Anthropological View." *Agriculture and Human Values* 2 (1985): 28–35.

Belden, Joseph N. *Dirt Rich, Dirt Poor: America's Food and Farm Crisis*. New York: Routledge and Kegan Paul, 1986.

228

Bender, Marty. "An Economic Comparison of Traditional and Conventional Agricultural Systems at a County Level." *American Journal of Alternative Agriculture* 16 (January 2001): 2–15.

———. "Industrial Versus Biological Traction on the Farm." In *Meeting the Expectations of the Land*, ed. Wes Jackson, Wendell Berry, and Marty Bender, 87–105. San Francisco: North Point Press, 1984.

Bentley, Jeffrey W., and Robert J. O'Neill. "On the Ethics of Biological Control of Insect Pests." *Agriculture and Human Values* 14 (1997): 283–89.

Berger, Fred R. "Gratitude." *Ethics* 85 (July 1975): 298–309.

Berry, Wendell. *The Gift of Good Land: Further Essays Cultural and Agricultural.* New York: North Point Press, 1981.

———. *The Unsettling of America: Culture and Agriculture.* 3rd ed. San Francisco: Sierra Club, 1996.

———. "Whose Head Is the Farmer Using? Whose Head Is Using the Farmer?" In *Meeting the Expectations of the Land*, ed. Wes Jackson, Wendell Berry, and Bruce Colman, 19–30. San Francisco: North Point Press, 1984.

Blake, Katharine V., Enrico A. Cardamone, Steven D. Hall, et al. "Modern Amish Farming as Ecological Agriculture." *Society and Natural Resources* 10 (1997): 143–59.

Boody, George M. "Agriculture as a Public Good." In *The Farm as Natural Habitat: Reconnecting Food Systems with Ecosystems*, ed. Dana L. Jackson and Laura L. Jackson, 261–75. Washington, D.C.: Island Press, 2002.

Borgmann, Albert. *Power Failure: Christianity in the Culture of Technology.* Grand Rapids: Brazos Press, 2003.

Bread for the World Institute. *Agriculture in the Global Economy: Hunger 2003.* Washington, D.C.: Bread for the World Institute, 2003.

Brewster, John M. "The Relevance of the Jeffersonian Dream Today." In *Land Use Policy and Problems in the United States*, ed. Howard W. Ottoson, 86–136. Lincoln: University of Nebraska Press, 1963.

Camenisch, Paul F. "Gift and Gratitude in Ethics." *Journal of Religious Ethics* 9 (Spring 1981): 1–34.

Canadian Institute for Environmental Law and Policy. "A Green Food and Agriculture Agenda for Ontario." 1999. Accessed at *www.cielap.org/infocent/research/agri.htm.*

Card, Claudia. "Gratitude and Obligation." *American Philosophical Quarterly* 25 (1988): 115–27.

Catechism of the Catholic Church. Mahwah, N.J.: Paulist Press, 1994.

Center for Rural Affairs. "Farm Bill Summary." 2002. Accessed at *www.cfra.org/resources/2002_FarmBill.htm.*

Childs, Brian. "Gratitude." In *Dictionary of Pastoral Care and Counseling*, ed. Rodney J. Hunter, 470–71. Nashville: Abingdon, 1990.

Cochrane, Willard W. *The Development of American Agriculture: An Historical Analysis.* Minneapolis: University of Minnesota Press, 1993.

Comstock, Gary L. *Vexing Nature? On the Ethical Case against Agricultural Biotechnology.* Boston: Kluwer Academic, 2000.

DeLind, Laura B. "Considerably More Than Vegetables, a Lot Less Than Community: The Dilemma of Community Supported Agriculture." In *Fighting for the Farm: Rural America Transformed*, ed. Jane Adams, 192–206. Philadelphia: University of Pennsylvania Press, 2003.

———. "Place, Work, and Civic Agriculture: Common Fields for Cultivation." *Agriculture and Human Values* 19 (2002): 217–24.

Douglass, Gordon, and Jane Douglass. "Creation, Reformed Faith, and Sustainable Food Systems." In *Reformed Faith and Economics*, ed. Robert L. Stivers, 117–44. Lanham, Md.: University Press of America, 1989.

Dudley, Kathryn Marie. "The Entrepreneurial Self: Identity and Morality in a Midwestern Farming Community." In *Fighting for the Farm: Rural America Transformed*, ed. Jane Adams, 175–91. Philadelphia: University of Pennsylvania Press, 2003.

Dundon, Stanislaus J. "Sources of First Principles for an Agricultural Ethic." In *Ethics and Agriculture: An Anthology on Current Issues in World Context*, ed. Charles V. Blatz, 63–74. Moscow: University of Idaho Press, 1991.

Duvick, Donald. "Biotechnology Is Compatible with Sustainable Agriculture." *Journal of Agricultural and Environmental Ethics* 8 (1995): 112–25.

———. "Genetic Diversity and Plant Breeding." In *Ethics and Agriculture: An Anthology on Current Issues in World Context*, ed. Charles V. Blatz, 492–98. Moscow: University of Idaho Press, 1991.

———. "Our Vision for the Agricultural Sciences Needs to Include Biotechnology." *Journal of Agricultural and Environmental Ethics* 4 (1991): 200–206.

Edwards, William R. "Agriculture and Wildlife in the Midwest." In *Sustainable Agriculture and the American Midwest*, ed. William R. Edwards and Gregory McIsaac, 95–123. Chicago: University of Illinois Press, 1994.

Eisenberg, Evan. *The Ecology of Eden.* New York: Vintage Books, 1998.

Ellul, Jacques. *The Technological Bluff.* Trans. Geoffrey W. Bromiley. Grand Rapids: William B. Eerdmans, 1990.

Evangelical Lutheran Church in America. "A Social Statement on Caring for Creation: Vision, Hope, and Justice." 1993. Accessed at *www.elca.org/dcs/environment/html.*

Farb, Peter. *Face of North America: The Natural History of a Continent.* New York: Harper & Row, 1963.

Ferré, Frederick. *Hellfire and Lightning Rods: Liberating Science, Technology, and Religion*. Maryknoll, N.Y.: Orbis Books, 1993.

Fitzgerald, Patrick. "Gratitude and Justice." *Ethics* 109 (October 1998): 119–53.

Flavin, Christopher. "The Heat Is On: The Greenhouse Effect." In *Environmental Ethics*, ed. Louis Pojman, 371–78. Boston: Jones and Bartlett, 1994.

Fletcher, Joseph. *Situation Ethics*. Philadelphia: Westminster Press, 1966.

Francis, Charles. "Research and Extension Agenda for Sustainable Agriculture." *American Journal of Alternative Agriculture* 3 (1988): 123–26.

Francis, David G. *Family Agriculture: Tradition and Transformation*. London: Earthscan Publications, 1994.

French, William C. "Ecological Security and Policies of Restraint." In *Christianity and Ecology*, ed. Dieter T. Hessel and Rosemary Radford Ruether, 473–91. Cambridge, Mass.: Harvard University Press, 2000.

Freudenberger, C. Dean. *Food for Tomorrow?* Minneapolis: Augsburg Publishing House, 1984.

———. *The Gift of Land: A Judeo-Christian Perspective on Value and Lifestyle Change in a Threatened World*. Los Angeles: Franciscan Communications, 1981.

———. *Global Dust Bowl: Can We Stop the Destruction of the Land Before It's Too Late?* Minneapolis: Augsburg Publishing House, 1990.

Funes, Fernando. "The Organic Farming Movement in Cuba." In *Sustainable Agriculture and Resistance: Transforming Food Production in Cuba*, ed. Fernando Funes, Luis García, Martin Bourque, Nilda Pérez, and Peter Rosset, 1–26. Oakland: Food First, 2002.

García, Luis. "Agroecological Education and Training." In *Sustainable Agriculture and Resistance: Transforming Food Production in Cuba*, ed. Fernando Funes, Luis García, Martin Bourque, Nilda Pérez, and Peter Rosset, 90–108. Oakland: Food First, 2002.

Gardner, B. Delworth. *Plowing Ground in Washington: The Political Economy of U.S. Agriculture*. San Francisco: Pacific Research Institute for Public Policy, 1995.

Gliessman, Stephen R. *Agroecosystem Sustainability: Developing Practical Strategies*. New York: CRC Press, 2000.

Goldschmidt, Walter. *As You Sow*. New York: Harcourt, Brace and Company, 1947.

Graham, Mark E. *Josef Fuchs on Natural Law*. Washington, D.C.: Georgetown University Press, 2002.

———. "Rethinking Morality's Relationship to Salvation: Josef Fuchs, S.J., on Moral Goodness." *Theological Studies* 64 (2003): 750–72.

Gula, Richard. *Reason Informed by Faith*. Mahwah, N.J.: Paulist Press, 1989.

Gustafson, James M. *Can Ethics Be Christian?* Chicago: University of Chicago Press, 1975.

———. *Ethics from a Theocentric Perspective.* Volume 1. *Theology and Ethics.* Chicago: University of Chicago Press, 1981.

Habel, Norman C. *The Land Is Mine.* Minneapolis: Fortress Press, 1995.

Hanson, Victor Davis. *The Other Greeks: The Family Farm and the Agrarian Roots of Western Civilization.* New York: Free Press, 1995.

Hargrove, Eugene C. "Anglo-American Land Use Attitudes." In *Environmental Ethics: Divergence and Convergence.* 3rd ed. Ed. Susan J. Armstrong and Richard G. Botzler, 164–76. New York: McGraw-Hill, 2004.

Hart, John. *The Spirit of the Earth.* New York: Paulist Press, 1984.

Hart, John Fraser. *The Land That Feeds Us.* New York: W. W. Norton, 1991.

Heffern, Jim. "Putting Local Food on the Table: Sustainable Rural Economy Depends on Keeping Regional Connections." *National Catholic Reporter* 38 (June 7, 2002): 1–7 (downloadable version).

Hilfiker, David. *Not All of Us Are Saints: A Doctor's Journey with the Poor.* New York: Ballantine Books, 1994.

Hillel, Daniel. *Out of the Earth: Civilization and the Life of the Soil.* Berkeley: University of California Press, 1991.

Hostetler, John A. *Amish Society.* 4th ed. Baltimore: Johns Hopkins University Press, 1993.

Hubbell, Bryan J., and Rick Welsh. "Transgenic Crops: Engineering a More Sustainable Agriculture?" *Agriculture and Human Values* 15 (1998): 43–56.

Hugo, Victor. *Les Misérables.* Trans. Lee Fahnestock and Norman MacAfee. New York: Penguin, 1987.

Hüttermann, Aloys. *The Ecological Message of the Torah.* Atlanta: Scholars Press, 1999.

Jackson, Wes. *Altars of Unhewn Stone: Science and the Earth.* New York: North Point Press, 1987.

———. *Becoming Native to This Place.* Washington, D.C.: Counterpoint, 1996.

———. "Ecosystem Agriculture: The Marriage of Ecology and Agriculture." In *Global Perspectives on Agroecology and Sustainable Agricultural Systems,* ed. Patricia Allen and Debra Van Dusen, 15–19. Santa Cruz: Agroecology Program, University of California, 1988.

———. *New Roots for Agriculture.* San Francisco: Friends of the Earth; Salina, Kans.: Land Institute, 1980.

———. "A Search for the Unifying Concept for Sustainable Agriculture." In *Meeting the Expectations of the Land,* ed. Wes Jackson, Wendell Berry, and Bruce Colman, 208–29. San Francisco: North Point Press, 1984.

———. "Why Natural Systems Agriculture?" January 2004. Accessed online at *www.landinstitute.org/vnews/display.v/ART/2000/08/01/37e288b43?in_archive=1.*

Jardine, Murray. *The Making and Unmaking of Technological Society: How Christianity Can Save Modernity from Itself.* Grand Rapids: Brazos Press, 2004.

Jenny, Hans. "The Making and Unmaking of a Fertile Soil." In *Meeting the Expectations of the Land,* ed. Wes Jackson, Wendell Berry, and Bruce Colman, 42–55. San Francisco: North Point Press, 1984.

John Paul II. "Address of John Paul II to the Participants in the World Conference on Agrarian Reform and Rural Development" 1979. Accessed at *www.Vatican.va/holy_father/john_paul_ii/speeches/1979/july/documents/hf?jp-ii_sp.htm.*

———. "God Has Destined the Earth for All Men." In *The Pope Speaks* 24 (1979): 339–42.

———. *Veritatis Splendor.* Vatican translation. Boston: St. Paul Books & Media, 1993.

Johnson, Mark. *Moral Imagination: Implications of Cognitive Science for Ethics.* Chicago: University of Chicago Press, 1993.

Jung, L. Shannon. "Agricultural Technology As If God Were Involved." *Reformed Review* 41 (Spring 1988): 200–213.

Kline, David. *Great Possessions: An Amish Farmer's Journal.* San Francisco: North Point Press, 1990.

———. "Great Possessions." In *The New Agrarianism: Land, Culture, and the Community of Life,* ed. Eric T. Freyfogle, 181–95. Washington, D.C.: Island Press, 2001.

———. *Scratching the Woodchuck: Nature on an Amish Farm.* Athens: University of Georgia Press, 1997.

Koch, Adrienne, and William Peden, eds. *The Life and Selected Writings of Thomas Jefferson.* New York: Random House, 1944.

Korten, David D. *When Corporations Rule the World.* San Francisco: Berret-Loehler, 1996.

Kozol, Jonathan. *Amazing Grace: The Lives of Children and the Conscience of a Nation.* New York: Crown, 1995.

Lappé, Francis Moore. *Diet for a Small Planet.* New York: Ballantine Books, 1982.

Lockeretz, William. "Open Questions in Sustainable Agriculture." *American Journal of Alternative Agriculture* 3 (1988): 174–81.

Logsdon, Gene. *At Nature's Pace: Farming and the American Dream.* New York: Pantheon Books, 1994.

Lovins, Amory, L. Hunter Lovins, and Marty Bender. "Energy and Agriculture." In *Meeting the Expectations of the Land,* ed. Wes Jackson, Wendell

Berry, and Bruce Colman, 68–86. San Francisco: North Point Press, 1984.

Lyson, Thomas A., and Annalisa Lewis Raymer. "Stalking the Wily Multinational: Power and Control in the US Food System." *Agriculture and Human Values* 17 (2000): 199–208.

Mander, Jerry. *In the Absence of the Sacred.* San Francisco: Sierra Club, 1991.

Manning, Richard. *Grassland: The History, Biology, Politics, and Promise of the American Prairie.* New York: Viking Penguin, 1995.

Marshall, Andrew. "Sustaining Sustainable Agriculture: The Rise and Fall of the Fund for Rural America." *Agriculture and Human Values* 17 (2000): 267–77.

Martin, Mike W. "Good Fortune Obligates." *Southern Journal of Philosophy* 37 (1999): 57–75.

McConnell, Terrance. *Gratitude.* Philadelphia: Temple University Press, 1993.

McDonagh, Enda. *Gift and Call.* St. Meinrad, Indiana: Abbey Press, 1975.

McKibben, Bill. *The End of Nature.* New York: Random House, 1989.

McMichael, Philip. "The Power of Food." *Agriculture and Human Values* (March 2000): 21-33.

Meaton, Julia, and David Morrice. "The Ethics and Politics of Private Automobile Use." *Environmental Ethics* 18 (1996): 39–54.

Meeks, M. Douglas. "God and Land." *Agriculture and Human Values* 2 (1985): 16–27.

Meilaender, Gilbert. *The Theory and Practice of Virtue.* Notre Dame, Ind.: University of Notre Dame Press, 1984.

Mendelson, Joseph. "Roundup: The World's Biggest-Selling Herbicide." *Ecologist* 28 (1998): 270–75.

Merrigan, Kathleen A. "Government Pathways to True Food Security." In *Visions of American Agriculture*, ed. William Lockeretz, 155–72. Ames: Iowa State University Press, 1997.

Moltmann, Jürgen. *God in Creation.* Minneapolis: Fortress Press, 1993.

Murphy, Catherine. *Cultivating Havana: Urban Agriculture and Food Security in the Years of Crisis.* Oakland: Food First, 1999.

National Catholic Rural Life Conference. "Agricultural Biotechnology: A Catholic Rural Life Perspective." June 2002. Accessed at *www.ncrlc.com/ NCRLC_GE_webstatement.html.*

———. "A Catholic Rural Ethic for Agriculture, Environment, Food, and Earth." N.d. Accessed at *www.ncrlc.com/ruralethic.htm.*

National Conference of Catholic Bishops. *The Challenge of Peace: God's Promise and Our Response.* Washington, D.C.: United States Catholic Conference, 1983.

———. "For I Was Hungry and You Gave Me Food." November 2003. Accessed at *www.usccb.org/bishops/agricultural.htm.*

National Research Council, Board on Agriculture. *Alternative Agriculture.* Washington, D.C.: National Academy Press, 1989.

Norberg-Hodge, Helena, Peter Goering, and John Page. "From Global to Local: Sowing the Seeds of Community." In *The Ethics of Food: A Reader for the 21st Century*, ed. Gregory E. Pence, 191–214. Lanham, Md.: Rowman and Littlefield, 2002.

———. *From the Ground Up: Rethinking Industrial Agriculture.* Rev. ed. New York: Zed Books, 2001.

North Dakota Catholic Conference. "Giving Thanks through Action: A Statement by the Roman Catholic Bishops of North Dakota on the Crisis in Rural Life." 1998. Accessed at *www.ndcatholic.org/ruralstmt.htm.*

Nova, Armando. "Cuban Agriculture before 1990." In *Sustainable Agriculture and Resistance: Transforming Food Production in Cuba*, ed. Fernando Funes, Luis García, Martin Bourque, Nilda Pérez, and Peter Rosset, 27–39. Oakland: Food First, 2002.

O'Brien, David J., and Thomas A. Shannon, eds. *Catholic Social Thought: The Documentary Heritage.* Maryknoll, N.Y.: Orbis Books, 1992.

Parfit, Derek. *Reasons and Persons.* Oxford: Clarendon Press, 1984.

Perfecto, Ivette. "Sustainable Agriculture Embedded in a Global Sustainable Future: Agriculture in the United States and Cuba." In *Environmental Justice: Issues, Policies, and Solutions*, ed. Bunyan Bryant, 172–86. Washington, D.C.: Island Press, 1995.

Peters, Christian J. "Genetic Engineering in Agriculture: Who Stands to Benefit?" *Journal of Agricultural and Environmental Ethics* 13 (2000): 313–27.

Pimentel, David, and Wen Dazhong. "Technological Changes in Energy Use in U.S. Agricultural Production." In *Agroecology*, ed. C. Ronald Carroll, John H. Vandermeer, and Peter Rosset, 147–64. New York: McGraw Hill Publishing, 1990.

Pinches, Charles R. *Theology and Action: After Theory in Christian Ethics.* Grand Rapids: William B. Eerdmans, 2002.

Pocock, J. G. A. *The Machiavellian Moment: Florentine Political Thought and the Atlantic Republican Tradition.* Princeton, N.J.: Princeton University Press, 1975.

Pollitt, Brian H. "The Transition to Socialist Agriculture in Cuba: Some Salient Features." *Bulletin of the Institute of Development Studies* 13 (1982): 12–22.

Pontifical Council for Justice and Peace. "Towards a Better Distribution of Land." November 1997. Accessed at *www.vatican.va/roman_curia/ pontifical_councils/justpeace/documents/rc_pc_justpeace_doc_12011998_ distribuzione_terra_en.html.*

Ponting, Clive. *A Green History of the World: The Environment and the Collapse of Great Civilizations.* New York: Penguin Books, 1991.

Pretty, Jules N. *Agri-Culture: Reconnecting People, Land and Nature.* London: Earthscan Publications, 2002.

———. *The Living Land: Agriculture, Food and Community Regeneration in Rural Europe.* London: Earthscan Publications, 1998.

———. "Supportive Policies and Practice for Scaling Up Sustainable Agriculture." In *Facilitating Sustainable Agriculture*, ed. N. G. Roling and M. A. E. Wagemakers, 23–45. Cambridge: Cambridge University Press, 1998.

Rahner, Karl. *Foundations of Christian Faith: An Introduction to the Idea of Christianity.* Trans. William V. Dych. New York: Crossroad, 1989.

Ratta, Annu, and Jac Smit. "Urban Agriculture: It's About Much More Than Food." *WHY Magazine* 13 (Summer 1993): 26–29.

Reichman, O. J. *Konza Prairie: A Tallgrass Natural History.* Lawrence: University Press of Kansas, 1987.

Rifkin, Jeremy. *Beyond Beef: The Rise and Fall of the Cattle Culture.* New York: Penguin Books, 1992.

———. *The Biotech Century: Harnessing the Gene and Remaking the World.* New York: Tarcher/Putnam, 1998.

Rissler, Jane, and Margaret Mellon. *The Ecological Risks of Engineered Crops.* Cambridge, Mass.: MIT Press, 1996.

Robinson, Kenneth L. *Farm and Food Policies and Their Consequences.* Englewood Cliffs, N.J.: Prentice Hall, 1989.

Rosset, Peter M. "Alternative Agriculture Works: The Case of Cuba." *Monthly Review* 50 (July–August 1998): 1–5.

———. "Cuba: Ethics, Biological Control, and Crisis." *Agriculture and Human Values* 14 (1997): 291–302.

———. "Cuba: A Successful Case Study of Sustainable Agriculture." In *Hungry for Profit*, ed. Fred Magdoff, John Bellamy Foster, and Frederick H. Buttel, 203–13. New York: Monthly Review Press, 2000.

Sampson, R. Neil. *Farmland or Wasteland: A Time to Choose.* Emmaus, Pa.: Rodale Press, 1981.

Santmire, H. Paul. *Nature Reborn: The Ecological and Cosmic Promise of Christian Theology.* Minneapolis: Fortress Press, 2000.

Schaller, Neill. "Sustainability and Public Policy." In *Sustainability in Agricultural and Rural Development*, ed. Gerard E. D'Souza, 155–70. Brookfield, Vt.: Ashgate, 1998.

Schockenhoff, Eberhard. *Natural Law and Human Dignity: Universal Ethics in an Historical World.* Trans. Brian McNeil. Washington, D.C.: Catholic University of America Press, 2003.

Shrader-Frechette, Kristin. "Pesticide Policy and Ethics." In *Ethics and Agriculture: An Anthology on Current Issues in World Context*, ed. Charles V. Blatz, 426–33. Moscow: University of Idaho Press, 1991.

Simmons, A. John. *Moral Principles and Political Obligations*. Princeton, N.J.: Princeton University Press, 1979.

Sommers, David G., and Ted L. Napier. "Comparison of Amish and Non-Amish Farmers: A Diffusion/Farm-Structure Perspective." *Rural Sociology* 58 (1993): 130–45.

Soule, Judith D., and Jon K. Piper. *Farming in Nature's Image: An Ecological Approach to Agriculture*. Washington, D.C.: Island Press, 1992.

Soule, Judy, Danielle Carré, and Wes Jackson. "Ecological Impact of Modern Agriculture." In *Agroecology*, ed. C. Ronald Carroll, John H. Vandermeer, and Peter Rosset, 165–88. New York: McGraw Hill, 1990.

Spohn, William C. *Go and Do Likewise: Jesus and Ethics*. New York: Continuum, 1999.

Staten, Jay. *The Embattled Farmer*. Golden, Colo.: Fulcrum, 1987.

Stauber, Karl. "Envisioning a Thriving Rural America through Agriculture." In *Visions of American Agriculture*, ed. William Lockeretz, 105–17. Ames: Iowa State University Press, 1997.

Stinner, Deborah H., M. G. Paoletti, and B. R. Stinner. "In Search of Traditional Farm Wisdom for a More Sustainable Agriculture: A Study of Amish Farming and Society." *Agriculture, Ecosystems, and Environment* 27 (1989): 77–90.

Strange, Marty. *Family Farming: A New Economic Vision*. Lincoln: University of Nebraska Press, 1988.

Thompson, Paul B. *The Spirit of the Soil: Agriculture and Environmental Ethics*. New York: Routledge, 1995.

———. "Thomas Jefferson and Agrarian Philosophy." In *The Agrarian Roots of Pragmatism*, ed. Paul B. Thompson and Thomas C. Hilde, 118–39. Nashville: Vanderbilt University Press, 2000.

Toolan, David. *At Home in the Cosmos*. Maryknoll, N.Y.: Orbis Books, 2001.

United Methodist Church. "U.S. Agriculture and Rural Communities in Crisis." 1996. *www.umc-gbcs.org/issues/resolutions.php?resolutionid=31.*

Vacek, Edward C. "Gifts, God, Generosity, and Gratitude." In *Spirituality and Moral Theology: Essays from a Pastoral Perspective*, ed. James Keating, 81–125. New York: Paulist, 2000.

van den Bosch, Robert. *The Pesticide Conspiracy*. Garden City, N.Y.: Doubleday, 1978.

Vogeler, Ingolf. *The Myth of the Family Farm: Agribusiness Dominance of U.S. Agriculture*. Boulder, Colo.: Westview Press, 1981.

———. "The Structure of U.S. Agriculture: Agribusiness or Family Farms?" In *Ethics and Agriculture: An Anthology on Current Issues in World Context*, ed. Charles V. Blatz, 144–59. Moscow: University of Idaho Press, 1991.

Walbert, David. *Garden Spot: Lancaster County, the Old Order Amish, and the Selling of Rural America*. New York: Oxford University Press, 2002.

Walker, A. D. M. "Gratefulness and Gratitude." *Proceedings of the Aristotelian Society* 81 (1981): 39–55.

Ward, Keith. *Religion and Creation*. Oxford: Clarendon Press, 1996.

Warner, Keith Douglass. *Questioning the Promise: Critical Reflections on Agricultural Biotechnology from the Perspective of Catholic Teaching*. Des Moines, Iowa: National Catholic Rural Life Conference, 2000.

Warren, Dennis Michael. "Indigenous Agricultural Knowledge, Technology, and Social Change." In *Sustainable Agriculture in the American Midwest*, ed. William R. Edwards and Gregory McIsaac, 35–53. Chicago: University of Illinois Press, 1994.

Warwick, Hugh. "Cuba's Organic Revolution." *Ecologist* 29 (1999): 457–60.

Weiss, Roslyn. "The Moral and Social Dimensions of Gratitude." *Southern Journal of Philosophy* 23 (1985): 491–501.

Wellman, Christopher Heath. "Gratitude as a Virtue." *Pacific Philosophical Quarterly* 80 (1999): 284–300.

Winner, Langdon. *Autonomous Technology: Technics-out-of-Control as a Theme in Political Thought*. Cambridge: Massachusetts Institute of Technology Press, 1977.

Wood, Ellen Meiksins. "The Agrarian Origins of Capitalism." In *Hungry for Profit*, ed. Fred Magdoff, John Bellamy Foster, and Frederick H. Buttel, 23–41. New York: Monthly Review Press, 2000.

Wright, Christopher J. H. *God's People in God's Land: Family, Land, and Property in the Old Testament*. Grand Rapids: William B. Eerdmans, 1990.

Zook, Lee. "The Amish Farm and Alternative Agriculture: A Comparison." *Journal of Sustainable Agriculture* 4 (1994): 21–30.

Index

239

CPSIA information can be obtained
at www.ICGtesting.com
Printed in the USA
LVHW010615260820
664209LV00012B/1174